Enterprise Engagement: The Textbook

A Roadmap to Achieving
Organizational Results Through People

Edited by Bruce Bolger, Richard Kern and Allan Schweyer, with contributions and insights from dozens of leading academics, corporate practitioners and engagement solution providers

Published for the Enterprise Engagement Alliance by
Engagement Enterprises LLC. © 2015
Edition 2.0

Copyright © 2015 by Engagement Enterprises LLC

All rights reserved, including the right of reproduction,
in whole or in part, in any form.

First printing: March 2014
Second printing: April 2015

ISBN: 978-0-9915843-1-4

Cover Design: B. Crispino

Enterprise Engagement: The Textbook

Essential Guide to an Emerging New Field

The power has shifted to the people. The Internet and social media have given consumers and employees unprecedented power to rapidly enhance or undermine an organization's brand, sales and reputation. Research proves that organizations that foster the proactive involvement of their people outperform those that don't over time.

Enterprise Engagement: The Textbook is the first known blue-print for implementing engagement principles across the organization to achieve both strategic and tactical goals in sales, marketing, human resources, vendor management, community and shareholder relations, and more. Edition 2.0 released in 2015 has been reviewed and updated by its contributors with the addition of new chapters on Trade Show Engagement, Workplace Engagement, and Travel Engagement.

Engagement isn't just about hiring a social media consultant or creating an exciting event or mobile app; it's a strategic approach that depends upon an organization's ability to manage all of the factors that foster customer and distribution partner loyalty, and employee, vendor and community engagement, across the organization.

Enterprise Engagement: the Textbook provides conclusive research on the connection between customer loyalty, employee engagement and financial results, as well as a practical, actionable framework for implementing an Enterprise Engagement strategy in any size organization to achieve concrete sales, marketing, and human resources goals. It's a strategy good for business and society because it provides a virtuous circle of prosperity.

Enterprise Engagement starts at the highest level of management, because it generates the best results when it redefines the brand and culture to touch and connect everyone involved with a business internally and externally, creating a level of alignment across organizations traditionally hampered by silos. It requires a redefinition of the brand to encompass everyone who touches the organization.

A number of great business minds over the past three decades have written and spoken about many of the subjects covered in this book, including Peter Drucker, Tom Peters, Don Peppers and Martha Rogers, Alfie Kohn, Fred Reichheld, Curt Coffman, Marcus Buckingham, and more recently John Smythe, Zenep Ton, John Fisher, Rajat Paharia, Kevin Sheridan and others.

Despite this impressive lineup, surprisingly few companies are following their advice. We believe the reason lies not only in the time it takes for industry to change, in this case from a process- to a people-focused management orientation, or because engagement isn't always critical to short-term success; it is also because none of the many experts in this area worked together, as did their counterparts in advertising, to create a cohesive field taught in schools with a formal framework and set of implementation principles that people generally agree with.

No two advertising agencies are alike, but they all begin with a general understanding of what they do and how they do it. Every organization we have encountered that has embarked on an engagement strategy describes the process as an arduous journey.

Enterprise Engagement: the Textbook is the first book to focus on the emerging new business of Enterprise Engagement that gathers together the collective research and wisdom of people who have researched and written about this concept and put its tenets into practice. Engagement is a new field that responds to the growing outcry for a more humane form of capitalism, while remaining true to capitalism's goal of maximizing profits, because it demonstrates that the two are not only compatible, but are actually better for shareholders over the long term.

This book contains information critical to CEOs and board members seeking to understand how the field of Enterprise Engagement can not only enhance their profitability, but also create a better society. Enterprise Engagement: the Textbook provides a practical guide for top management in marketing, sales, channel management, human resources, finance, community relations and other related areas who seek to understand how engagement is transforming business and how they can apply it to their organizations, their jobs and their careers. These principles apply equally to government and not-for-profit organizations.

We understand that many readers will be experts in one or more areas of engagement, and that some chapters will read like basic information to them. The idea is not to make everyone experts on every aspect of engagement through this book, but to define the general tactical components of this new field and the essential information on how they inter-relate in a way that can dramatically improve results and lower costs, but which is still radically different from the way many businesses operate today.

The goal of Enterprise Engagement: the Textbook is to provide organizations and people with the skills and expertise required to achieve organizational goals through the engagement of people critical to success, offering a clear framework and tactical roadmap for translating that vision into a measurable and profitable process. It will be continually updated with new chapters and revisions of current chapters to remain up to date.

Enterprise Engagement: The Textbook

▶ **Curriculum Directors**
Allan Schweyer, President, TMGov.org and Partner/Principal, Center for Human Capital Innovation
Gary Rhoads, Academic Director, Stephen Mack Covey Professor of Marketing & Entrepreneurship, Department of Business Management, Brigham Young University

▶ **Co-Directors, Curriculum and Certification Development**
Bruce Bolger, Principal, Engagement Enterprises LLC
Melanie Lewis, Senior Consultant, Enterprise Engagement Alliance
Rodger Stotz, Chief Research Officer, Incentive Research Foundation and Principal, Delta Qi Consulting

▶ **Faculty Advisors**
Dr. Laurie Bassi, CEO, McBassi & Co.
Curt Coffman, Sr. Partner and Chief Science Officer, The Coffman Organization
Susan Forgie, Director, Customer Experience Mgt., McAfee Inc.
Barbara Porter, Executive Director, Advisory, Customer Practice, Ernst & Young LLP
Roy Saunderson, Chief Learning Officer, Rideau Recognition Management Institute
Kevin Sheridan, author, speaker, and consultant on employee engagement and founder of an engagement survey company.
Dr. Kathie Sorensen, Partner, The Coffman Organization
Gina Valenti, Vice President Owner Services Hilton Worldwide and VP Brand Culture and Internal Messaging, Hampton Hotels

▶ **Academic Advisors**
Comila Shahani-Denning, Associate Professor of Industrial & Organizational Psychology, Hofstra University
Dr. Terri Shapiro, Associate Professor, Hofstra M.A. Program in Industrial & Organizational Psychology

Enterprise Engagement: The Textbook

▶ **Curriculum Contributors**
Brad Callahan, VP, Business Solutions, Marketing Innovators
Sandra Daniel, Principal and Founder, FIRE Light Group
Paul Hebert, Vice President, Solution Design, Symbolist
Robert Hughes, Principal, The Hughes Group
William Keenan Jr., business writer specializing in marketing, HR, management and engagement
Richard Kern, Editorial Director, Enterprise Engagement Alliance
Paul Kiewiet, Executive Director, Michigan Promotional Products Association and past chairman of PPAI
Amy Kramer, Solution Design Strategist, Maritz Motivation Solutions
Paula Masters, CEO and President, Fatboy USA
Ira Ozer, Founder and President, Engagement Partners
Patty Pae, VP Business Development, Employee Vacations, American Express Travelink
Rajat Paharia, Founder and Chief Product Officer, Bunchball
Charles Scherbaum, Associate Professor, Baruch College, and Owner, Cielo Management Consulting, LLC
Eric Tejeda, Director of Product Marketing, PossibleNOW and board director and sponsorship chairman for American Marketing Association

▶ **Founding Sponsors**
The following organizations provided funding and support for the original Enterprise Engagement textbook strategy:
Dittman Incentive Marketing
EGR International

▶ **General Content and Topic Sponsors**
The following companies have provided general support for the development of the comprehensive textbook:
Canon USA
The Engagement Agency
FIRE Light Group
Nikon
Performance Enhancement Incentives
PossibleNOW
Rideau
Symbolist
Travel and Transport, Loyalty Services

Enterprise Engagement: The Textbook

Table of Contents

PART I INTRODUCTION TO ENGAGEMENT 1

AN INTRODUCTION TO ENTERPRISE ENGAGEMENT 3
CHAPTER 1 PRINCIPLES OF ENTERPRISE ENGAGEMENT 5
CHAPTER 2 ECONOMICS OF ENTERPRISE ENGAGEMENT 9
CHAPTER 3 CULTURE AND THE ENTERPRISE BRAND 17
CHAPTER 4 BREAKING DOWN ORGANIZATIONAL SILOS 23
CHAPTER 5 CASE STUDY: HAMPTON HOTELS 27

PART II AUDIENCES OF ENGAGEMENT 29

INTRO: THE AUDIENCE CHALLENGE 31
CHAPTER 6 CUSTOMER ENGAGEMENT 33
CHAPTER 7 CHANNEL PARTNER ENGAGEMENT 43
CHAPTER 8 EMPLOYEE ENGAGEMENT 49
CHAPTER 9 VOLUNTEER & COMMUNITY ENGAGEMENT 57
CHAPTER 10 VENDOR ENGAGEMENT 67
CHAPTER 11 THE EMPLOYEE/CUSTOMER LINK 73
CHAPTER 12 CASE STUDY: AMERICAN AIRLINES 79

PART III TOOLS OF ENGAGEMENT 83

INTRO: TOOLS AND TACTICS 85
CHAPTER 13 EMPLOYEE ASSESSMENT 87
CHAPTER 14 COMMUNICATION 93

CHAPTER 15 PREFERENCE MANAGEMENT 105

CHAPTER 16 CONTENT MARKETING 111

CHAPTER 17 LEARNING AND TRAINING 115

CHAPTER 18 GAMIFICATION 121

CHAPTER 19 COLLABORATION AND INNOVATION 127

CHAPTER 20 REWARDS & RECOGNITION 133

CHAPTER 21 LOYALTY 139

CHAPTER 22 SOCIAL RECOGNITION 145

CHAPTER 23 WELLNESS 153

CHAPTER 24 MEETINGS AND MOTIVATIONAL EVENTS 159

CHAPTER 25 THE ROLE OF TRAVEL IN ENGAGEMENT 167

CHAPTER 26 DESIGNING AN ENGAGING ENVIRONMENT 177

CHAPTER 27 TRADE SHOWS & CONFERENCES ENGAGING THE STAKEHOLDERS 183

CHAPTER 28 ENGAGEMENT TECHNOLOGY 191

CHAPTER 29 MEASURING ENTERPRISE ENGAGEMENT AND PERFORMANCE 197

CHAPTER 30 BIG DATA AND ANALYTICS 201

CHAPTER 31 CASE STUDY: UNITEDHEALTH GROUP 209

PART IV APPLICATIONS OF ENGAGEMENT 213

INTRO: THE ENTERPRISE ENGAGEMENT FRAMEWORK 215

CHAPTER 32 KEYS TO IMPLEMENTATION 217

CHAPTER 33 BUDGETING AND ROI 225

CHAPTER 34 ENGAGEMENT CAREERS 229

CHAPTER 35 ENGAGEMENT AND NONPROFITS 233

CHAPTER 36 IMPLICATIONS FOR GOVERNMENT 237

NOTES AND ACKNOWLEDGMENTS 245

Part I
Introduction to Engagement

Enterprise Engagement: The Textbook

An Introduction to Enterprise Engagement

It's not every year that a new profession bursts on to the business scene. The rise of the new field of Enterprise Engagement is the result of profound changes in business that have forced organizations to rethink the way they define their brands and their cultures, and how they manage their relationships with customers, employees, distribution partners and even their vendors and communities.

Years of research demonstrate that organizations able to build greater loyalty and engagement with their communities outperform those that don't, and social networking has given organizations even more reason to focus on engagement now that consumers and employees can so easily affect an organization's brand image and reputation. As a result, more organizations are putting top management in charge of engagement initiatives for customers, distribution partners and employees, as well as developing formal strategies to translate engagement principles into organizational success. The challenge is that no formal framework or roadmap exists, so organizations waste countless hours finding their way.

Enterprise Engagement is to the 21st century what advertising was to the 20th century. It promises to transform the way we do business and means that management, agencies and consultants will need to acquire an entirely new combination of skills. It requires an understanding of branding and culture from an enterprise-wide perspective, knowledge of an organization's many audiences – not just customers – and an approach that links the external marketing message to all constituencies to ensure that the brand promise gets fulfilled and delivered.

For the purposes of this book, engagement is defined as fostering the proactive of involvement of people to achieve an organization's goals. According to a 2006 Conference Board report, engaged customers have "a heightened emotional connection that a customer feels for his/her brand, that influences him/her to exert greater discretionary effort to buy or promote."

According to the 2008 *State of Employee Engagement* global research study, engaged employees aren't just committed. They aren't just passionate or proud. They have a line-of-sight on their own future and on the organization's mission and goals. They are "enthused" and "in gear," using their talents and discretionary effort to make a difference in their employer's quest for sustainable business success.

Enterprise Engagement: The Textbook

Chapter 1

Principles of Enterprise Engagement

Disengagement costs American industry hundreds of billions of dollars per year in lost productivity and reduced sales. At the same time, extensive research proves that organizations with proactively involved customers, distribution partners, employees and suppliers consistently outperform their competitors in earnings and growth. Until recently, only a few major companies have had engagement strategies or anyone specifically in charge of engagement.

This is changing rapidly. Over the past several years, hundreds of leading companies have put top management in charge of customer and employee engagement strategies designed to find ways to increase customer loyalty and employee quality and productivity. More and more of these executives have the word "engagement" in their titles; for others it's internal branding or customer experience or employee engagement. Organizations are spending more and more on outside experts, some now known as engagement agencies or consultants, who understand and/or can implement all of the elements that go into engaging any audience.

Enterprise Engagement is about achieving goals by fostering the proactive involvement of each and every customer, distribution partner, employee, vendor, or community member whose actions can affect results. Enterprise Engagement reflects the shift in emphasis from mass marketing to one-to-one-marketing. Driving the change is the growing ability of organizations to measure the impact of engagement through customer relationship management (CRM) and social networking, and the increasing recognition by top management that engagement can provide a competitive advantage. The Internet, combined with the ability for almost any organization to manufacture offshore, has reduced the traditional cost and service differentials between organizations. Today, even a little company can find a niche amidst the giants.

A MORE HUMANE CAPITALISM
The Occupy Wall Street movement and the popular television series *Undercover Boss* reflected other social undercurrents driving the emergence of Enterprise Engagement. The world is asking for a more humane form of capitalism that values people. Many Americans enjoy watching episodes of *Undercover Boss* that show top management being awakened to the importance of – and personal needs of – customers and employees. One of the world's most popular companies, Apple Computer, faced an

outcry when it became clear its iPad was being built by hundreds of thousands of Chinese working in conditions almost no Americans would tolerate. It subsequently changed its business practices.

For decades, it was easy to ignore the issue of engagement because engagement was hard to define and almost impossible to measure. But for a growing number of organizations, the question now isn't if engagement matters, but how to make it happen. The business of measuring customer and employee engagement has become a billion-dollar business, yet organizations are often left grappling with ever-changing engagement issues with no single resource to call upon.

For organizations dedicated to engagement, which include the likes of McDonalds, the New York Stock Exchange, Whole Foods, the Container Store, Southwest Airlines, Stew Leonard's and many others, it's more of a journey than a science because business books and media provide so little guidance on how to proceed, and so few traditional agencies and consultants take a holistic approach to helping organizations do whatever's necessary to direct everyone's energies to those tasks that yield organizational success.

THE LEADERSHIP/ENGAGEMENT CONNECTION
It's easy to confuse leadership with engagement. Leadership, of course, is essential to engagement. It describes the personal skills required of people who manage at any level, including the ability to create a culture based on providing clear direction, support, learning opportunities, enthusiasm, a sense of mission, constructive feedback, ability to recruit, etc. Yet leadership is only the first element of Enterprise Engagement.

The larger the organization – the more consumers, distribution partners, employees, volunteers, vendors and others are involved – the more complex it becomes to engage. The process requires more than leadership and a general goal. It requires informing people of the mission and how they can contribute or benefit. It requires providing people with the capability or skills to contribute and foster an emotional connection that makes them want to become involved, share and collaborate. It's about translating leadership into results through an appropriate framework of tools and tactics based on the specific organization, culture and marketplace. It requires not only making promises, but also delivering on them every step of the way.

Engagement is to the 21st century what advertising was to the 20th. It's a new field based on a new set of skills that integrate an understanding of leadership; an organization's different audiences; the tactics that can affect engagement (communication, learning, collaboration, rewards and recognition, etc.); and measuring the impact of these activities on the bottom line.

Enterprise Engagement involves many issues foreign to the typical advertising executive. Advertising focuses on selling; engagement requires a willingness to stop selling and instead focus on helping and enabling. This means marketing that informs instead of hypes. Advertisers routinely distort; engagement requires total sincerity, a commitment to fulfilling marketing promises. Few people believe advertising, and yet it continues to thrive; engagement cannot work unless it's 100% sincere, because otherwise people see through it.

Engagement requires an understanding not just of customers, but of the link between all organizational audiences, external and internal. Engagement requires an understanding of the tactics and tools necessary for learning, collaboration, rewards and recognition, all alien to traditional advertising experts. Enterprise Engagement requires the ability to align strategies across organizational and tactical silos so all functions and constituencies mesh with an organization's people and goals.

THE ORGANIZATIONAL CHALLENGE
The emergence of Enterprise Engagement is evidenced by the emergence of new titles that incorporate the concept of engagement, including people in charge of customer engagement or experience, as well as employee engagement. The concept is still so new that organizations aren't quite sure of the skill sets required and are putting people with diverse backgrounds into such positions.

Implementing engagement at any level is a journey, not only because there are no textbooks (until now), but because traditional business consultants, no matter how prestigious, don't provide all the answers. The typical consulting practice is broken up into different silos that reflect those of their clients – benefits, compensation, assessment, organizational design, organizational development, talent management, process management, recruitment, etc. But by focusing on the needs of customers and all of the people required to serve customers, Enterprise Engagement challenges organizations to break the old management style that focuses more on processes than people.

Enterprise Engagement: The Textbook

Chapter 2

Economics of Enterprise Engagement

The research is clear: Engagement provides a long-term competitive advantage. In 2005, a milestone book, *The Enthusiastic Employee: How Companies Profit by Giving Workers What They Want,* by Dr David Sirota made headlines across corporate America. Sirota gathered never-before-published case studies, more than 30 years of employee attitude research, and data from 920,000 employees from 28 multinational companies. This data showed that the share prices of firms with highly engaged employees increased an average of 16% in 2004, compared with an industry average of 6%. Stock prices of companies with high morale outperformed similar companies in the same industries by more than 2½-to-1 during 2004, while the stock prices of companies with low morale lagged behind their industry competitors by almost 5-to-1.

A Towers Perrin study in August 2005 looked at 85,000 people employed in large and midsize companies in 16 countries on four continents. It showed there is a vast reserve of untapped "employee performance potential" that can drive better financial results if companies can successfully tap into this reserve. The study also showed that highly engaged workers believe they contribute more directly to business results than less engaged employees. For instance:

- 84% of highly engaged employees believe they can positively impact the quality of their company's products, compared with 31% of disengaged workers.
- 72% of the highly engaged believe they can positively affect customer service, vs. only 27% of the disengaged.
- 68% of the highly engaged believe they can positively impact costs in their job or unit, vs. just 19% of the disengaged.

Watson Wyatt researchers quantified this relationship by performing an analysis to explain current financial performance (measured as the market premium) as a function of various factors. They found a significant relationship between current financial performance and past engagement, even after controlling for past financial performance, industry and other considerations, to wit: A significant (one standard deviation) increase in the level of past employee engagement is associated with a 1.5% increase in current market premium, all other factors including past market premium constant. For the typical company in the sample with a market value of $14 billion, that represents an increase in market value of 1.7%, or more than $230 million.

Based on more than five years of data involving several million responses, the Federal Government's Office of Personnel Management stated in 2014 that "Employee engagement has been linked to important outcomes, including agency performance, sick leave usage, EEO complaints and turnover. Engaged employees are less likely to leave their agency, while those who are unengaged will likely start to look for opportunities elsewhere."[1]

> **Research has clearly and consistently proved the direct link between employee engagement, customer satisfaction and revenue growth.**
>
> **– Harvard Business Review**

Employee engagement data is today broadly accepted as a leading indicator of actions and behaviors that trigger near-term future financial performance. Thus, applied correctly, engagement data can act as an early warning system, allowing organizations to right the ship before the conditions causing a decline in employee engagement translate into a hit on revenue and profits.

THE EVIDENCE IS MOUNTING

In 2008, the Human Capital Institute and IBM partnered in a global research study into the adoption and impact of Integrated Talent Management practices. In part one of the study, the three-year financial track records (2004-2007) of 287 publicly-traded U.S. companies were examined (a subset of the 1,900 organizations surveyed in the study).

Across the board, those that invested more in talent management performed better financially. However, researchers found that those who were able to do two things in particular – focus on measuring and addressing employee engagement and aligning incentives to business goals – were more likely to outperform other organizations in their industry than by pursuing any other talent management initiatives.

In 2013, The Winters Group published research that demonstrated correlations between inclusion and engagement ranging around .8 amongst many of the organizations they studied.[2] The deliberate act of including employees in decisions and respecting their ideas and opinions counts as another leading driver of engagement and performance.

THE PEOPLE CONNECTION

In 1996, Theresa Welbourne and Alice Andrews published the results of research they had been conducting into the success of start-ups over the previous eight years. They analyzed the five-year survival rates of 136 companies that had made initial public offerings in 1988, finding that companies which emphasized the importance of their people and shared rewards broadly survived at a much higher rate than those that didn't.

Similarly, Bilmes, Struven and Wetzker of the Boston Consulting Group conducted research over an eight-year span to understand the characteristics of top performing companies (48 in Germany and 36 in the U.S.). In every case, each of the high performing companies had unusually progressive policies toward their employees.

In 1999, Stanford Business School professors Michael T. Hannan and James N. Baron published research they had done on the success rates of Silicon Valley start-ups in the

---

[1] *Strategic Plan FY 2014-2018*, U.S. Office of Personnel Management
[2] *The Global D&I Tipping Point: 9 Key Trends in Diversity & Inclusion (2013)*, The Winters Group, Inc.

1990s. In their research, they discovered five models of human resource management (normally driven by the start-up's founder and/or CEO). They labeled them: Star, Commitment, Engineering, Autocracy and Bureaucracy. The Star model centers on recruitment – get the best people "on the bus" and they'll take you where you need to go. The Commitment model emphasizes engagement and a family-like work environment characterized by caring and trust. The Engineering model emphasizes performance, challenging work, self-motivation and teamwork. The Autocracy model emphasizes top-down command and control, and the Bureaucracy model emphasizes process, procedure and rigor.

Hannan & Baron found that the Commitment model resulted in start-ups that were most likely/fastest to go public. All other things being equal, the Commitment firms were also significantly less likely to fail. And while Star firms have the largest post-IPO increases in market cap, they're followed closely by Commitment firms. Not surprisingly, Autocracy firms perform the worst, followed by firms without a clear model.

FUNDAMENTAL CONDITIONS
There are some fundamental conditions that must be in place in order to make employee engagement possible. Whether the engagement diagnostic is from Gallup, Towers Perrin or other sources, questions about the quality of the employee's relationship with the organization, supervisors and colleagues are invariably included. From its 2008 global engagement study of 90,000+ workers worldwide, Towers Perrin concluded that, while the impact of the immediate boss on employee engagement is large, the top single driver of discretionary effort is "senior management's sincere interest in employee well being." In other words, does senior management consistently demonstrate that it truly cares about front-line employees? The Great Place to Work Institute (GPTWI), a San Francisco-based organization that produces *Fortune* magazine's "100 Best places To Work" list each year, boils this down to the following:

...a great workplace is measured by the quality of three, interconnected relationships that exist there:
- The relationship between employees and management
- The relationship between employees and their jobs/company
- The relationship between employees and other employees.

In determining who makes *Fortune*'s annual 100 Best Places to Work list, GPTWI surveys at least 400 individuals from every company nominated each year. The employees rate the organization on elements of trust and workplace relationships, and their assessments lead to the final selection of the top 100.

Since 1998, the first year of the *Fortune* 100 Best Places to Work List, the publicly-traded organizations on the list have significantly outperformed the average S&P 500 company and the Russell 3000 index. Indeed, if an investor bought stock only in companies that made the top 100 list from 1998 to 2006, his investment would have been worth more than double an identical investment in the S&P 500 or Russell 3000 companies.

Employee engagement in the top 100 companies is high, leading to better performance, sales and customer retention. But it's also reflected in turnover data. Over an eight year period, turnover in GPTWI Top 100 companies is much lower than the industry average across a range of sectors. Given the enormous cost of turnover, this is another of the key reasons for better financial performance among the top 100 organizations on *Fortune*'s annual list.

THE COSTCO ADVANTAGE

As in the GPTWI example above, the fundamentals are pretty basic. Organizations that can establish trust between the workforce and management, and between co-workers, stand to gain an engaged workforce and the benefits that go along with it. But how does one build that trust? In large part, trust is established by treating employees well and consistently through good times and bad.

In the big-box retail sector, competition is fierce and margins are thin, yet Costco Co-founder and former CEO Jim Sinegal bucked the low-wage, high-turnover approach to the workforce several years ago and showed that it pays off in numerous ways. At Costco, employees have learned to trust that the following will be true (as of 2010) regardless of the business cycle:

- At least $10/hour starting wage (avg. $17/hour – 42% more than Wal-Mart)
- After 4 years, cashiers earn roughly $44,000, including bonuses
- 94% of healthcare costs are covered by Costco
- Generous & compassionate family leave policies
- CEO pay is 10 times that of the average employee vs. a national average of 531 times.

The results are eye-popping:
- 23% turnover vs. 66.1% industry average
- 7% labor costs vs. industry average of about 16%
- Sales (2003 through Aug.) on 312 U.S. stores: $34.4 B vs. Sam's Club $32.9 B with 532 U.S. stores, as well as higher productivity and higher profitability
- On average, Costco stores generate nearly double the revenue of Sam's Club stores ($112 million vs. $63 million) and more per sq. ft.
- Reduced employee theft: 0.2% vs. an industry average of 2%.

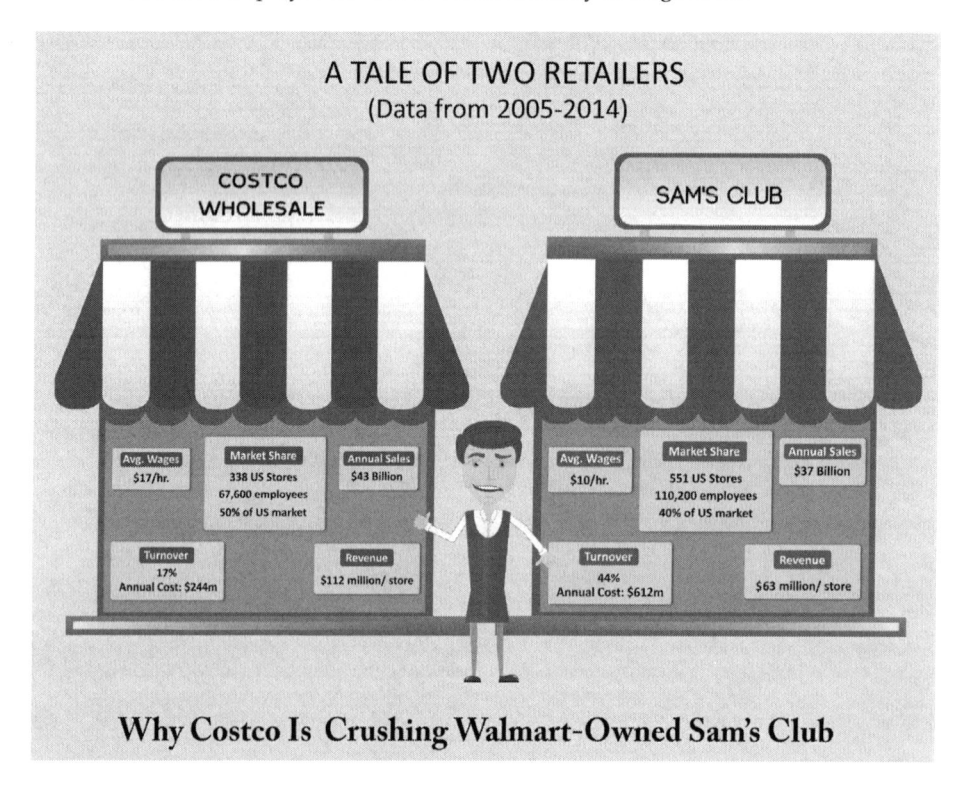

A TALE OF TWO RETAILERS
(Data from 2005-2014)

	COSTCO WHOLESALE	SAM'S CLUB
Avg. Wages	$17/hr.	$10/hr.
Market Share	338 US Stores, 67,600 employees, 50% of US market	551 US Stores, 110,200 employees, 40% of US market
Annual Sales	$43 Billion	$37 Billion
Turnover	17% Annual Cost: $244m	44% Annual Cost: $612m
Revenue	$112 million/ store	$63 million/ store

Why Costco Is Crushing Walmart-Owned Sam's Club

As Patricia Edwards, Managing Director of Wentworth Hauser and Violich (a San Francisco investment firm that owns 785,000 shares of Costco) says, "These guys have bucked Wall Street as far as taking care of their employees, yet their return last year was pretty darn good." Indeed, in 2003, Costco's sales topped sales at Sam's Club by 21%, even though Sam's had 28% more stores. Costco stock was up 34% for calendar 2004; Wal-Mart's stayed about even.

RETURN ON ENGAGEMENT

Much evidence exists that demonstrates the importance of employee engagement to the success of modern organizations. The examples above are just a few of a vast and growing body of case studies and research that make the point convincingly and consistently across all industries and countries. But engagement-related initiatives need to be all-encompassing – and they aren't cheap.

The initial capital outlay to begin pursuing such initiatives may be modest, but to change or improve an organization's culture so employees better trust their leaders, so that leaders are instilled with a talent mindset and commit themselves to the daily practices of coaching, rewarding, managing performance and talent planning, requires patience, perseverance and investment of both time and money.

As such, convincing senior leaders in an organization to make engagement a priority is sometimes difficult. Those in charge of planning and implementing an Enterprise Engagement strategy must demonstrate the expected Return on Investment (ROI) in a convincing and credible manner. Fortunately, tools and expertise are available to make the business case for engagement using bottom-line language that CEOs and CFOs understand. Here are some examples of how firms are measuring "Return on Engagement."

> **By enabling employees to see the implications of their actions, it changed the way everyone at Sears thought and acted. The bottom line reflected this changed behavior. The merchandising group, for example, went from a loss of nearly $3 billion in 1992 to a net income of $752 million in 1993.**
>
> **– Harvard Business Review**

SEARS

Though the organization has faltered in recent years, Sears was a trailblazer in measuring Return on Engagement. During the recession of the early 1990s, Sears – at that time the world's largest retailer – was losing billions of dollars a year. But losses didn't make the company unique. Competitors, as well as firms in almost every other industry, were also suffering from the recession, and mass layoffs were the order of the day. Despite such losses, Sears chose not to downsize. Instead, executives decided to invest more in their workforce, particularly in measures aimed at employee engagement. Sears hypothesized that better employee engagement would lead to better customer engagement, leading to more sales, revenue and profits. The result:

On the face of it, Sears' dramatic financial turnaround correlates strongly with their employee engagement initiatives. But Sears went much further. In fact, they came as close to proving the link between employee engagement, customer satisfaction/engagement and profits as any study before or since.

Within two years of the launch of the program, Sears was able to use employee engagement data as an almost perfect "leading indicator" of financial performance in its stores. For example, a store manager whose engagement scores increased by 5 units could expect a 1.3 unit increase in customer impression (satisfaction), followed by a .5% increase in revenue growth.

The work done at Sears has led to similar use and refinements of their toolset in other organizations and became a precursor to research done by Gallup more than a decade later. In HR circles, Gallup is best known for its "Q12" employee engagement diagnostic. Derived from millions of interviews and extensive data sets, Gallup researchers have boiled the measurement of employee engagement down to just 12 questions. The Q12 is likely the most utilized index of its kind in the world.

More recently, Gallup introduced a new tool, the "CE11," designed to test customer engagement. Taken together, the Q12 and the CE11 form the basis for what Gallup researchers call "Human Sigma," a measurement of the employee/customer encounter and the subject of a 2007 book by the same name, authored by Gallup researchers John H. Fleming and Jim Apslund.

On page 35, the authors state: "In our own research, we have observed that building a critical mass of engaged employees contributes significantly to the bottom line. In a recent study of 89 companies, we found that the companies that build this critical mass of engagement grew earnings per share (EPS) at 2.6 times the rate of companies who do not."[7]

Gallup research has regularly added to the evidence linking employee engagement to organizational performance, revenue and profits. Its most recent work provides evidence of the importance of customer engagement and the link between the two types of engagement.

Gallup has shown that "rationally satisfied" customers – those that have no or few complaints – behave no differently toward their providers than dissatisfied customers. Even if a company satisfies a customer with good pricing, quality on-time delivery, etc., he or she is no more likely to reward them with loyalty or increased business than a customer who feels let down and disappointed.

On the other hand, Gallup's research points out that "emotionally engaged" customers aren't only more loyal and spend more, they're far more tolerant of mistakes and minor disappointments than either dissatisfied or rationally satisfied customers.

Each of the 10 companies and 1,979 business units Gallup studied as part of its initial Human Sigma research undertook initiatives to strengthen the employee/customer encounter. The result? These companies outperformed their five largest competitors in 2003 by 26% in gross margin and 85% in sales. Again, Gallup found that in order for companies to realize outstanding financial benefits, they had to be better than average in *both* employee and customer engagement.

Gallup's Fleming and Apslund argue that engagement, whether employee or customer, is highly local. In other words, variation from store to store (in the case of a retailer, for example) is such that an employer might be a "Best Place to Work" in Phoenix and a miserable employer in Boston. Customers might be engaged and loyal in Denver but fleeing in droves in Chicago. Not surprisingly, they argue that both forms of engagement must be locally driven and managers held accountable at the most local levels possible.

Gallup has introduced a formula to calculate what it calls an organization's "Human Sigma" (HS) score. The formula takes each business unit's mean scores on the G12 and CE11 and turns them into percentages. Gallup then uses the results to place their clients in one of six HS bands. At the higher ends, HS5 and HS6, business units within organizations have managed to optimize employee engagement and customer engagement, leading to "financial results that are about 3.5 times as good as HS1 and HS2 unit's results."

With Human Sigma, Gallup has shed more light on the critical links between employee and customer engagement, demonstrating that initiatives designed only to drive high employee engagement can be too inwardly focused; despite happy employees, they can still fail to engage customers. On the other hand, organizations that focus only on their customers may succeed temporarily, but the results won't be sustainable unless employees are also engaged.

CENTER FOR TALENT SOLUTIONS
The Center for Talent Solutions (formerly the Center for Talent Retention) has added to the quantification of engagement in a different and equally important manner. For most of the past decade, CTS has been working with firms around the world to increase the engagement levels of their employees. In this time it has amassed a lot of valuable data on the measures of engagement and, more importantly, the costs versus the benefits of improved employee engagement.

Over the years, CTS has found that employees it terms "fully engaged" deliver, on average, 22% better performance than so-called "normally engaged" employees. Employees who are "somewhat engaged" are, on average, only about 75% as productive as normally engaged employees, and those it terms "disengaged employees" perform at only about half the value of normally engaged employees.

As an illustration, let's look at an organization before specific engagement-related activities are undertaken. In this case, let's say 10% of the company's employees are fully engaged and 65% are normally engaged, leaving 20% only somewhat engaged and 5% disengaged.

Based on this organization's performance management data, fully engaged workers are estimated to deliver 25% higher levels of productivity than engaged workers. The somewhat engaged and disengaged are at minus 25% and minus 50%, respectively. CTS estimates that this organization is losing over $112 million annually due to its less-than-engaged workers.

The organization's next step was to determine specific actions that would lead to better engagement. An employee questionnaire was used to better understand where solutions and/or improvements were most necessary.

Based on this information, the organization then undertook the actions, assigning clear responsibility and scheduling weekly meetings to discuss the actions taken and outcomes to date. Managers were held accountable and were expected to have something to report at weekly meetings.

Within seven months, the size of the fully engaged group doubled to 20%, the normally engaged group grew from 65% to 70%, the somewhat engaged were reduced by 50% (to 10%) and the disengaged were eliminated entirely. As a result, the organization was able to turn its $112 million loss into a $56 million gain.

Intuitively, good managers have understood the Return on Engagement for decades. More recently, research that quantifies those returns has been available to leaders and managers. Today, valid tools exist to measure and predict the ROI in engagement related initiatives. Yet, as Gallup and others point out in their studies year after year,

> **Research has shown that engaged employees are more productive employees. Research also proves that engaged employees are more profitable, more customer-focused, safer and more likely to with-stand temptations to leave. Many have long suspected the connection between an employee's level of engagement and the level and quality of his or her performance. Our research has laid the matter to rest.**
>
> **– Gallup, 2009**

the American workforce remains a place where less than one-third of employees can be truly described as "engaged."

SUMMARY

The cost of disengagement is enormous – hundreds of billions of dollars are lost in the U.S. economy alone each year. So why don't more organizations do something about it – particularly now, when every dollar counts?

Employee engagement and customer engagement are both driven by the fundamentals in organizations. For both levels to be high and stay high, an organization needs a solid culture and value system that supports the ingredients necessary for engagement. Senior leaders have to drive the process, "walk the walk" to demonstrate their commitment to engagement. Managers must be selected and developed with employee (and customer) engagement in mind, and they need to be held accountable through a total rewards and performance management strategy that aligns their desired behaviors, goals and outcomes with those of the organization. Most importantly, employees must be made partners in the effort.

In most organizations, both the challenges of engagement and the remedies to improve it are daunting. But the payoff is enormous, and beyond the bottom line it's clear that in the near future an engaged workforce will be a necessity for survival. Ask yourself: Who would continue to drag themselves into work every day for a paycheck when they can have the paycheck *and* be highly engaged in their work at the same time.

One key reason many organizations may overlook engagement as a strategic management tool is because it takes time to deliver results. The Enterprise Engagement Alliance Good Company Stock Index has found that organizations with low engagement can outperform their competitors in the stock market for up to a three-year time frame, after which companies with high engagement have the advantage.

Enterprise Engagement: The Textbook

Chapter 3

Culture and the Enterprise Brand

By Dr. Kathie Sorensen

Why is culture so critical to organizations and their brand proposition? What is the best way to understand it, measure it and manage it to a sustainable competitive advantage?

Creating the right strategy garners a huge amount of organizational attention because it represents the best set of assumptions, expectations and plans we can create to guide our decision-making and business development. It's the rational description of how we'll go about growing our business. This approach creates an "enterprise brand" that addresses every audience.

The translation of strategy into goals, steps and actions further adds to the highly rational way in which we approach the achievement of our goals. The process is orderly and effective…until we get around to executing those goals.

PEOPLE ARE MESSY
Research suggests that only about 14% of goals we set actually achieve the desired outcome. Why? Because the rational plans we make are implemented by human beings, and people are messy.

The gap between our painstakingly crafted goals and our desired performance outcomes is the province of culture, and the brand organizations use to encapsulate it. The people are the culture and, as a result, culture is highly emotional. Organizational culture delivers the human energy available to power our goals and must be evaluated in the context of the organization's primary performance outcome – sustainable growth.

Our organizational interests aren't well serviced by describing all cultures, but rather by understanding the factors that create high performance culture – i.e., cultures that drive sustainable growth by fulfilling the expectations of the brand. High performance cultures are best understood in three levels: MicroCulture, MacroCulture and BridgeCulture. Of these, MicroCulture is the most critical, because that's where human energy is applied to goals.

MICROCULTURE
To understand MicroCulture, you have to understand its inherently personal nature. Have you ever experienced a moment – a place in time – you wished you could bottle up and preserve for the future? In that instance, the world around you conspired to bring out the best in who you are and what you were working to achieve. Some people refer to it as being "in the zone."

If we're fortunate, those moments happen frequently enough that we come to expect them from our workplace. That's what great culture feels like to the "actively engaged" people within it – a place that brings out the best in them. Research suggests that 42% of people are actively engaged at work. Day to day, these individuals believe their opinions count, their talents are well utilized and their team members and manager trust and support them.

In contrast, what about those moments when we mutter to ourselves "beam me up, Scotty"? We don't care to where; we just want to be lifted out of the spiralling pit of despair. These are usually the 35% of people who feel "actively disengaged" at work. They're stuck in a cycle that diminishes their sense of value and worth, curtails their development and disconnects them from the people they need the most (their team members, customers and manager).

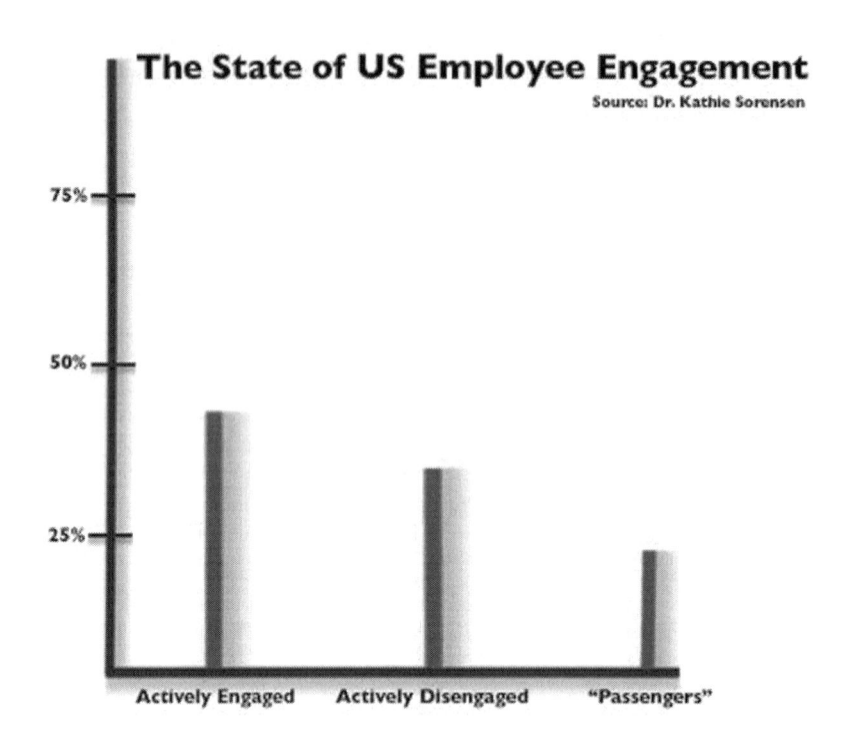

The State of US Employee Engagement
Source: Dr. Kathie Sorensen

[Bar chart showing: Actively Engaged (~42%), Actively Disengaged (~35%), "Passengers" (~23%)]

Perhaps you're stuck in the middle of this cultural continuum, on the balancing board between terrible and great, afraid to move. We refer to this group of employees as "passengers" – people along for the ride. And in the U.S., this describes about 23% of employees at work.

Culture is personal. Its pull on us is directly dependent upon our desire to belong. If we don't care, it doesn't matter. So to measure an organizational culture's vitality, we must measure the MicroCulture from the perspective of each individual. The quality of the immediate work unit has the greatest influence, because that's how people connect and where they focus their energy at work.

When people are Actively Engaged at work, they're working at approximately 82% of capacity, compared to Passengers (65% of capacity) and the Actively Disengaged, who are working at only 27% of capacity.

MACROCULTURE
High performance MicroCultures maximizes the productive energy available for work in the overall organization – what we call MacroCulture. For that energy to be productive to the organization, it must in one way or another support the organization's brand proposition and related business objectives.

Because of the "strategy gap" and growing pressure to produce, leaders are increasingly concerned about the overall culture of their organization and its alignment to their brand promise. This concern most often translates into actions to clarify vision and values. Unfortunately, about 75% of organizations share the same values (integrity, service, respect), but their cultures are completely unique.

The MacroCulture of an organization isn't one single thing. It's more like a force in motion, constantly evolving, whether we intend it or not. Without our deliberate and intentional focus, our cultures drift with the prevailing currents. And these movements can damage the integrity of the culture overall and its connection to the brand.

In the U.S. today we're seeing organizational MacroCultures splitting into two dominant camps, which we earlier referred to as the Actively Engaged and the Actively Disengaged. As people become more polarized in their attitudes about work, the normal curve is being replaced by a "well curve" so named because the central tendency has been depleted and people are being forced to the sides.

The most vivid example of the well curve of MacroCulture is the American political scene, where the so-called "Red" and "Blue" states have dominated decision-making long after the terms have gone into disuse. Most Americans acknowledge the political split that forces people into camps of "us and them" on almost every decision point. Each side relies on its own experts and estimates and eschews the other side's data. Compromise isn't based on merit, but around trading "my X for your Y."

This cultural fracture creates more problems than it solves, and the same is true for the fracturing of organizational culture. Yet leaders seldom recognize the fracturing of their organizational culture because of the way in which culture has been measured and described.

The tendency to rely upon averages to describe the complexity of organizational culture is problematic. Consider an organization with an "average" engagement score, according to a national benchmark. This means that about half of the companies in the U.S. have better average engagement and half have worse engagement, as reported by their employees. Given this, most executive teams would be prepared to make plans to address the overall organization.

However, looking closer at the distribution tells a completely different story – one of both excellence and failure. Inside the "average" culture (or MacroCulture) in one organization, we found MicroCultures operating at the 90th percentile and above and MicroCultures that were functioning at the 10th percentile and below. Executive action in such a case should be distinctly different for the high performing MicroCultures versus those in a chronic 911 (desperate and disillusioned) state.

That's the second lesson in developing a high performance culture: you can't describe MacroCulture via averages; it obscures the glimmers of excellence within. And leaders can't force a MacroCulture by driving it from the top – they can only identify and encourage the strengths already present within it.

BRIDGECULTURE

There are three critical snapshots for understanding the elements of high performance culture. We've discussed the elements of healthy MicroCultures and the thematic movement of the MacroCulture, but high performance culture depends on the effectiveness of the bridge between the two.

> **Helping each person have a strong line-of-sight to the customer means that every person and team understands how what they do attracts and retains customers.**

The BridgeCulture is the connective tissue between the MicroCultures where people work and the MacroCulture where vision and strategy are defined. The most effective bridges connect people to the brand proposition, the values it reflects, and a specific purpose. They link and direct the energy that people bring to work in a way that maximizes line-of-sight with the customer and fulfillment of the brand promise. This, in turn, creates sustainable growth.

The most significant element in BridgeCulture effectiveness is the manager, whose efforts provide the catalyst for healthy MicroCultures and the connection that these people have to vision and strategy and the customer and brand. The best managers reduce internal, procedural barriers that create frustration and inefficiencies and encourage action and partnership in the interest of the real outcomes desired. Helping each person have a strong line-of-sight to the customer means that every person and team understands how what they do attracts and retains customers.

THE NEXUS POINT

Organizational culture is a collision between rational goals, procedures and expectations and the people who are responsible for carrying them out through the delivery of the brand promise. Bringing human energy into focus is the nexus point that delivers competitive advantage.

Cultures are as unique as the people within them. But high performance Micro, Macro and Bridge Cultures engage people in the following ways:

- They are successful. People have work they feel is meaningful and that "fits" their talents and abilities.
- They belong. People feel connected to one another, supported and understood by their managers.
- They are customer-focused and empowered to act. People see a clear line-of-sight to the customer and the brand promise and how what they do helps their organization acquire and keep customers.
- They have "servant" managers. Managers see their role in helping each person develop, become more productive and make decisions in the interests of the customer and company.
- They are relentlessly interested in their people. Leaders focus on the inherent strengths of their people and find ways to draw out the best within.

Organizational culture is energy in motion. It needs to fuel organizational goals and objectives and must be judiciously assessed in relationship with its desired outcomes.

MicroCulture must be addressed first, because people connect to the larger enterprise through the people and managers with whom they work.

Secondly, the MacroCulture must inspire confidence and resonate with the brand.

Third, the Bridge Culture offers the final piece of the cultural puzzle; the Nexus point that connects human energy to the priorities of the business and delivers the brand promise.

Enterprise Engagement: The Textbook

Chapter 4

Breaking Down Organizational Silos

By Susan Forgie

Every organization, no matter how forward-looking it believes itself to be, has silos. It's a business paradox that can stop real change in its tracks if not recognized and given proper consideration in any plans that affect the enterprise.

Taking that first step to break down silos is often the hardest because they are not always readily evident. After all, silos have a purpose, which is why they exist in the first place. There are the obvious departmental silos such as Human Resources and Legal. These sections of an organization have very specific job functions that can be unlike others. The sharing of information isn't only unnecessary in some cases, but prohibitive as well. Having this type of information restraints can be considered a silo. But for the sake of this chapter, the silos we're referring to are the people of cross-functional departments that have a need and/or desire for joint partnership to meet objectives or realize success on various initiatives.

Altering a company's core DNA to become more customer-focused sounds like a no-brainer. Many would say this has always been the case. But let's look at it from another point of view. At your company, is the customer experience just as important as the sale or the product? Does your Customer Service or Technical Support department get the same amount of "air time" as Sales or Engineering? Is the success of one interdependent on the other? Intuitively, you may believe that it is, but if your company has built up multiple silos over the years, it would be very difficult to understand why or how.

There are five basic steps that can prove successful in breaking down such silos:

1. First, do your homework. Talk to people. Understand their struggles and their successes. Learn their business objectives; they're likely very similar to your own. By showing a genuine interest in what's important to them, you're investing in them and, more importantly, building a relationship.
2. Look for what's already there. Is there something you already know or have discovered in these "interviews" that will help another department with a challenge they're facing? Be the catalyst in bringing them together.

3. If you've managed to loosen the foundation of the silo by building these relationships, don't leave it alone. Stay visible and relevant by communicating often.
4. Attention to detail is important. Credibility is essential to keeping a silo from being resurrected. If you don't know or understand the facts, find out or get help.
5. Show them how it will help them. Just telling someone how important something is usually isn't enough. For businesses, it's often about the money, but not always. Whatever it is, show them the benefits of tearing down the silo and letting you in.

BUILDING TRUST
If there's one thing above all else that's required to start breaking down organizational silos, it's building a relationship. The trust that comes with a strong relationship is what allows you to have a voice in a world where you may not have the expertise or experience specific to that department or function.

You don't have to be a coder or electrical engineer or talk "geek" to have a business relationship with Engineering. You have to have trust. But as with every relationship, trust is hard to earn – and even harder to keep. It's true that trust can build over the years, but if you don't have years to cultivate the relationship to that level, there are other ways to weaken the walls of the silo and to keep that relationship strong.

BECOME AN INFORMATION BROKER
We've all likely heard someone talk of the "quick win" or the "low-hanging fruit" that offers a quick and easy solution or is easy to implement. Now take that idea and grow it. All of the low-hanging fruit that's plucked at the right time will make up a bountiful harvest.

Do the same within your organization. Look for information that would be helpful to another part of the company. And don't limit yourself to finding a problem with a solution that can be implemented or a process that can be changed. Information is just as powerful and can help someone else come up with that improvement opportunity. By sharing any and all information that's germane, you're contributing to the relationship with that department.

MAKE SURE IT'S RELEVANT
Another part of building a solid relationship is communication. Silos weaken with intentional focus, but neglect will allow them to fortify, and you may find yourself starting from square one again.

Communicating at regular intervals will help strengthen the relationship, as long as it's relevant. Relevance is critical to the success or failure of your communication strategy. Sending out trivial information is more likely to hurt the relationship than if you hadn't sent anything at all. Pertinent information should be shared as often as necessary, but don't waste people's time. Uninformative and unsolicited meetings, phone calls, or emails are just as annoying as telemarketing calls while you're having dinner.

A critical piece of your communication strategy is to ensure your information, insights, and feedback are accurate and fact-based. Having the type of relationship that ensures silos stay down requires making sure your attention to detail is always evident. Making careless mistakes can damage the relationship and the trust you've earned. That's not to say that an honest mistake will void what's been built up, but your creditability may be at stake if it happens too often. One way to help circumvent mistakes is to ensure you have a clear understanding of the information you're providing.

REINFORCE THROUGH VALUE
Now that you've begun to replace the framework of the silo with a solid relationship-based foundation, it's time to seal the deal, so to speak. By this time you should have a good understanding of what's important to a particular functional group or department. Make it a priority to understand what you bring to the table and how it will benefit them. Be concrete and realistic. Show them the impact to them.

Maybe it's sales leads; maybe it's insights into a potential marketing campaign; a customer profile on your website usage. Whatever it is, deliver it in a way that enables your audience to draw a specific conclusion. You shouldn't have to lead this horse to water; it should be thirsty enough to go there on its own.

BUILDING A NEW FOUNDATION
Remember that a silo is a protective barrier, and in business it's the people in a department or functional group that comprise that barrier. It's effective for those that are in the silo, and thus resistance to breaking the silo down is something that you'll have to take into account.

> **Remember that a silo is a protective barrier, and in business it's the people in a department or functional group that comprise that barrier.**

By showing interest and being an active participant in their business, you can start to break the silo down. Through relative and timely communication, you'll continue to chip away at the walls. It won't happen overnight, and it won't happen with every person that makes up the silo. Like a wrecking ball tearing down a building, making strategic strikes to the walls will bring the entire building down over time.

Building a new relationship in its place is just as important. By ensuring your information is meaningful and accurate, you build the trust that will help cement the relationship. Showing the value or benefits of the relationship will strengthen that bond.

Going back to our earlier statement about the importance of customer experience at your company, we can start to answer those questions posed if you have clear line of sight into what's important to another department and what are part of those success measurements. With the silos down and relationships built up in their place, when change is needed it'll be a joint effort. The benefit of the relationship is two-way. You have more people working with you, and the chances of success are much greater.

Enterprise Engagement: The Textbook

Chapter 5

Case Study: Hampton Hotels

Dictionary.com defines corporate culture as "the distinctive ethos of an organization that influences the level of formality, loyalty and general behavior of its employees."

This definition probably doesn't come as a surprise. After all, "corporate culture" is a common phrase these days. Yet, corporate culture isn't completely understood in the business world. Just ask the more than 54% of employees who have felt frustrated at work or the 40% who say they don't get a company's vision or have never seen it.

But there is hope. Many organizations are doing culture right, such as Hampton Hotels, a brand that has knocked down its walls to unleash its culture – both internally and externally.

ORGANIC AND INTERNAL
You may have heard the term "Hamptonality" or seen it used as a tagline in the brand's television commercials and print ads. What makes Hampton different from many other brands is that this isn't a catchy term dreamt up by a team of ad execs and tacked onto a campaign. It's the organic internal culture of Hampton blossoming into its external campaign. Hamptonality is truly the essence of the Hampton brand; it's the spirit and authentic personalities of the 60,000 employees (known throughout the company as Team Members) who work in Hampton hotels in 16 countries worldwide.

So, what exactly is Hamptonality? "Hamptonality is the manifestation of where hospitality meets unique personalities," says Gina Valenti, Vice President of Owner Services and Hampton Brand Culture and Internal Communications for Hilton Worldwide. "It isn't a tagline. This is our culture being turned inside-out." Hamptonality is a classic example of an "enterprise brand" that touches the entire organization, internally and externally.

> **Hamptonality is a classic example of an "enterprise brand" that touches the entire organization, internally and externally.**

A CONSISTENT EXPERIENCE
With tens of thousands of Team Members serving guests around the world, Hamptonality unifies and connects hotels from state to state and continent to continent. It's Hamptonality that ensures the

consistent experience Hampton guests expect – no matter if they check into a hotel in West Berlin, Germany or Atlanta, Georgia.

There's a twist in the story, however. Hampton is 99% franchised – so hotel Team Members aren't Hampton employees. Any efforts to engage Team Members and inspire culture in hotels must be accomplished through positive influence of the owners/operators and general managers who formally manage individual properties. No mandates or edicts from Corporate.

So how exactly do Valenti and her team inspire Hamptonality across more than 2,000 hotels in 16 countries and territories? The answer is in encouraging individual strengths and personalities to shine.

"Ultimately, the job we get paid to do is to build more hotels. The best way to do that is to have loyal owners who continue to invest in our brand and our sister brands at Hilton Worldwide," says Valenti. "To keep our owners loyal, we have to have loyal guests who keep our hotels full. Creating memorable, Hamptonality-filled experiences that inspire our guests to return and recommend us to others is where Hamptonality and culture directly impact the bottom line."

STRENGTHS-BASED CULTURE
In 2006, the brand began promoting a strengths-based culture, thanks to direction from The Marcus Buckingham Company. Together with Root Learning, they developed a series of 45- to 60-minute eLearning modules based on Marcus Buckingham's "Simply Strengths" concepts. The learning modules helped Hampton Team Members to identify personal strengths and apply them so they can be more productive and fulfilled.

As individuals identify their competitive edge, they realize what makes them unique and what makes them shine. Then they bring that to their role at work – whether they're in housekeeping, at the front desk, etc. The result is a hotel full of engaged Team Members who exhibit the Hampton values – Friendly, Authentic, Caring, and Thoughtful – in every interaction with guests.

And Hampton doesn't stop there. The activities are varied, and the suite of tools is expansive. From songs and videos (with Team Members literally leaping over front desks) to engaging eLearning programs and tangible Root Strategic Learning Map modules, Hampton teaches and communicates with Team Members in ways that work for this on-the-go group. It's not about being kitschy or fancy; it's about developing and delivering consumable, effective tools that resonate with Hampton's busy, multi-tasking Team Members.

RESULTS AND REWARDS
Hampton's intentional and dedicated focus on culture and people works, as evidenced by numerous awards and accolades. Hampton has been recognized by *Entrepreneur* magazine as the number one franchise for four of the last five years, and the brand was honored at the J.D. Power and Associates Customer Service Roundtable as a 2012 Customer Service Champion. Need more proof? 70% of new Hampton franchise deals come from existing owners.

Strong, successful company cultures exist beyond the storied walls of Google, Southwest Airlines and Zappos. Yes, it takes time and energy to execute. Yes, it must be a mindset that lives at the top and is embraced all the way through. But it's worth it. Culture helps business bloom and makes employees feel valued, inspired, and energized. Culture differentiates your brand and connects it to performance.

Part II
Audiences of Engagement

Enterprise Engagement: The Textbook

Intro: The Audience Challenge

The emergence of any new business field challenges old ways of thinking. One of the greatest obstacles to Enterprise Engagement is the traditional way that organizations view their audiences.

In the traditional world of "process-oriented" management, audiences are put into separate buckets, each one managed and treated quite differently from audiences in other buckets. In the world of Enterprise Engagement – in which all actions are aligned toward identifying customer or community needs and the best ways to meet them to the benefit of all – audiences are viewed as part of an organization's overall community linked by common goals, values and principles.

The traditional organization creates a wide management gulf between customers and distribution partners on the one hand, and sales and other employees on the other, each often managed by its own executives, management team and staff whose main aim is to focus on the needs of their own particular audience. This is most apparent in traditional marketing, where the brand proposition almost always focuses on a promise to the customer, not to the organization's entire community.

The Enterprise Engagement Audience

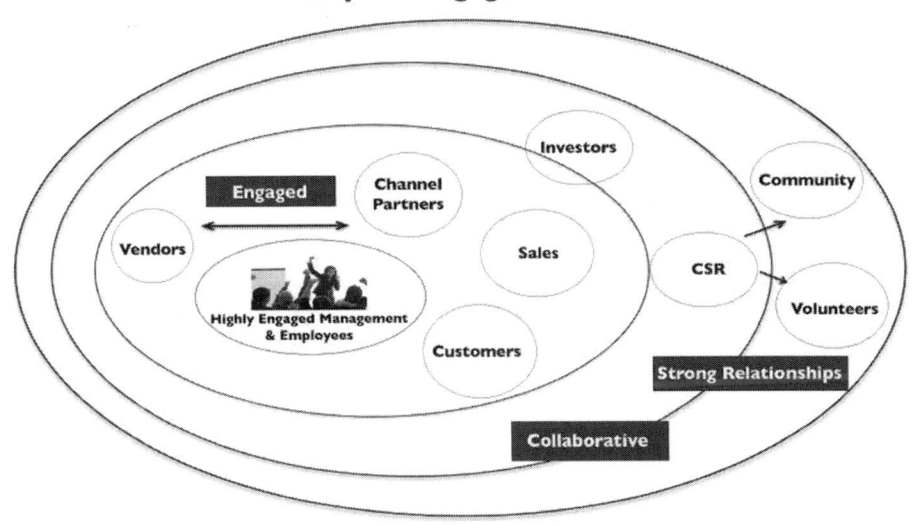

Research related to Enterprise Engagement has identified a fundamental link between an organization's different communities that often is overlooked at many organizations. Enterprise Engagement seeks to profit by aligning the interests of all of an organization's constituents under a similar vision, values and goals in order to increase chances that expectations are consistently met.

A key takeaway from the following section is to understand the interrelationships between audiences. The goal isn't to make anyone an expert on the finer points of engaging all of these audiences, as one could easily build an entire career as a specialist in any single audience, external or internal. And, generally speaking, organizations will continue to require experts to engage specific audiences. The objective is to help those who deal with customers, distribution partners, sales, operations, human resources and finance better understand how their audiences interrelate with others, and how they can adjust their strategies accordingly with better effect.

Ideally, organizations start by creating an "enterprise brand" (see Chapter 3) that applies to all of their audiences, not just customers, developing strategies that cascade from there by putting in place leadership coaching, communications and rewards strategies and other tactics that reinforce the brand proposition and business objectives.

In the meantime, department heads and managers at the front lines can apply these principles to formulating their own plans related to specific loyalty, distributor engagement, sales force or other employees objectives, no matter how siloed their organization might currently be. In developing any type of traditional initiative to achieve a specific goal over time, it pays to identify exterior circumstances, such as the influence of the shipping department, customer service team, manufacturing, production, etc., whose people can have as much impact on revenues as salespeople.

Enterprise Engagement: The Textbook

Chapter 6

Customer Engagement

Most organizations in the United States – even if they haven't considered their broader stakeholders, such as vendors, channel partners, volunteers and the community itself – utilize at least some components of customer and employee engagement. The great majority, however, approach their employee and customer engagement strategies haphazardly and piecemeal. Inconsistent application of initiatives intended to drive customer engagement are combined with multiple accountabilities throughout the organization. The only result can be inconsistent experiences among customers and a negative impact on the brand.

The theme of this chapter is consistent with the theme of the book. Enterprise Engagement must be a deliberate, cross-departmental exercise that recognizes the direct and dependent relationships between customer, employee, vendor and partner engagement, extending to volunteers, investors, regulators and the broader community.

The specific focus of this chapter is customer engagement, yet you must engage your employees – particularly those who touch customers most – before you can engage customers. And customers must become engaged in order for employees to avoid the negative experiences with them that may lead to their own disengagement. It's a dependent, symbiotic relationship that must be managed holistically, so that employees become more engaged and, in turn, customers enjoy better relationships with them, becoming more engaged themselves.

A CULTURE OF ENGAGEMENT
Customer Engagement is dependent – like the engagement of any stakeholder – on whether a culture of engagement exists in your organization. Everyone has to be responsible for engaging customers. For that to occur, it has to be embedded in your values and culture so that it comes as naturally as breathing.

Clearly, this level of customer engagement is impossible to reach in the absence of employee engagement, and easier to reach the broader your engagement strategy, (i.e., to include vendors, channel partners and other key stakeholders).

Customer engagement occurs when customers become fans – willing and even eager to refer their family, friends and colleagues to you. Only when a customer is emotionally engaged will they spend even a very small amount of their unpaid time promoting a commercial brand – think Harley Davidson, Apple, many colleges and universities, even certain banks and airlines. There's a place beyond the point where customers simply say yes to your product or service and become "Raving Fans."

> **Gallup studied organizations across various industries. What they found was that even when a customer is rationally satisfied – where price, quality and on-time delivery are all good – they're no more likely to stay with the company than a customer who is unsatisfied.**

The benefit of reaching this level of connection with customers is profound. In their 2007 book, *Human Sigma*, Gallup studied organizations across various industries. What they found was that when a customer is rationally satisfied – i.e., against price, quality, delivery, etc. – they're no more likely to stay or spend more money with a company than is a customer who is dissatisfied.

However, when a customer becomes emotionally engaged, they're tremendously more likely to be retained and to spend more[1].

Merely satisfying your customers is an old-world proposition; today you must engage them at an emotional level to gain their loyalty and a greater share of their spending. Indeed, it's not a stretch to say that customer connections today are built on emotion, not reason. You must connect with customers at a level that taps their feelings.

As Gallup advised in *Human Sigma*, your company probably isn't what you think it is; it's what your *customers feel it is*. Remember that 60% to 80% of customers who defect to a competitor say they're satisfied or very satisfied on the survey just prior to their defection.[2] It shouldn't surprise you that your customers are often irrational. All of us, except perhaps extreme sociopaths and psychopaths, make irrational decisions more frequently than we do rational ones.[3] We act based on how we feel; it's what defines us as humans. Accept this and you're on your way to better customer relationships, connections and engagement.

RATIONAL VS. EMOTIONAL
Why would someone spend their free, unpaid time promoting a commercial brand? Today, it's often because they're emotionally engaged with that brand. The benefits of reaching this level of connection with customers are startling. In *Human Sigma*, Gallup studied organizations across various industries. What they found was that even when a customer is rationally satisfied – where price, quality and on-time delivery are all good – they're no more likely to stay with the company than a customer who is unsatisfied.[4] They are more likely to spend more money if they're rationally satisfied, but when a customer becomes *emotionally engaged*, they're tremendously more likely to be retained and spend even more.

If, as many suggest, 80% of sales are driven by 20% of customers, then "market share" is not the whole picture. Marketing and sales will drive market share, but what drives customer share? Engagement is the key. An engaged customer says good things about the organization, stays as a customer and spends more with that organization. Engaged customers have a positive involvement with the brand. They take actions, make recommendations and do things that impact the relationship. They're proactive in their

---

[1] Gallup Consulting (2009), Customer Engagement: What's your engagement ratio? – Gallup: available at www.gallup.com
[2] See: http://www.loyaltyrules.com/loyaltyrules/BB_Loyalty_effect_essay_5_Satisfaction_trap.pdf
[3] Dan Ariely, Predictably Irrational, Harper Collins, 2008
[4] John Fleming and Jim Apslund, Human Sigma, Gallup Press, 2007

involvement – initiating, not just responding – and they are, most importantly, emotionally connected to the brand, identifying with your employees and other customers.

Gallup found that customers who are fully engaged represent an average 23% premium in terms of "share-of-wallet," profitability, revenue and relationship growth than the average customer. Actively disengaged customers represent a 13% discount in those same measures. Gallup concludes that the great organizations focus on maximizing their customer relationships – organizations that optimize engagement have outperformed their competitors by 26% in gross margin and 85% in sales growth. Their customers buy more, spend more, return more often and stay longer.[5] But customer engagement must be continually nurtured because, now more than ever, involved, proactive, emotionally connected individuals who are negative can be your worst nightmare!

ARE YOUR CUSTOMERS ENGAGED?
In 2003, Baylor University neuroscientist Read Montague conducted an experiment[6] involving subjects doing blind tastings of Coke and Pepsi while connected to an MRI. By a margin of 5 to 1, subjects' pleasure centers in their brains lit up when they tasted Pepsi versus Coke, strongly suggesting – as Pepsi has always attested – that the great majority of people prefer the taste of Pepsi. Yet Coke consistently outsells Pepsi by a margin of at least two to one. Even Diet Coke sells significantly more product than regular or diet Pepsi.[7]

Amazingly, the test subjects, who had moments before chosen Pepsi, declared their preference for Coke once they were told the identity of the samples. This comes from emotional attachments to the brand, pride in being associated with it and the irrational loyalty that goes along with it. Coke's continuing victory in the cola wars is planned and deliberate. For almost three decades it has focused on building a brand around family, friendships and warm, emotional associations. The lesson is crystal clear.

Ask yourself: Are your customers proud to be associated with your brand? Is it tattooed on their shoulder as it is with many Harley Davidson customers? Have some of them shaved it into their hairdos as Apple customers have done? More practically, do they wear your t-shirt and sing your praises on social forums? Do they volunteer their time to give you feedback, rate your products and services, and encourage other people to become your customers? You might have a long way to go to get to these levels of engagement with your customers, but it's worth it – and almost certainly necessary if you intend to thrive in today's markets.

Consider some fundamental questions about the way your organization treats customers. Do you always deliver on promises to customers and do all that you can to earn their trust? Do you solve their problems quickly when things go wrong and always treat them fairly? These are the basic "musts" in building your brand over time. They are the tenets of good customer service, and customer service is still the dominant component of customer engagement.

Every interaction with a customer, by you or anyone in your organization, results in an increase or a decrease in their engagement with you. In the vast majority of companies, inconsistent service and interactions are the norm, but a customer's ups and downs –

---

5 Ibid
6 See: www.pbs.org/wgbh/pages/frontline/shows/persuaders/etc/neuro.html
7 See: www.slate.com/articles/business/rivalries/2013/08/pepsi_paradox_why_people_prefer_coke_even_though_pepsi_wins_in_taste_tests.html

characterized by good experiences followed by mediocre, then bad and back to good – frustrates them and damages your brand immensely. The lesson: Be consistent.

ENTERPRISE ENGAGEMENT
The tactics used to increase customer engagement are many, but those that emphasize customer service, rewards and branding are the mainstays. Tactics that are aligned and integrated across the organization, as well as with other stakeholders, stand the greatest chance of success, longevity and of realizing the "multiplier" effect of multi-stakeholder engagement.

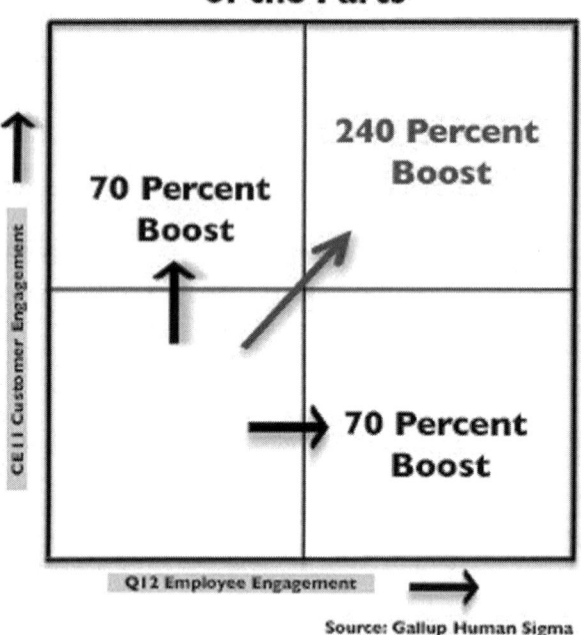

Combined Employee & Customer Engagement: Greater than the Sum of the Parts

- 70 Percent Boost (CE11 Customer Engagement axis)
- 240 Percent Boost (combined)
- 70 Percent Boost (Q12 Employee Engagement axis)

Source: Gallup Human Sigma

In the next several pages are two vignettes that illustrate these tactics with an emphasis on Enterprise Engagement – the combination of the main elements of engagement and driving consistency of its application across the enterprise.

The first thing you need to do is identify and engage all of the people critical to achieving your goals. With them, develop and implement a formal Enterprise Engagement plan that integrates all of the tactics necessary to engage customers and your other key stakeholders.

As noted above, Enterprise Engagement focuses on creating alignment across the organization to consistently deliver positive interactions between employees and customers, as well as with other stakeholders. Obviously, this consistency is difficult to achieve in complex, large and far-flung organizations.

Meet regularly to discuss customer engagement, even organize conferences on the theme in which critical people are assembled from across the organization. An enterprise-wide approach is key in reaching and maintaining the level of consistency you need.

TACTIC: CUSTOMER SERVICE
According to the Gartner Group, 68% of all customers defect because of poor service.[8] It stands to reason, then, that addressing customer needs and service preferences more adequately can be highly profitable.

Ensure that customer needs are continually identified and consistently delivered upon. To do this, bring the people who can affect results on board. Defeat the typical corporate structure where customer interactions and accountabilities are managed discretely by separate groups – marketing, sales, customer service, tech support, etc. Instead, try to see it from the customer's perspective, where all of their contact with your company adds up to their impression. After all, customers don't generally rate companies based on their experiences with its sub-components.

This viewpoint may allow your teams to come up with better solutions to enhance the customer experience and their level of engagement. Whoever is in the best position to aid and delight a customer should be empowered to do so.

In most organizations, sales and customer service have the most contact with customers, so start there. But don't wait for complaints from customers to figure out what's most broken.

Research shows that, on average, only about 4% of customers will complain about bad service.[9] Foster an environment in which customers and employees feel encouraged to contribute ideas and continually communicate. Make it easy to contribute, and reward contributions.

Customers typically want:

- The ability for a customer service agent to assist with all their needs, not be passed on through a chain, put on hold and made to wait
- The ability to discuss problems with knowledgeable customer service agents rather than untrained call center generalists
- Their problems solved or questions answered in a reasonable amount of time
- Credible, quality responses
- A respectful manner and approach from customer service agents.

Customers may often be wrong, but it no longer matters. As workplace dynamics guru Dan Pink points out in his latest book, *To Sell is Human*, product and pricing information is ubiquitous, along with customer ratings and detailed information about the product. Today, customers have as much information as companies; there's no advantage or knowledge mismatch to exploit.

Pink suggests that even attempting to solve your customers' problems is a dated approach. Instead, you must identify their problems *before* they do. Pink cites Perfetti Van Melle, the candy company than makes Mentos. Its salespeople visit convenience stores with the hope of placing more Mentos on store shelves. But this practice also gives the company knowledge and insight into candy in general, such that it can offer valuable advice to store owners about the kinds of products they should be selling. This

---

[8] See: http://www.amdocs.com/Whitepapers/wp_CEBreport_0709.pdf
[9] See: http://businesscard2.com/resources/taking-care-of-customers-is-taking-care-of-business

sometimes leads to recommendations that the store stock fewer brands of Mentos, and even that they offer more of Mentos' competitor brands! The tradeoff is trust, access, loyalty and a relationship that will pay off in spades over a longer timeframe.

Organizations that sell things have to become customer-centric. Learn about your customers, track their changing preferences in real-time to the extent possible. Listen attentively to their problems so you can identify solutions and even uncover opportunities they didn't know about. Strive to make their businesses and/or their lives better.

To put yourself and your team in the right mindset, re-draft your organizational chart so the top box says "customers." Underneath this, include boxes for everyone that serves them – which should be everyone in the organization. Companies like Zappos and Amazon illustrate this ethos well. Zappos used to make a video feed of its meetings available to anyone who wanted to tune in. At Amazon, CEO Jeff Bezos places an empty chair at meetings for what he calls the most important person in the room – the customer.

Products often fail because they don't consider the customer enough in their development. For example, a hotel might lead with its amenities and hospitality in advertising, but Booz & Company research suggests that cleanliness trumps all else in pleasing customers.[10] Put the customer in the room at meetings, during product development and in determining marketing strategy.

Another simple tactic is to try to say "yes" to customers as much as possible. Discount Tire, for example, says yes to people who want flat tires fixed at no charge – even if they bought their tires from another supplier. When you say yes, you empower your staff members to engage with your customers. Becoming a "yes" company isn't difficult, but like engagement in general, you have to encourage your people to get into the habit.

Finally, don't forget the power of purpose. TOMS Shoes famously gives a pair of new shoes to a child in need for every pair purchased in its stores on via its website. TOMS is in business "to help change lives," an ambitious mission for a shoe company. But by giving shoes to more than a million kids in 60 countries around the world, it's changing lives for the better, and customers (as well as employees and other stakeholders) are responding.

More than ever, customers today want to be associated with causes. CSR (Corporate Social Responsibility) is a growing component of reputation and brand-building through serving others. It's also a competitive advantage. In their 2013 book, *The Why Axis*, economists Uri Gneezy and John List conducted field experiments to determine what causes people to spend more and give. They found that matching programs, like that at TOMS, in which sales are combined with donations, result in 20% more sales, on average.[11]

This business philosophy of putting customers first, treating them fairly, charging reasonably, providing excellent customer service combined with empathy – thinking like the customer, trying to make customers' lives better, solving and identifying their problems and CSR activities – provides the balance between reason and emotion that can build lasting and strong customer engagement. It brings the "what" together with the "why" and appeals to customers' need for tangible and intangible reasons for doing business with you.

---

[10] See: http://travel.usatoday.com/hotels/story/2012-05-30/CSI-hotel-room-Best-Western-goes-high-tech-to-clean/55270430/1
[11] John A. List and Uri Gneezy, The Why Axis, PublicAffairs, 2013

When your company operates with a customer-centric mindset, you engage with them and improve their experience. This is the best way to establish an individualized brand and optimize the value you offer.

TACTIC: REWARDS & RECOGNITION
Incentives and rewards are important to win and keep customers, just as they're important to motivation in just about every aspect of life. Incentives, rewards and recognition are also essential to keep customers and earn their "share of wallet" – they're important tactics in the overall approach to sales and marketing and, ultimately, customer engagement.

Your strategy may be to get males age 25-40 to identify with a shoe brand. This might include tactics such as a free movie coupon for each pair of shoes sold, contributing to sales. But ask yourself what appeals to your demographic – for example, extreme sports, fitness, attractiveness, etc., You might also sponsor events, endorse specific athletes, etc. to cause your customers to better identify with and "live" your brand. This is an element of recognition and one of the keys to long-term customer engagement. When your customers use your brand to portray themselves the way they wish to be seen, you've touched them at an emotional level.

Customer loyalty programs are effective ways to build lasting loyalty. Example: Shell Oil overbuilt gas stations in Canada in the early 1990s, and many of them didn't meet customer expectations. Shell wanted to reduce its 2,500 Canadian stations to approximately 2,000. It planned to spruce up the outlets it kept open, turning many of them into more profitable self-service operations, and it planned to manage this complicated project without losing any market share.

Shell partnered with the Air Miles reward program, a loyalty program that provided it comprehensive information about its customers. By analyzing this valuable customer data, Shell determined which locations to close and which ones to renovate. The program's customer sales data helped Shell develop a marketing program to convince existing Shell customers to fill up at the company's new locations. Given the program's extensive data about customers' purchasing habits, analysts could define Shell's target market precisely. This probe of consumer behavior enabled it to predict the specific gas stations that Air Miles members would be inclined to use when Shell closed other stations. Direct mail and in-store marketing told these customers about the renovated locations and alerted them to the nearest (and most likely) alternate site.

To convince these buyers to stay with Shell during the transition period, the company promised loyalty members double air miles for their purchases at the recommended stations. When the renovations were complete, Shell promoted the newly redone stations with "site-reopening" ads and "welcome-back teasers" offering to double and even triple consumers' miles.

Customer loyalty takes two forms: "behavioral loyalty" springs from pricing and convenience, while "emotional loyalty" represents a remarkably strong bond between customer and company. The bond of emotional loyalty can overcome compelling offers from the competition. Emotionally engaged customers spend more money with the businesses they like and are more intensely loyal than other customers. Companies' loyalty programs should offer rewards that are appealing enough to entice customers and then keep them with recognition-type benefits like prestige access to airline lounges or VIP access to concerts, for example, to touch the emotional side of their customers and thus

> **Emotionally engaged customers spend more money with the businesses they like and are more intensely loyal than other customers.**

move them from a rational (price-based) reason for their loyalty to a more complex and unpredictable, but far more rewarding, emotional attachment.

TACTIC: BRANDING
Branding used to be about "mindshare." Today it aims at "heartshare." This is important for two reasons. First, for all the factors related to emotional engagement outlined above, and second, because today your customers can do you much greater damage if you alienate them. Your customers have powerful new platforms – global social media stages – where they can tell their friends, family, neighbors, colleagues and even strangers what they think and feel about the products and services they buy and the companies that sell to them.

On the positive side, you can use the same platforms to interact with customers more intimately and less expensively than in the past. Find out how and why your customers choose particular communication platforms. Leverage each platform by taking an active role, soliciting or monitoring feedback, answering questions and building your reputation. Through these channels, you have an unprecedented ability to learn about how your products and services impact customers and prospects, and the chance to collect ideas from customers on how to make your services and products better.

Create an enterprise brand that connects customers, distribution partners, employees, vendors and communities to the organization by ensuring:

- people know the true benefits of your brands
- they feel they are part of your community
- they're getting the information they need or want rather than just being sold to
- they know what they need to know
- your employees have the ability to deliver promises.

As part of a broader customer engagement strategy, social media is usually an effective and cost-efficient marketing, sales, service, insight and retention tool. Recent research reveals that customers who engage with companies over social media spend 20% to 40% more with those companies than other customers.[12] They also demonstrate a deeper emotional commitment to the companies.

More than 60% of Internet-connected individuals in the U.S. now engage on social media platforms every day.[13] The speed and access to information they've come to appreciate has made them more demanding customers. For example, many now expect real-time customer service and quick responses to their online feedback. Hyper-connected individuals regularly broadcast their opinions. And they rely on their friends and social networks for news, reviews and recommendations for products and businesses.

Social media leaders understand and appreciate the magnitude of the shift in customer empowerment and the opportunities and risks these tools create. As a result, they approach their social media efforts differently.

While the average company may maintain Facebook and Twitter accounts and have other discrete programs run by their marketing or customer service teams, these efforts tend to be uncoordinated, with different business units, brands or geographies conducting their own social media experiments.

---

[12] See: http://www.bain.com/publications/articles/putting-social-media-to-work.aspx
[13] See: http://callcenterinfo.tmcnet.com/news/2013/12/21/7605273.htm

Social media shouldn't be viewed as a mere channel for marketing or public relations, or just an effective customer service tool. While many companies begin using social media to get the word out about products, the most successful have significantly expanded their efforts to engage their customers at every step of the "customer corridor," touchpoints that start when a potential customer first learns of a product and extending through the moment they opt to make repeat purchases. It means helping by becoming a source of useful information, not just selling. See Chapter 16 on Content Marketing.

While a company's products are important, only 40% of people's willingness to recommend that company is determined by their perceptions of products, and 60% is determined by their perceptions – the brand – of the company itself. "Though a company can no longer control the dialogue surrounding their company, they can definitely pay attention to it and shape it in the best light possible."[14] Bottom line: You no longer win by pursuing sales alone; you must build an active, online community around your brand.

TACTIC: ENGAGEMENT CONNECTIVITY
Customer loyalty depends on employee loyalty. The blending of customer and employee engagement through enterprise branding is a vital tactic discussed briefly above and seen more and more among large organizations.

General Electric, for example uses national media campaigns to link its production of high-tech aircraft engines and other products to the commitment and passion of its employees.

Intel succeeded in elevating a commodity (microprocessor chips) to a global brand. Its Intel Inside® campaign[15] largely convinced consumers that their choice of microprocessor manufacturer for their laptop or computer is important. More recently, Intel extended the campaign to include another differentiator, the employees Inside Intel.

By airing commercials, erecting billboards and constructing elaborate websites about the "Rock Stars" at Intel, it very effectively integrates consumer and employer branding and uses a very clever tactic to drive employee engagement through recognition.

Moreover, as witnessed by hundreds of comments on YouTube, the campaign has been effective in endearing consumers to the brand through a very human and emotional connection to its people.

Remember that connectivity and integration are key. After all, how can customer engagement improve if the people responsible for employees almost never talk to the people responsible for customers, or to those in charge of vendor management and partner relationships?

While it's beyond the control of almost anyone in the organization, save its leaders, a select few organizations are appointing Chief Engagement Officers who are charged with tearing down silos and bringing employees, customers, vendors and partners together. This is a tactic whose time has come, yet instances are still rare.

---

[14] See: http://www.marketingtechblog.com/marketing-sales-service-new-rules-customer-engagement/
[15] See: http://www.intel.com/consumer/tomorrow/innovators/index.htm

> **How can customer engagement improve if the people responsible for employees almost never talk to the people responsible for customers, or to those in charge of vendor management and partner relationships?**

While creating a new 'C' level position may be impractical for most, the idea is key. There must be cross-organizational responsibility for customer and Enterprise Engagement.

In many cases, this might mean forming those responsible for different disciplines into an executive committee or group to champion, sponsor and drive the Enterprise Engagement initiative. While it will take time to integrate engagement across the enterprise for all of your key stakeholders, you should start by combining employee and customer engagement.

Again, referring to Gallup's work in *Human Sigma*, about a decade ago Gallup charted the progress of a bank that pursued a combined employee/customer engagement strategy over the course of several years.

The bank combined branding efforts in a manner similar to Intel. It used employee and customer engagement surveys and tracked, compared and correlated the results of front-line manager engagement initiatives and focused separate, intensive efforts on front-line sales and customer service employees – employees who interacted with customers most frequently.

According to the bank, more than $1 billion in additional deposits resulted from the effort. Yet, in a recent study in the U.S., only 21% of front-line staff of the top 100 companies could clearly articulate what their company does for customers and what role they play in it strategically.[16]

The integration of employee and customer engagement through a simple program such as Capri Casino's *See.Say.Smile* initiative demonstrates the synergistic relationship between the two. Studies going back as far as 1999 have established the strong, consistent connection between employee commitment, customer engagement and increased profits (see *The Employee-Customer-Profit Chain at Sears*, Harvard Business Review, 1999). In *Human Sigma*, researchers found that integrated customer and employee engagement results don't just double the benefit of one or the other (as might be expected); they more than *triple* the returns.[17]

SUMMARY

A customer engagement strategy in the absence of an Enterprise Engagement strategy, and most importantly, one that includes employee engagement, is bound to produce disappointing returns. In the context of a broader engagement strategy, customer engagement initiatives must recognize that social media is shifting power to consumers and employees; that communication is moving from mass to one-to-one; that the customer experience has become the competitive edge; and that employees are critical to the brand equation.

The C-suite is beginning to see the connection between engagement across the organization and among stakeholder groups, largely because of the overwhelming evidence that companies with engaged audiences outperform their competitors in the stock market.

---

[16] See: http://www.mycustomer.com/topic/customer-experience/business-unusual-falling-loyalty-all-bad-news-customer-engagement/127816
[17] Fleming, John.H and Asplund, Jim. Human Sigma, Gallup press, 2007. P. 207

Enterprise Engagement: The Textbook

Chapter 7

Channel Partner Engagement

Not every business has distributors or resellers, but every business has collaborators, advisors and others who help them succeed in ways that complement the activities of customers, employees and vendors. While this segment of the curriculum refers mainly to sales and marketing partners, the advantages of engaging all key constituents, including partners, are universal. Whatever the role of a partner, they're an important part of your success and must be engaged like all other constituents.

In many industries and businesses, channel partners are key links between employees and customers – a weak link if they're ignored, an important source of strength if they are engaged. The stakes are high. Channel partner impact can be enormous in terms of sales volume, market share, brand reputation and "share of customer." Indeed, channel partners are often the sole link to the customer. But channel partners can also impact employee engagement, especially when they fail to deliver. Conversely, channel partner engagement is directly affected by the employees who manage them and who produce the products and services.

> **Most businesses succeed only to the degree that symbiotic relationships exist between employees, customers, channel partners and vendors.**

In short, most businesses succeed only to the degree that symbiotic relationships exist between employees, customers, channel partners and vendors. This is the basis upon which "Enterprise Engagement" is built. In this chapter, we focus on channel partners as a key constituent of organizational success and offer practical strategies and tactics to engage them.

DRIVERS AND EMOTIONS
Employee and customer engagement have become high management priorities over the past several years, and rightly so. But while organizations concentrate on making customers and employees happy, they sometimes take partners for granted. It's important to remember that channel partners are subject to the same drivers and emotions as employees and customers; in fact they have added distractions. They work with many source manufactures or service providers ("primes") and naturally will favor some over others. Being low on the priority list for your channel partners is not a winning strategy.

As with customers, the reasons channel partners favor some relationships more highly than others is based on a variety of factors. Financial motivations are certainly among them. Yet just as the lowest price can't be the only customer engagement strategy (or the most effective) "spiffs" and margins aren't the only ingredients to an engaged relationship with partners.

Organizations should actively nurture a culture of partner engagement so that, like employees and customers, channel partners become emotionally engaged and are more likely to take an active interest in the organization's success. You can't expect a disengaged channel partner to build engagement around your brand. They may meet monthly goals and be able to accurately describe the benefits of your product, but they'll be far less effective if they're emotionally detached. Their detachment vs. enthusiastic engagement is also bound to have an impact on your employees, just as unenthusiastic, disengaged employees will have a negative impact on any channel partners they interact with. The goal is to assist in the development of an "emotionally engaged" channel partner.

PROACTIVE PARTNERS
It isn't difficult to spot an engaged channel partner. They are *involved* with the brand – they take action, make recommendations and do things that positively impact the relationship. Engaged channel partners are *proactive,* they initiate brand development and don't simply react or respond. For most companies that sell through channels, the typical 80-20 rule applies, meaning that 80% of their business comes through 20% of their distributors. The objective is to get more share from the 80% who are not as engaged wherever you can.

Are your channel partners talking up your brand? Do they appear proud of the association with you? Are they making suggestions or identifying innovative ways to extend your brand and boost sales? Are they delivering your brand promise? Their strength of engagement has a direct correlation to the strength of your brand.

Think about Apple and Harley Davidson; their customers are fully engaged, but so are their employees, suppliers and channel partners. People like being associated with great brands, and that attraction, in turn, creates more brand value – a kind of virtuous cycle or "channel ecosystem."

FIGHTING AGAINST DISENGAGEMENT
Since your sale is going through an intermediary, i.e., an agent, channel partner, distributor, broker or reseller, your channel ecosystem is the mix of paths to the consumer and how they are aligned and integrated. Whether the ecosystem is harmonious or in conflict depends a great deal on engagement. Disengagement among channel partners stems from things that are within your power to correct, such as:

- **Channel Conflict.** Channel conflict exists where direct and indirect sales channels are misaligned. Problems often start in the pre-sales cycle – whose prospect is it? In the actual buying cycle, if a reseller invests months working with a prospect only to see the final sale go direct or through another channel, they won't be as enthusiastic about selling that product or service in the future. Misalignment can occur post-sale as well, where the sale may have been direct, for example, yet the channel partner is expected to provide service even though they didn't benefit from the sale.

- **Ease of Doing Business.** A common mistake in organizations is to assume that resellers know the product or service as well as the manufacturer. The fact is, resellers represent many products; they don't necessarily know all of them thoroughly or equally. Resellers also often deal with disparate systems in order to interact with their partners. Different sales databases, different ERPs, different processes, rules and procedures. People and organizations tend to follow the path of least resistance. A culture of partner engagement requires thinking like a partner.

- **Channel Strategy.** Obviously, any organization would sell their goods or services directly if that were always the most efficient means to market. A channel strategy is created to efficiently drive the flow of goods to the consumer and to align that with how and where your consumer prefers to buy. Efficiency is key. For example, Coke would love to have a person in every convenience store to direct consumers to their products and away from those of rivals. But that would be grossly inefficient. The more sophisticated the product, the more vital the channel partner relationship.

- **Channel Culture.** To what degree are you embracing your channel partners and making them engaged and happy throughout the process? Recognize that you don't have the same type of control over partners as you do in your own organization. This make-or-break understanding is at the core of channel engagement. Always remember that partners are independent and have their own agendas. Also, ask yourself how you can build individual relationships with the dealer's sales team or other employees.

FOUR REQUIREMENTS

Now that you understand the fundamentals, how do you build a successful channel partner culture and process? The main requirements for channel engagement are Recruitment, Enablement, Management and Reward.

Requirements for Channel Engagement

- Recruitment
- Enablement
- Management
- Reward

1. RECRUITMENT

First, know what kind of partners you should be pursuing. This will depend on your position in the market, your brand strength and the reach of your internal sales and marketing capabilities. To what extent does your channel partner have a sales strategy aligned with your own – types of consumers, values, etc.? Do they already have a broad clientele you can leverage, or do you have to help them build it? What kind of services do you expect your partners to provide – are they adding configuration, service, installation, etc.? Are they selling competitive products? If so, is that acceptable? And if it is, is your value to them going to be compelling enough so you get your share of their attention?

When recruiting channel partners, avoid setting yourself up for channel conflict. Consider delineating audience segments and geographical boundaries. If you sell to both the private and public sectors, for example, look for partners with expertise to target segments within those sectors and avoid channel conflict by granting exclusivity (tied to performance) in those areas. Also, clearly delineate where your channel partner picks up and where you leave off in the marketing/sales cycle.

2. ENABLEMENT

Now that you have the right channel partners on board, you should change your focus to reducing the time it takes them to become productive on your behalf. In the spirit of engagement and building a harmonious Channel Ecosystem, think less about their obligations and more about how you can offer support to get them up and running with minimal effort on their part.

A great deal of this will be accomplished by assigning a strong partner advocate to work with them. You might also provide qualified leads, offer co-marketing programs and product or technology/sales & marketing training. Some organizations provide channel partners an "MDF" (Market Development Fund) which is an allowance provided to partners to offset marketing costs and/or go toward demonstration equipment, customer events, training, etc. It's extremely important to enable the actual people interfacing with the customer, not necessarily the dealer principal, who values organizations that help train his/her sales team to be more effective.

3. MANAGEMENT

Part of creating a positive channel partner culture is making sure that you're easy to do business with. Your complexities may be understood internally, but remember your product is probably one of many your channel partner represents.

For example, do you require multiple log-ins to systems they have to interact with? How fast can they get answers to their questions about products, prices and new features? How many steps are there in the sales process; how much bureaucracy impedes the process? Management is where the relationship succeeds or fails. Again, both parties should have an individual who is committed to the other partner's success – an advocate.

Organizations with a positive channel partner culture naturally think more about how they can drive the success of the channel partner and less about how they can squeeze the most out of the relationship for themselves. This, in turn, drives engagement and better results for both partners over time. Finally, you should also realize that channel partners have a lifecycle. Your engagement process will be different

> **Organizations with a positive channel partner culture naturally think more about how they can drive the success of the channel partner and less about how they can squeeze the most out of the relationship for themselves.**

depending on where your partner is in that cycle – i.e., whether you're onboarding them, ramping them up, or in long-term maintenance mode.

4. REWARD

Margins and commissions are not enough. Companies that implement non-cash reward and recognition programs for their channel partners report annual revenue increases averaging 9.6%, compared to an average of only 3% for all other companies, according to research from Aberdeen Group and the Incentive Research Foundation (IRF) in 2011. In fact, the Aberdeen/IRF study suggests that organizations that implement non-cash reward and recognition programs tend to outperform other organizations across several major business indicators, and not just in terms of revenue growth. According to IRF Chief Research Officer, Rodger Stotz, "Perhaps the greatest lesson to be learned from this study is that professional sales staff tend to respond to measurable rewards and recognition much like other employees, so it's not surprising to find that companies using such programs post better sales results."

Again, it's critical to make sure your reward programs target the people who are helping you achieve your goals. Many dealer principals value having their partners provide extra rewards for their sales team. Marketers have to understand the behaviors they want to encourage; these could be different for a distributor as opposed to a reseller, for example. You have to motivate differently to get mindshare. In addition to margins and equity rebates, consider non-cash rewards for meeting and exceeding goals.

Creative rewards can have a significant impact on relationships, but a culture of partner engagement requires more to build true emotional engagement. Tangible rewards must be combined with regular, verbal recognition and acknowledgement of your partners.

SHAPING AND REINFORCING

The principles of engagement are the same between constituent groups. After all, people are people. Everyone craves recognition and feedback; everyone wants to be treated with respect and no one can resist favoring a person or organization with which it has established an emotional connection.

Organizations should take care and caution in recruiting the right partners. Next, they should onboard those partners proactively and methodically to reduce that partner's "time to contribution." A management structure should be in place where a channel partner mindset is encouraged (in which partner success is at least as important as your success). It's important to address both the dealer principals and their employees, as it's often the employees who can make the difference.

Any serious channel partner engagement strategy should start with a well-designed web portal that provides useful information, news, the opportunity to share success stories or issues, knowledge tests, surveys, rewards and recognition, performance measures and more.

Enterprise Engagement: The Textbook

Chapter 8

Employee Engagement

A great deal has been written and said about employee engagement over the past two decades or so, and for good reason. Beyond satisfaction, the extent to which an employee identifies with the organization, embraces its values and commits discretionary effort are perhaps the most important determining factors of individual and organizational performance.

Today, the debate has shifted away from *whether* employee engagement is critical. Very few leaders dispute the direct connection between employee engagement, customer engagement and financial outcomes (see Chapter 2: Economics of Enterprise Engagement). Leaders now seek managerial constructs, strategies and tactics that will raise the level of engagement in their workforce quickly and sustainably.

In its 2013 global engagement study, Gallup found that only 18% of the world's workers are engaged, including just 29% of workers in the U.S. and Canada.[1] The rest are just going through the motions – or worse. According to the research, almost one in five North American workers are "actively disengaged," meaning they're uninvolved and unenthusiastic about their jobs and frequently tell others how bad things are. Indeed, many actively disengaged employees are actually doing harm in the workplace either by not performing their basic job duties – and forcing others to pick up the slack – or by attempting to sabotage the organization in some way.

BASIC ENGAGEMENT
Beyond a small minority of workers, pay and other tangible benefits do not drive great performances. Compensation must be competitive, or most talented individuals will disengage and eventually leave your organization, thereby rendering engagement a moot point. In situations where pay, benefits and tangible rewards are better than an employee might find in most other places, you effectively remove compensation from the equation for most people.

Employees are typically satisfied at work when their rational needs are met. Fair pay, security, safety (mainly from toxic bosses and co-workers), adequate resources, equipment, space, etc. And while each of these is critical for a properly functioning

---
1 - See: http://www.gallup.com/poll/165719/northern-america-leads-world-workplace-engagement.aspx?ref=more

organization, they don't inspire committed effort and great performance. The missing ingredient – emotion.

The American Workforce
Engaged, Disengaged, Actively Disengaged

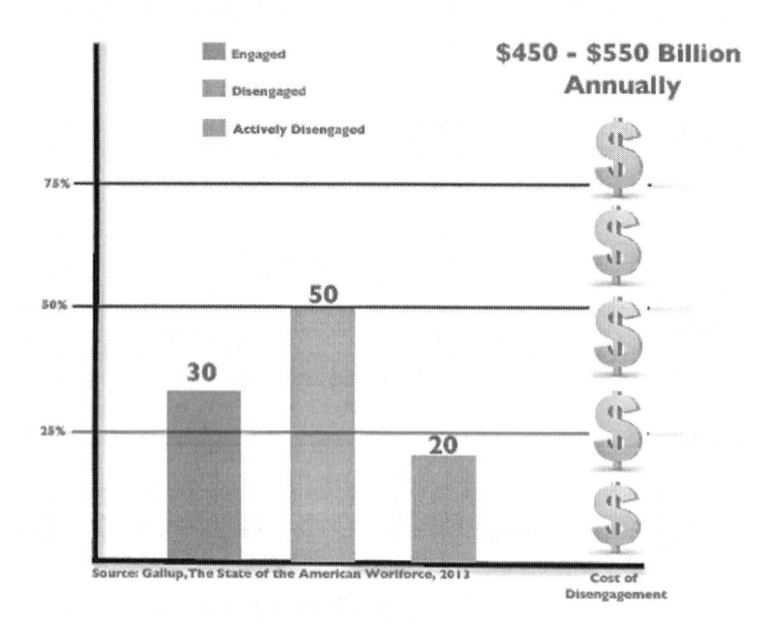

- Engaged: 30
- Disengaged: 50
- Actively Disengaged: 20

$450 - $550 Billion Annually — Cost of Disengagement

Source: Gallup, The State of the American Workforce, 2013

Employees want more than money. They crave purpose and pride. The reputation of their organization is also increasingly important, especially among younger workers. Employees want growth, career opportunities and good management that recognizes them for the work they do. In short, they want a great place to work.

Making your organization such a place requires developing trust, generating enthusiasm and instilling a shared sense of mission, all of which are part of what might be called the *emotional* paycheck. By forging an emotional connection to the organization – to colleagues, customers and partners – employees become committed to the organization's success. At that stage performance potential is boundless.

RECOGNIZING ENGAGEMENT
Employee engagement involves a heightened connection between employees and their work, their organization and the people they work for/with. Engaged employees find personal meaning in their work, take pride in what they do (and where they do it) and believe that their organization values them. According to Gallup, engaged employees are those that work with passion and feel a profound connection to their firm. They drive innovation and move the organization forward.

When you engage employees, they become ambassadors for the organization. Instead of conveying a negative – and ultimately corrosive – attitude about their employer, they are enthusiastic supporters. This doesn't mean they've completely conformed or capitulated to your will – after all, we also want employees to engage when they see something negative. Engaged employees are more likely to share their ideas on how to improve things, and are more likely to be positive about the organization with prospective customers, employees, suppliers, partners and the community as a whole.

They also tend to stay with the organization. Turnover, especially when it involves a valued employee, is very costly and disruptive. Most importantly, engaged employees strive. That is, they put forth more discretionary effort, beyond what it takes just to keep their jobs. The result – when multiplied across the workforce – is enormous productivity gains.

GETTING TO 'WANT'
When organizations truly make employee engagement a company-wide priority and commit the time and resources needed to monitor and maintain their human capital, the financial results can be spectacular.

A study by Wharton Finance Professor Alex Edmans casts an interesting light. He found that companies on *Fortune* magazine's "100 Best Places to Work" list (companies that obviously take good care of their employees) outperformed the market between 1998 and 2005 by a margin of 14% growth in share value vs. 6% overall.[2] The important difference between employees who are skilled enough to do something and know what needs to be done versus those that actually get it done is the "want."

We all agree that employees must know *what* to do, that they must know *how* to do it and they must be *equipped* to do it. But for greater performance and competitive advantage, organizations need to give them reasons to *want* to do it as well. The *want* is what engagement is all about.

TACTICS OF EMPLOYEE ENGAGEMENT
There are thousands of initiatives, programs, incentives and other tactics available to leaders who seek to inspire their employees to greater performance. Fortunately, most can be classified into a few categories. Your most effective levers in driving employee engagement are through better management and leadership, incentives, rewards & recognition and through a category we'll call "The Primacy of Purpose."

These key tactics are best illustrated using real examples across a number of situations and industries. The three vignettes below offer multiple, practical solutions that virtually any organization can implement to drive higher levels of employee engagement.

THE USS BENFOLD
The U.S. Navy is a tradition-bound organization in which command and control management techniques and an extremely hierarchical structure are firmly entrenched.

As the new commander of the USS Benfold in 1997, Captain Mike Abrashoff inherited one of the worst ships in the Navy. The USS Benfold's performance ranked nearly last in the world's largest naval fleet. It was a situation that screamed for a strong leader, yet Abrashoff had no power to hire, fire, promote or even transfer personnel.

In taking command, Abrashoff's first experience was to participate in the formal ceremony in which the departing commander leaves and the new one takes over. Full of pomp and circumstance, the ceremony takes place on the deck of the ship and includes the entire crew, as well as the family of the incoming and outgoing commanders. As a Naval band plays, the outgoing commander walks between the

---

2 - Alex Edmans, Journal of Financial Economics 101(3), 621-640, September 2011

columns of his crew, over the gangway and off the ship. The worst insult the crew can give the outgoing commander is to turn their backs on him as he passes. The gesture is extremely rare and undoubtedly painful for any commander that experiences it. As Abrashoff observed this happening to his predecessor, he vowed he would do anything to avoid the same experience when he left the ship in eighteen months time.

What separates Abrashoff from so many leaders is that he concentrated on the possible rather than the obstacles. The Benfold's culture mirrored the Navy's command and control traditions. But Abrashoff knew that the commander he was succeeding had little success with that style, so he crafted an entirely new approach – a style and method he calls "Grassroots Leadership." Crew members became empowered leaders. Abrashoff met with each and every one of his crew individually to get to know something about all of them – why they had joined the Navy, their aspirations, etc. To each he repeated his mantra: It's your ship, your responsibility; what can you do to make it better?

Abrashoff followed up with action. He empowered the crew to make suggestions and implement them. In one case, a sailor questioned the wisdom of repainting the ship every year at great expense of both time and money. Abrashoff asked how they would avoid the ugly rust stains that cover the sides of ship, as bolts and nuts rust and discolor the ship over time. The sailor's suggestion was simple: replace the thousands of nuts and bolts on the ship with stainless steel ones. Abrashoff used his Navy credit card to get the hardware that day. It worked, and since then every ship in the Navy has been refitted.

Without the power to promote crew members or even offer tangible rewards, Abrashoff had limited means of recognition. He was allowed to hand out merit citations, yet in the culture of the Navy, where merit citations can make the difference in the trajectory of one's career, they were awarded very sparingly. Abrashoff found no rules limiting the number of these awards he could make. Accordingly, he walked the decks looking for what was going *right* as opposed to what was going wrong and handed out the badges unsparingly.

Before long, the crew became engaged; engagement boosted ideas and performance, which lifted the Benfold to recognition as the best ship in the U.S. Pacific Fleet – one of the Navy's top performing ships – less than 18 months after Abrashoff took command. In other words, Abrashoff went against Navy traditions, changed the culture of the ship and won one of the Navy's top performance awards, all during his short assignment on the Benfold. His principles of autonomy *with* results generated engaged, self-led teams that took more pride in their ship and its accomplishments.

A brilliant example of this pride comes from an email Abrashoff received from an Admiral days after earning recognition as the best ship in the Pacific Fleet. The email congratulated Abrashoff on the award, but boasted that the Benfold would never break the Admiral's long-standing record for gunner accuracy. Abrashoff said nothing to his gunnery crew; he simply posted the email on the Ship's Mess Bulletin Board.

The next month, at the annual competition, the Benfold shattered the record for gunnery accuracy, a record that stands to this day. Abrashoff's engaged crew figured it out for themselves with no special urging or training.

As commander of a Navy destroyer, Abrashoff used engagement and leadership techniques and turned one of the most under-performing warships in the U.S. Fleet into perhaps the best performing ship in the Navy. Commander Abrashoff took the same team he inherited – a dispirited bunch of sailors and officers that had wanted to transfer off the ship as soon as they could – and made them a high performing, high functioning team.

JOHN DEERE CREDIT

Leaders and managers can drive appreciable improvements in engagement by a variety of techniques and behaviors. Knowing this, John Deere Credit (JDC), a division of John Deere (now John Deere Financial), sought to improve its managers' capabilities as related to employee engagement.

First, JDC surveyed its organization of about 800 employees. Though much like an engagement survey, this survey focused on those things most impacted by a person's direct manager or supervisor. Analyzing the results, JDC could see what managers were doing relatively well and relatively poorly. Manager strengths were documented and shared, as were their weaknesses. This gave the organization (and managers themselves) a benchmark and guidance for where improvements might have the most impact.

Related to their strengths and weaknesses, managers were asked to choose two activities that would drive higher engagement among their teams. Each would lead and be accountable for these initiatives with their reports. The interventions were simple and cost effective – for example, developing individual learning plans with each team member, scheduling weekly one-to-one coaching sessions, finding the time to recognize people regularly for their contributions. Monthly meetings were scheduled to review progress and hold all managers accountable for following through with their plans.

JDC's next employee engagement survey took place about eight months after the program was initiated. Not surprisingly, it revealed tremendous gains. While it wasn't possible for JDC to isolate the impact of the management initiative alone, they felt the initiative contributed to the lion's share of improvements. Those assessed as "Fully Engaged" rose from 18.2% to 25.6%. "Engaged" workers rose from 49.8% to 55%. Those previously deemed "Somewhat Engaged" and "Disengaged" dropped from 24% to 17.3% and 10.1% to 3.2%, respectively.

So what do these numbers mean? Using their previous engagement survey results, JDC determined it lost over $6 million per year due to the 34% of it employees who were either Somewhat Engaged or Disengaged. After the intervention, they produced the following profile using data and recommendations from the Center for Talent Solutions (CTS), a firm that has been assisting organizations worldwide with employee engagement for the past 15 years.[4]

- 800 employees
- Average salary: $78,000
- Average benefits: 28%
- "Fully Engaged" = 122% performance
- "Engaged" = 100% performance

> 'There's nothing magical about it. In most organizations today, ideas still come from the top. Soon after arriving at this command, I realized that the young folks on this ship are smart and talented. And I realized that my job was to listen aggressively – to pick up all of the ideas that they had for improving how we operate. The most important thing that a Captain can do is to see the ship from the eyes of the crew.'
>
> ~ Capt. Mike Abrashoff, author of It's Your Ship.[3]

---

[3] Mike Abrashoff, It's Your Ship, Business Plus, 2007
[4] - See: www.keeppeople.com

- "Somewhat Engaged" = 71% performance
- "Disengaged" = 40% engaged

By multiplying the number of employees by average salary plus benefits ($99,840), managers arrived at an ideal "performance number" if all employees were engaged: $79,872,000. However, because 25.6% of its employees are now Fully Engaged, it received an annual performance boost of $4,498,391.04. Unfortunately, despite decreasing the number of Somewhat Engaged and Disengaged employees, it is still losing money in terms of performance. The 17.3% of its employees who are still Somewhat Engaged cost JDC $4,007,178.24 each year, and the 3.2% that are Disengaged cost it $1,222,041.60.

Yet by taking the simple, inexpensive actions they did, JDC reduced its net annual performance loss from roughly $6,000,000 per year to roughly $731,000 – a drop of more than $5.2 million.

Consider whether these numbers appear credible to you. Does the Center for Talent Solutions use inflated or conservative calculations in your opinion? Is it a stretch to say that Fully Engaged employees contribute 122% of their compensation, while Disengaged workers contribute only 49%? The actual numbers will differ between industries and organizations, but most experts believe the CTS calculations are extremely conservative. In any case, the potential hard dollar savings in driving higher employee engagement are enormous.

A U.S. INTELLIGENCE AGENCY
Imagine you're an analyst for a government intelligence agency. You're watching TV one Sunday evening when a breaking news item appears:

The Island of Quadraat has just suffered a major earthquake. You immediately sit up and pay attention because Quadraat is one of the nations you're responsible for as an intelligence analyst.

Using a secure network site and your tablet, you draft a fast report based on the initial information you're able to glean online. You tag it with keywords and press "send." The system automatically routes your report to your direct manager and to the in-boxes of every analyst, specialist, agent and operative who matches your keyword.

Within hours you receive an update from the system. Already, more than a thousand people throughout the nation's network of thirteen intelligence agencies has received your briefing, and some have already added their own insights.

By sharing your briefing, you've set in motion a system that taps the collective insights of dozens of experts. They are able to combine satellite images of Quadraat with intelligence about potentially sensitive materials located on the island. By Monday morning, they've alerted the Director of the agency that a breech in a chemical plant caused by the earthquake is a potential source of "controlled materials" that terrorist networks known to be operating in the area may try to get their hands on.

By noon on Monday, the system reports back to you with a summary of the impact your briefing has had so far. Seeing the results, you feel connected and gratified that you played a part in identifying a potentially dangerous situation. That evening, the Director decides the situation is serious enough that it should go into the following morning's Security Briefing to the President. The Director recommends that a Navy Seal team parachute onto the island to secure the facility as quickly as possible, while awaiting a Marine guard contingent and construction repair crews. On Tuesday morning, the system alerts you that your briefing has made its way into the President's daily Briefing. You beam with pride knowing that you've made a difference. The system is fully integrated with the agency's performance-management system, meaning you'll have a record of it when performance review time comes around.

The intelligence analyst in this example is very likely underpaid versus her counterparts with similar experience and education in the private sector. But she works for a cause and purpose that are important to her and her colleagues and co-workers. The technology, based on sound principles of motivation, is perfectly suited to her key drivers of engagement.

But it's important to keep in mind that nearly everyone shares a similar need for a sense of purpose in what they do.

'PRIMACY OF PURPOSE'
Thinkers, philosophers and theorists have told us for thousands of years that purpose is essential to leading meaningful and contented lives.

It's not enough to say that you want to be a wealthy and important executive, or even that you want to be a wealthy but compassionate and generous executive. You have to be able to answer "why?" – in other words, you'll use being a wealthy and important executive for what purpose? And the "what" must amount to something greater than yourself. Knowing your purpose, you can more easily define the values that will help you achieve it and thereby give meaning to everything you do and accomplish.

Most people, absent this purpose, will find their accomplishments either unsustainable or hollow – or both. You can avoid this fate for yourself and your employees by practicing the tenets of Self Determination Theory (SDT)[5] which prescribes three elements for your best approach to sustained, intrinsic motivation and subsequent development as a human being:

1. **Autonomy** – You decide. You choose your work, how you live, the way you behave and your goals.
2. **Mastery/Competence** – After you've chosen what you do, you naturally crave the ability to do it well. You are happy and thrive in the application, practice and learning involved in its pursuit.
3. **Relatedness of Purpose** – You must link your pursuits to a purpose involving connection with, and service to, others.

As a leader, strive to ensure that your employees can achieve autonomy, mastery and purpose. This might develop in different way and in different people over the course of many years, but as long as they're on the path they stand a much better chance of being happy and engaged at work.

THE EMOTIONAL CONNECTION
Gallup stands above all other organizations in the depth and breadth of its research into the drivers of engagement. Over the decades, it has come to a very solid (if intuitively obvious) conclusion about what makes people connect to another person, an employer, a seller or a community. In studying customers across industries, it found that those who are emotionally engaged are far more valuable that those who are rationally engaged.

---

[5] - See: http://en.wikipedia.org/wiki/Self-determination_theory

For example, if you have a customer who has experienced nothing but positive service (i.e. great price, great quality, responsiveness, etc.) in their dealings with you, congratulations; you're very likely to have a rationally satisfied customer. If, on the other hand, you have a customer who deeply identifies with your products, services or brand – even if they pay more and even if they occasionally experience poor quality and bad service – you likely have an emotionally engaged customer.

Despite experiencing the same (or worse) treatment as a customer, someone who is emotionally engaged is far more likely to remain your customer and spend more money with you over time.[6]

This runs completely counter to the field of classical economics, which is based on the assumption that consumers act rationally. But where classical economics gets it wrong is that people very often *do not* act rationally; they act on emotion and they never engage on a rational basis. They only engage on an emotional level.

Think about your own behaviors. If you always act rationally, you'll always buy the lowest cost car with the longest and best warranty. Some manufacturers go after that market, but many others – especially the luxury brands – succeed in winning your business with other carefully crafted messages that resonate with you emotionally and that make you want to be identified with that brand. The very same thing applies to employees. We have to get their *emotional* commitment, we need to make them *want* to stay, perform well and see the organization succeed.

CHOOSE THE RIGHT LEADERS
If you get only one thing right, make sure it's your leaders – especially front-line managers and supervisors. Don't let bad leaders impact your workforce. Remember that not everyone should be a leader or wants to be a leader. Get it right in your organization by knowing the difference between a high performing individual contributor (IC) and one with the potential to be a leader. ICs with leadership potential tend to exhibit common traits. They perform at high levels, but they also demonstrate cognitive and emotional intelligence; a willingness to work with, assist and share recognition with others; a commitment to learning; and they do what they say they'll do. Most importantly, they inspire high commitment and high performance in others. In other words, they get things done through other people.

Great managers and leaders are motivated to lead. Too many organizations provide only one path for employees to achieve the prestige and high pay that talented individuals seek – the management track. Smart organizations create a second career ladder for those who prefer to remain technical experts, great salespeople or brilliant researchers but still want to be promoted, respected and rewarded without being forced into leadership roles.

With the right leaders in place – either through selection, development or both – the path to a highly engaged workforce is largely free of obstacles. You'll still need a sense of purpose and the right incentives, but great leaders will deliver both seamlessly.

---

6 - John H. Fleming and Jim Apslund, Human Sigma, Gallup Press, 2007

Enterprise Engagement: The Textbook

Chapter 9

Volunteer & Community Engagement

For most organizations today, community involvement – whether it's a small business sponsoring a local soccer team, a law firm donating pro-bono services or a multinational corporation contributing to education efforts in poor countries – has become essential to the development of a positive brand image, as well as to recruiting and retaining top talent. In the U.S. alone, giving exceeds $300 billion each year.[1]

Corporate involvement in improving communities and societies has a long history. In the U.S., industrialists such as Henry Ford, John D. Rockefeller, Andrew Carnegie and others built institutions of learning and foundations that are still contributing to the betterment of society today – in some cases more than a century after they were started.

Dating back as far as the 1970s, however, the focus and practice of corporate philanthropy has been in a state of flux. The practice of corporate foundations funding worthy proposals by writing checks alone has evolved into a more active and, it is hoped, more sustainable, form of giving.

Today, corporate philanthropy and volunteerism is often referred to under the blanket term Corporate Social Responsibility (CSR), emphasizing the linkage of community needs with business values to produce sustainability. In other words, where corporate giving and volunteering is integrated – benefiting both the community *and* the employer – it is more likely to continue and grow than if money were merely handed out in support of good causes.

Corporate Social Responsibility encompasses a broader strategy of giving centered on engagement. CSR initiatives aim to engage the community so the organization is viewed in a positive light, and to engage employees, who want to "do good" and be associated with a company that gives back. CSR also engages customers and consumers who want to support responsible companies and be associated with positive brands.

There's little doubt that tremendous value can be created when an organization's business goals and strategy are linked to (and integrated with) community priorities,

---

1 - See: http://www.american.com/archive/2008/march-april-magazine-contents/a-nation-of-givers

including social welfare (human and animal), jobs, growth, education, the environment and goals such as community health, safety and improved educational performance.

ACTIVE PHILANTHROPY
Companies have always understood the benefits of maintaining good relationships with the communities in which they operate, but *active* philanthropy deepens the connections as employees representing the firm work side by side with staff and other volunteers in nonprofits, schools, hospitals and elsewhere. In turn, organizations benefit from the increased engagement and skill-building of their employees and the stable and healthy communities they contribute to.

The meaning of "good corporate citizenry" has changed over the years, as has the concept of community and volunteer engagement. In the past decade or so, the definition of "community" – which once meant the local communities in which organizations did business – has expanded tremendously. With social media and the explosion of online and virtual communities, organizations must be careful to nurture their image wherever they sell their products and services (or hope to), not just where they make them or where they happen to have offices or factories. Most large organizations monitor and manage their reputations and image online as much as they do in the physical world, and in many cases are even more active in online communities than local ones.

For large companies like Microsoft, the world is literally their community, including the online world. While not a part of the Microsoft Corporation, the Bill & Melinda Gates Foundation is nonetheless associated with the company, contributing billions of dollars worldwide each year for education, healthcare and other programs while involving leaders and employees of dozens of companies (including Microsoft) in helping deliver those programs.

Volunteer engagement, which was once almost exclusively the domain of nonprofits, has expanded to include a wide swath of the for-profit sector. Today, corporate volunteers in the U.S. alone number in the hundreds of thousands – employees who contribute their time each year to fundraisers, schools, nonprofits and other initiatives, both at home and abroad, while on the payroll of their firms.

Arguably, the definition of volunteer can also be broadened to include unpaid internships and other "corporate in-house volunteers," and certainly to encompass the millions of individuals who are engaged in rating, recommending, reviewing, summarizing and providing feedback on commercial products and services ranging from books to software, hotels, restaurants, cars and just about everything else. In many cases, informal volunteers spend countless hours online, helping other users of commercial products with tips and solutions, some of which are unavailable even from the providers themselves.

The broader community in which you do business, whether you're a for-profit company, a government agency or a nonprofit, is an increasingly important stakeholder. Within those physical and virtual communities are volunteers and potential volunteers who exist alongside detractors and potential detractors. Most organizations can no longer afford to think only locally when engaging their communities, nor can they fail to think about volunteers in a broader context.

Engagement with the Community pays off to the Bottom Line

64%
Corporate Giving Up Since Recession

Companies that have increased giving by more than 10% since 2010 also increased median revenues by 11% from 2010 to 2013

In this chapter, volunteer and community engagement is discussed in the context of corporate volunteers and volunteering, as well as Corporate Social Responsibility and contributions to the community. Traditional "volunteer engagement" in the nonprofit sector, while similar in many respects, is the domain of numerous other books and articles.

ALIGNING THE ORGANIZATION'S MISSION

Organizations that excel in employee and customer engagement understand the vital connection to Corporate Social Responsibility (CSR) which includes aligning the organization's mission with causes, being a good corporate citizen in terms of the environment and other social causes, and giving back wherever possible to communities and people. In its *Talent Report: What Workers Want in 2012*, Net Impact found that workers who are able to make a social or environmental impact on the job are more satisfied than other employees by a margin of 2:1. Moreover, the report found that 71% felt more positive about their company.

Many organizations address community and volunteer engagement by combining the two – allowing their employees to take paid volunteer time where they may work locally or even globally and/or contribute online to causes virtually anywhere. Each year, the number of formal corporate volunteer programs increases, as does the amount invested per employee. Volunteers contribute to causes ranging from food shelters and literacy programs to aid work and special projects in developing countries. One corporate volunteer program called "A Billion + Change," for example, has secured commitments worth more than $1.7 billion from 160 companies as of 2012.[2] This represents about twelve million hours of corporate volunteer time in nonprofits.

LBG Associates' 2012 study of employee volunteerism found that 52% of companies are operating hybrid volunteer programs (in which volunteer events and activities are organized, planned and run jointly by the company and employees) versus just 36% in 2004, when it published its *Measuring Corporate Volunteerism* study. It also found that service on boards is more prevalent – a full 93% of respondents to its 2012 survey

---

[2] - See: http://www.causecast.com/blog/bid/166457/In-a-Tough-Economy-Pro-Bono-Employee-Volunteering-Takes-on-New-Importance

encourage executives to serve on boards of nonprofits, an increase of about six percentage points compared with similar data gathered in 2004.[3]

REAL WORLD EXAMPLES
Campbell Soup Company encourages employee volunteers by paying their salary while they volunteer, a practice that more and more organizations are adopting every year. To entice employees even further, Campbell takes the unusual step of topping up that contribution by adding $20 per hour in cash to nonprofits for every hour its employees volunteer, including hours contributed on Campbell time and after hours.

At Microsoft, ongoing employee volunteering and giving now surpasses $100 million each year and benefits about 20,000 organizations worldwide. Since 1983, Microsoft employees have raised more than $1 billion for charities,[4] and the company matches each hour of employees' volunteer time with $17 in cash. Similarly, Kraft runs an annual Week of Service that raises almost $3 million in addition to the time Kraft employees spend volunteering with nonprofits nationwide.

Since 2008, IBM has deployed more than 100 teams and 1,000 of its employees to communities in need worldwide through just one of its corporate volunteer programs. Entitled Corporate Service Corps (CSC), the program selects only from IBM's highest performing and most promising associates. Competition to be selected for the program is intense – it's among the most sought-after rewards for top performers at IBM – with less than one in a hundred applicants selected each year.[5] IBM's CSC teams include roughly 5-10 employees and their assignments last about six months, including more than two months in preparation, a month or more on-site and another two months concluding their projects back home. The impact of the program has been felt in dozens of countries so far.

According to Harvard professor Chris Marquis, the volunteers generate tremendous value for the recipient countries. For IBM, which has spent well over $50 million on the program already, there are also big returns. CSC participants become more engaged, stay with the company longer and develop very valuable skills.[6] The CSC projects build goodwill in communities worldwide, occasionally leading to paid assignments. For IBM, the positive brand-building and deep connections made in emerging nations constitute a long-term investment that is bound to pay off as those nations grow and develop.

To meet its goal of creating shared value, IBM operates the program for a variety of reasons.

- It's part of IBM's rewards and recognition for high achievers and high potentials – being admitted to the program is clear evidence of an associate's value to the company.
- It's a valuable tool for associate development, teaching future leadership skills that would be more expensive and more risky to obtain through typical expatriate assignments.
- As noted above, the program generates enormous goodwill and positive brand association for IBM.
- Applicants are attracted to the program because it offers them both tangible and intangible rewards.

---

[3] - See: http://www.lbg-associates.com/publications/
[4] - See: http://doublethedonation.com/blog/2013/01/spotlight-on-microsoft-a-leader-in-corporate-giving/
[5] - See: http://www.businessweek.com/stories/2009-03-11/the-world-is-ibms-classroom
[6] - Ibid

- It's good for their development and career trajectory, and it appeals to their need for meaningful work and to make a contribution.

In short, there's as much in it for IBM as there is for the communities that host the projects. And that also means the program is much less likely to be cut when business is slack or when different leadership takes the helm.

Pfizer Pharmaceuticals is also a pioneer in corporate volunteerism. Since 2003, hundreds of employees worldwide have participated in its corporate volunteer programs. Like IBM, Pfizer pays its employee volunteers' salary while they're working for aid organizations and nonprofits. Also like IBM, Pfizer aligns its projects to its business and the skills and knowledge of its volunteers.

At outdoor apparel company Patagonia, employee salaries and benefits are paid for one month while on assignment to nonprofit environmental groups worldwide. Again, the projects leverage employees' knowledge and interests. Where organizations can donate employee time toward projects that tap their skills and passions, the results can be many times more impactful than those made by typical volunteers.

According to the *2011 Volunteerism ROI Tracker* study, employee volunteers can be significantly more effective than traditional volunteers, in part because of the alignment between the projects they volunteer for and their skill sets and interests.

From the perspective of the nonprofit beneficiary, the skills and talents of corporate volunteers can be as much as 500% more valuable than what traditional volunteers bring."[7] For the company, the report states that "skills-based volunteers are 142% more likely to report job-related skills gains than traditional volunteers, 47% are more likely to report high satisfaction from volunteering than traditional volunteers, and 82% are more likely to report that volunteerism generated new recruits for their company versus traditional volunteers.[8] Clearly, employee volunteer programs generate engagement at an emotional level for both employees and the community.

TACTICS OF VOLUNTEER ENGAGEMENT

Volunteers are the lifeblood of any successful corporate volunteer program. Causecast, which describes itself as the "Complete Corporate Philanthropy and Employee Volunteering Platform," notes on its website that corporate volunteer and giving campaigns can be beautifully conceived with the best of intentions, "but their oxygen is engagement. Without employee buy-in, cause campaigns die a slow, embarrassing death, leaving a trail of bitter disappointment in their wake that only makes it more difficult to launch other campaigns in the future."

Taking participation for granted is a mistake many organizations make in their initial efforts. Employees are busy and may have their own causes to which they donate time and money. Given this, there are several important ingredients and tactics necessary to launching and sustaining a successful program.

PLANNING

Start by planning what kind of volunteer program you want to offer the community. Ideally, it will align with the skills and knowledge of your employees and support the brand your organization wants to be known for. It should also be something your organization understands well so that you can contribute with the shortest learning curve and most impact.

---

[7] - See: http://www.trueimpact.com/blog/bid/74811/Key-Findings-from-the-Volunteerism-ROI-Tracker
[8] - Ibid

For example, a local hardware store might align with the local chapter of Habitat for Humanity, a veterinary clinic might donate employees' time to the local SPCA or Humane Society. For a large national publisher or educator, online literacy programs, including tutoring, might be a good choice. Whatever the cause, ensure that employees can get involved easily and that it's something worthy – look for the biggest bang within the constraints you'll be operating under. This can mean being selective about which causes already show promise and those which are unlikely to be able to sustain the benefits after your program ends.

> **Nearly two-thirds of students entering the job market today expect to make a social and environmental impact through their work, and 45% indicated they would be willing to take a pay cut to do so. In fact, students say this is more important than having children, a prestigious career, being wealthy, or being a community leader, ranking only below financial security and marriage.**
>
> **~ What Workers Want in 2012, Net Impact[9]**

Think about the intrinsic value a volunteer opportunity might bring participants and the amount of time it requires. Can it be completed in one day, or is it a longer commitment like IBM's Corporate Service Corps? Will it be something volunteers will do for a few hours a day on an ongoing basis or for a defined period of time? Think about what works better with volunteers' schedules and the needs of the organization(s) you'll be helping. Consider employees' other work objectives and your own requirements on their time.

Once you've selected a program and cause and the nonprofit or community organization it will benefit has agreed, give yourself time to plan and promote the program before it launches. Two to three months is a good cushion, depending on the length, size and complexity of your program (i.e., local, overseas, online) Remember there are likely to be logistical challenges, including transportation, catering and supplies, in addition to scheduling, promotions and planning the project work itself.

RECRUITING & RECOGNITION

How many employees are likely to participate? How will you get the word out? Consider the incentives you'll use to entice volunteers. The intangible or intrinsic incentives are obvious and compelling if you've picked the right causes, but will you also offer tangible (extrinsic) rewards? As noted above, paid time off to volunteer is fairly standard, but how much and how often? Will you offer awards or prizes for the most committed volunteers? Will you contribute matching cash donations on top of volunteer time? All of these tactics are used frequently by organizations, sometimes to generate competition among employee volunteers, and other times to promote teamwork and a sense of shared accomplishment.

Also frame the programs as developmental and learning rewards. When volunteer programs are aligned with the organization's competencies, employees should see volunteering as a learning opportunity and career-enhancing activity. Demonstrate the value you place on volunteering by integrating your corporate volunteer program with performance management & reviews, succession planning and leadership identification activities. When employees link volunteering to improved prospects for promotion, they'll be even more motivated to participate because they'll know the company takes it seriously.

Beyond rewards, volunteers should be frequently recognized for their efforts and participation. The right recognition tactics can get employees excited about volunteering, including simple communication tools such as articles and pictures in

---

9 - See: https://netimpact.org/blog/what-workers-want-in-2012-introducing-net-impacts-talent-report

corporate newsletters and email circulars, or even running ads to recognize your employees' contributions in the local newspaper (which combines employee recognition with positive community brand-building). Of course, recognition of skills developed or knowledge learned is also critical. This can be formalized through individual learning plans and in performance reviews.

POST-PROGRAM
Recognition of volunteers might include a team celebration after the program. Certificates of Participation might be distributed at the event, along with a speech by the CEO and/or the leader of the beneficiary organization summarizing the value and impact the program generated. Remember to use your newsletters and website to showcase the program and include it in official corporate publications such as your annual report.

Seek to share the good work of your employee volunteers within the organization and externally in your communities and among your stakeholders in ways that communicate accomplishment and recognition. Avoid self-serving advertisements that praise the company itself or glorify the use of its products in volunteer efforts. The focus should be on the volunteers and those they helped.

Think about your next program as you conclude the most recent one. Will it be repeated or become an ongoing program with the same beneficiaries? Should it be expanded? What can be improved? Now is the time to learn from your efforts, maximize their impact and plan for your next program.

SOCIAL COMMUNITIES AND ONLINE ENGAGEMENT
Today, community engagement includes a major dimension that wasn't on the radar of most organizations just 15 years ago. Online social networks and communities have become new and powerful places for organizations to develop followings – even volunteers – for their commercial interests. At the same time, they represent great risk to reputation and brand for many companies.

Hyper-connected customers can be extremely active and influential in their support or criticism of your products, services, actions or inactions as a company. Positive reviews on Amazon, Yelp, TripAdvisor, Twitter or Facebook can generate hundreds or thousands of potential new customers in days or even hours. When Oreo cookies sent out a simple tweet "You can still dunk in the dark," during a blackout in the 2013 Super Bowl, it was quickly re-tweeted to 15,811 people and generated 2,200 new twitter followers for Oreo.[10]

Just as a positive review can go viral, so can a negative one, oftentimes even faster and with devastating consequences. In 2012, a woman entered a David's Bridal store in Sioux Falls, SD, looking for a wedding gown. According to her subsequent Facebook post, she was abandoned and left unattended after an associate discovered she had tattoos on her back. According to an article in *Forbes*, her post attracted more than 125,000 likes and thousands of comments within days, including many who claimed to have had similar experiences at other David's locations. The company's response – David's Bridal claims to be the largest bridal retailer in the world – didn't appear until a week after the incident and didn't directly apologize.

This fumbled attempt to manage a rapidly worsening situation itself attracted more than 1,000 additional, mostly negative, comments. *Forbes* described it as a "social media

---
10 - See: http://www.huffingtonpost.com/jose-costa/brand-building_b_3950341.html

disaster" that led to loss of business and a boycott, all organized by angry online communities.[11]

The impact of negative reviews on retailers and others types of businesses (i.e., hotels, restaurants and most personal services businesses) may be the single-most vital element to their success. In a sense, their community is both physical and virtual, and it may consist of "volunteers" from all corners of the globe.

Regardless of industry, most companies today can gain or lose by engaging (or failing to engage) online communities and volunteers. Coca-Cola, for example, is the world's most recognizable brand,[12] but its engaged customers (aka, volunteers) help make it a cool brand in social media. Coke was once in a neck-and-neck race with Pepsi for dominance in the soft drink industry, but today both Coke and Diet Coke lead the industry by a comfortable margin, leaving Pepsi in third place.[13]

Obviously, we don't know what part social media has played in Coke's dominance, but we do know that Coke has embraced customer involvement with its online brand. A visit to Coke's homepage is evidence enough. The page is dominated by social media – "tell a friend," post to Facebook, twitter, etc. Furthermore, Coke integrates its traditional advertising with its social media strategy. For example, its marketing and product placement on shows such as American Idol is made interactive, allowing Coke's customers to go online to influence the programming on the show itself.[14]

Not long ago, Coke, like most companies, had no idea of the eventual impact of sites like Facebook. In this period, volunteers – supportive fans of a company or of its products or services – often started Facebook fan pages without the involvement or knowledge of the company. For Coke, the story is posted on its Facebook page and goes like this: *"Once upon a time, while searching for the official Coca-Cola Facebook page, a young man named Dusty discovered there wasn't one. Feeling inspired, he enlisted the help of his friend Michael, found the perfect image of a Coke and created this page. The rest, as they say, is history."*

Today, most organizations monitor their social media brands very carefully – if you don't already have a business profile page on Facebook, for example, you should. But because companies have little control over what is said (and would be very unwise to censor such postings[15]), their strategies and tactics must recognize that the customer – or volunteer – is really the one in charge these days.

People become fans of brands and companies on Facebook mainly because they're customers (or would be customers if the right incentives were offered) and because they want to tell others they like the brand. Ideally, they can be enticed to form an emotional attachment and connection with the brand and want to be associated with it as well. However, with millions of companies competing for online fans, incentives and rewards have become an important tactic in building online communities.

First, make sure that your website and social media pages offer compelling and useful content for visitors. Then, encourage your employees, friends, family and current customers to "like" you online and build your following from there. Often, companies

---

11 - See: http://www.forbes.com/sites/kellyclay/2012/08/06/why-this-facebook-post-could-destroy-a-business/
12 - See: http://www.interbrand.com/en/best-global-brands/2013/Coca-Cola
13 - See: http://online.wsj.com/news/articles/SB10001424052748703899704576204933906436332
14 - See: http://adage.com/article/cmo-strategy/coke-crowdsources-song-american-idol-finale/241282/
15 - For a case study in how not to manage a social media presence, see: https://www.techdirt.com/articles/20131218/11581925605/kleargear-sued-destroying-credit-couple-who-wrote-negative-review.shtml

run contests in which people can enter by "liking" them on Facebook.[16] The "likes" become the basis for a growing community of fans that might also become customers. Moneysaver, for example, ran a contest in which people who "liked" their page would be entered to win one of several $50 Outback Restaurant gift cards.

Fans were further incentivized to forward the contest details to their friends and enter comments about why they like Moneysaver. Within a nine-month timeframe, this simple and cost-effective tactic quadrupled Moneysaver's number of fans and almost doubled its email list.[17]

Alignment is also important in developing your social media strategy. Florida-based Toojays Restaurant doesn't simply ask fans to "like" them on Facebook, it asks them to take pictures of the menu items they like best, along with the location of the restaurant. In this way Toojays appears on hundreds of people's Facebook forum pages with pictures of its food and recommendations from their friends.

These tactics – restaurant gift cards, movie coupons, etc. – are further enhanced when combined with an emotional component. An athletic shoe brand, for example, might reward followers with chances to win tickets to a pro sporting event. If combined with efforts to align the brand with a lifestyle or personal image, it stands to make a much greater impact because the emotional connection is more likely to lead to lasting engagement. The brand might also sponsor events or endorse specific athletes to cause their customers to better identify with and "live the brand."

The combination of tactics described above entices people to the brand with social-media-based contests and will keep them if it can establish an emotional connection. Central to this achievement will be combining community and volunteer engagement strategies. Such integration requires a clear vision of the brand architecture (external & internal) and consistency across communications mediums.

In essence, to manage their online brands effectively and to engage virtual communities, organizations need to become marketing vehicles, and the marketing organization itself needs to become the engagement engine, responsible for establishing priorities and stimulating dialogue throughout the social media as it seeks to design, build, operate and renew cutting-edge community and volunteer engagement approaches.

Clearly, the tactics used in corporate volunteerism and physical community engagement differ tremendously from those deployed in the virtual, social media world. The underlying principles, however, are the same:

- Communities and volunteers, no matter who they are or where they are, must be engaged at an emotional level.
- Organizations must develop integrated, organization-wide strategies to align their efforts with their values and goals and to ensure consistency across all divisions of the organization and across all mediums in which the brand is being promoted.
- Community and Volunteer engagement, whether physical or online, are intertwined with customer, employee and other stakeholder engagement. Efforts in one or the other are profoundly less successful if they're not enveloped in a broader Enterprise Engagement strategy.

---

16 - Note that Facebook has some restrictions on the running of contests and promotions on its site. See: https://www.facebook.com/business/news/page-promotions-terms

17 - http://blogs.constantcontact.com/product-blogs/social-media-marketing/facebook-contests

Enterprise Engagement: The Textbook

Chapter 10

Vendor Engagement

Of all our stakeholders, vendors and suppliers are often the most challenging. It's natural to think that if you select a supplier and pay their fees, they should be happy and provide sound customer service. But suppliers are just as human as customers, employees and other stakeholders. To get the most from them, you have to treat them with the respect, trust and emotional intelligence they deserve.

The relationships with those in the supply chain can represent the greatest risk of all to a business. Unlike customers, vendors might remain even when they're treated poorly. But as with employees, financial incentives alone won't engage them to the point where a real relationship is created. Absent emotional engagement with your suppliers, you can never become a "customer of choice." And when your suppliers see you only as a paycheck, they're not emotionally invested in your success. This can be a crippling disadvantage that's especially fraught with risk because it lurks just below the surface – invisible until a crisis occurs and a trusting partnership with a supplier is needed, but it's not there.

Benefits of Vendor Engagement

Lower Costs / Better Service / Referrals = **Vendor Engagement** = Higher Quality / More Supply & Availability / Ideas/Feedback & Insights

STEAK AND PRODUCE
Consider the advantages that an engaged vendor brings. Imagine you're a restaurant owner in a small college town that specializes in local fare. You've been in business for a year and things are looking very promising. You have one main competitor who is also supplied by the only organic farm in the area, just outside town. The busy fall

season is approaching, parents will be arriving with their kids and everyone is looking for a nice place to have dinner (students are especially conscious about food and the environment).

Suppose prime cuts of beef are suddenly in short supply and the vegetable growing season was cut short by an early autumn cold snap. There's simply not enough organic beef and produce to meet demand. Will your restaurant be the one offering steaks and local farm-to-table produce? Or will you be running blue-plate specials on pasta and burgers? It likely depends on your relationship with your suppliers.

> **Many of our frequent and recurring failures in organizations are a consequence of not comprehending the importance of relationships. We approach major organizational issues – mergers, accountability, knowledge management, implementation and change – as if they were engineering issues.**
>
> ~ Meg Wheatley

Suppose you're told that your allotment of steak and produce will be far less than what you need. How do you react? Do you threaten to remove them as a supplier if they don't come up with what you need? Do you threaten to withhold monies you might owe them for past deliveries? Either response is typical of what suppliers encounter all the time. But think about your competitor – the restaurant across town that is getting all the steaks and produce it needs. Why? Maybe they pay a premium, but it's more likely due to the type of relationship they have with the supplier. Their suppliers are treated more like partners, with trust, transparency, respectful interactions, perhaps even incentives and certainly plenty of recognition.

Your competitor goes on to have record revenues for the next two weeks. In fact, you lose two of your top wait staff to them (perhaps your employee engagement practices are also in need of adjustment). Your competitor wins some of your customer base, and your relationship with your supplier is worse than ever.

Of course, nothing comes without cost. Your competitor spent time and money ensuring that their relationship with the supplier was grounded both in the rational and the emotional. In addition to paying on time and agreeing to a fair price, your competitor shows appreciation for the supplier, she visits the farm on occasional weekends with her family and invites the owners and staff to her restaurant. She features recipes with the farm's products in her monthly newsletter, promoting them alongside the restaurant itself. She recognizes exceptional customer service by thanking farm staff and praising them to the farm's owners.

In August, well ahead of the fall crush, she met with the farm. She explained the importance of the two weeks in mid-September that could make or break her business. By sharing this information, she made herself vulnerable to the farm raising prices – after all, it has her over a barrel. But because the relationship is strong and built on trust, and because the farm owners genuinely care about her restaurant's success, jacking up prices doesn't even cross their minds. Indeed, they bend over backward to help her prepare. And when the unexpected cold snap occurs and their beef supply drops at the same time, they take care of her…to your detriment.

TREMENDOUS RISK
In 2012, Gallup published a white paper on supplier engagement entitled *Creating Strategic Advantage through Superior Supplier Engagement*.[1] The authors, Leslie Rowlands and John H. Fleming, found that organizations face tremendous risk in their supply

---

1 - See: http://www.gallup.com/strategicconsulting/159326/creating-strategic-advantage-superior-supplier-engagement.aspx for the full report.

chains due to numerous factors, but key among them is the absence of an "emotional connection" in most of their relationships with vendors.

The paper goes on to advise leaders that they should actively measure supplier engagement and strive to become a "customers of choice." Doing so, they argue, requires more than the rational elements associated with paying vendors for their goods and services. Instead, leaders should seek a blend of the rational and emotional drivers that create deep, enduring and resilient connections.

The reward is better customer service, first access to the latest improvements and innovations created by the vendor, vendors who speak highly of your organization and recommend you to others, and, as in the example above, access to goods and services when demand exceeds supply.

The closer you get to your vendors, the more they trust you and the more you might learn about your industry and the competition. While you should not attempt to turn your suppliers into spies, they're a terrific source of intelligence about what's selling and what might be coming next. As Rowlands and Fleming note: "…suppliers will go above and beyond for one customer over another, yielding advantages for the customer of choice."

> **Many fear their companies are only as strong as the weakest link in their supply chain.**
>
> **~ Gallup, 2012**

Bestselling author Dan Pink echoes this sentiment. In his book, *To Sell is Human*, he describes a new world of selling in which suppliers no longer have an information advantage over buyers. He refers to "problem-finding" as the new value suppliers can offer their customers and uses Mentos Mints as an example. Today, Mentos' parent company, Perfetti Van Melle, emphasizes a new frontier in sales by helping customers understand their businesses better.

According to Pink: "Using a mix of number-crunching and their own knowledge and expertise, the Perfetti salespeople tell retailers what assortment of candy is best for them to make the most money. That could mean offering five flavors of Mentos rather than seven. And it almost always means including products from competitors."

Pink cites a Perfetti VP as saying his best salespeople think of their jobs not so much as selling candy but as "selling insights about the confectionary business."[2] Imagine a world in which your suppliers' market insights give you the intelligence and vision you needed to stay a step ahead!

BEST PRACTICES AND TACTICS
Gallup suggests that organizations follow a structured process for vendor engagement. All suppliers are not equal in terms of their importance or risk to your business, so it makes sense to evaluate them – including whether you have the right vendors and the right number of vendors. While it's likely you'll have two or more tiers of vendor – and you'll focus more of your engagement effort on some rather than others – good relationships should be sought with all.

BASIC SATISFACTION
It's important to draw a distinction between vendor management and vendor *engagement*. A good definition of the former comes from Frank Nuegebauer, CIO of United Educators, who calls supplier relationship management "an all-inclusive

---

2 - Dan Pink, To Sell is Human, Riverhead Books, 2012. P.131

approach to managing the affairs and interactions with the organizations that supply your company with goods and services. This includes communications, business practices, negotiations, methodologies and software that is used to establish and maintain a relationship with a supplier. Benefits include lower costs, higher quality, better forecasting and less tension between the two entities that result in a win-win relationship."

Naturally, good supplier relationship management is a necessary foundation for supplier engagement; it's akin to employee or customer satisfaction but on the vendor side. But satisfaction maps only to the rational elements Gallup addressed in the white paper referenced above. While they're all necessary, they won't endear you to a supplier on an emotional level, and therefore won't confer maximum competitive advantage.

Strategically and tactically, then, it's essential that solid supplier relationship management has been established – including rigorous processes for vendor selection, clear service level agreements, communications, dispute resolutions and vendor evaluation. Once those fundamentals are in place, vendor *engagement* can build a deeper, more resilient relationship. Of course, there's no reason that vendor management and vendor engagement capabilities can't or shouldn't be built simultaneously.

> **The real potential comes in the collaborative, mutually supportive relationships you establish with the suppliers whose capabilities best fit your needs. By building trust and transparency with these companies, you can eliminate inefficiencies, collaborate on innovations, and take advantage of each other's strengths.**
>
> **~ Paul W. Schroder and David M. Powell**

ENGAGEMENT

Eliminate elements of your culture that encourage or tolerate adversarial relationships with suppliers. Make it a policy that money isn't to be used to drive better vendor performance, or the withholding of money used as a threat. Pay fairly and on time for goods and services that are delivered according to Service Level Agreements (SLAs). Even consider financial bonuses for exceeding SLAs, but avoid threats to withhold money owed and avoid policies to always choose the low-cost supplier. At the same time, resist offering premiums only when you're in desperate need.

Cultivate relationships that move beyond a transactional mindset. Be sure not to treat vendors maliciously or with "benign neglect" – both are dangerous. By being engaged in projects outsourced to vendors, you demonstrate their importance and make it possible for vendors to be engaged in turn. We all carry some responsibility for being engaged, so that our employees, those who sell to us, our partners, customers and others can more easily make the effort to truly connect to our goals – and our success.

Most leaders know that one of the benefits of engaged employees is greater creativity and innovation. Engaged employees, by definition, trust their employers. Because they trust and because they're happy at work, they can take risks, offer suggestions and innovate. Likewise, vendors should be made to feel secure and trusted so that they offer suggestions, give feedback and provide information. After all, few stakeholders are better positioned to understand your industry (and your competitors) than your suppliers, and few invest more time and effort in their understanding. They can be a natural and invaluable ally.

COMMUNICATION
Strive for transparency in your relationships with suppliers. Communicate frequently and disclose fully. A partnership without transparency is a dysfunctional one that cannot leverage information and strengths. Where your organization relies on a web of suppliers, withholding vital information creates chokepoints, leading to slow responses and errors. Transparency, on the other hand, allows for easier orchestration of the many moving parts in your supply chain. Of course, some information must be held secret, but in general the tendency to be open and share is the superior culture.

As with employees, try to make all interactions positive. In situations where the vendor isn't performing and you feel the situation cannot be corrected (or it would take inordinate time or resources to do so), respectfully end the arrangement, much as you would with an employee who cannot or will not do the job.

REWARDS & RECOGNITION
Use recognition widely, it's free and has an enormous impact. From praising vendor employees to sending thank-you notes when expectations are exceeded to recommending your supplier to other potential customers (or acting as a reference), the bonds are strengthened and the emotional commitment deepened. Even an acknowledgement on the bottom of an email about unrelated business can have a powerful impact. It can go a long way toward building good will, and it only costs you a few seconds of your time.

> **All relationships in an enterprise system are connected, including the vital living and emotional connections between stakeholders.**
>
> ~ Jeremy Scrivens[3]

Consider tangible rewards where appropriate. Bonuses for exceeding SLAs, gain-shares for completing a project ahead of schedule or under budget – even contract extensions recognizing excellent work – are legitimate drivers of engagement. But more powerful still are rewards with a personal touch. The restaurant owner inviting supplier employees for a free dinner. The CEO taking an executive from a vendor company out golfing or sailing. The tangible reward value may be small, but the impact is often immeasurably large and long-lasting.

RELATIONSHIP-BUILDING
Choose those who lead your vendor engagement efforts carefully – as you would supervisors and managers of your employees. In addition to domain knowledge, project management, communications, problem-solving, negotiating and contractual skills, they should possess sufficient emotional intelligence to build and maintain the kind of trusting, transparent relationships described above.

Engagement beyond employees and customers is still a fairly radical idea, which makes its early adopters ripe for realizing a competitive advantage. People want to be engaged, but you still have to give them reasons to *become* engaged. Whether they're employees, customers, partners, vendors, volunteers or members of the community, people want to be inspired and feel like they're a part of something meaningful. What is elegant and immensely attractive about engagement is that it offers so little resistance.

Why not build convivial, trusting relationships with suppliers and stakeholders? Conversely, why would you either deliberately create caustic relationships or allow them to develop with the people you rely on most to make your business successful – whether they be employees, customers, partners or suppliers?

---

3 - See: http://www.businessdnaresources.com/Articles/The%20Emotional%20Economy%20-%20White%20Paper%20200.pdf

Enterprise Engagement: The Textbook

Chapter 11

The Employee/Customer Link

By Barbara Porter

Rapidly changing customer needs and adoption of new technologies, combined with increased pressure on short-term financial results, has forced companies to look for a model that aligns business priorities with those of employees, customers and stakeholders. The one element that most influences the ability to deliver sustained results is the culture you create for your organization linking employees and customers.

The challenge of many executives is how to deliver both an improved customer experience and improved financial metrics. To address this, many executives and managers turn to cutting costs and headcount or increasing pricing to achieve the necessary results. But this tends to ignore the importance of employees as the most effective means they have to deliver both a defined customer experience and sustained business improvement.

Traditionally, organizations have addressed the customer experience in two ways:

1. They look at customer experience from an internal perspective using silos. When this happens, many managers look at how they can reduce their costs and improve or change processes based upon their internal knowledge. Each business unit focuses on their respective departments and begins to make decisions on how they can reduce costs, change or improve processes. Unfortunately, this is done without taking into account how their decisions may affect other parts of the organization or, most importantly, the customer.

2. They look at customer experience from an external perspective. These organizations collect and use customer survey data, yet the majority use this customer feedback to improve processes or change policies. The risk of this "outside-in" view is it can cause havoc in an organization if employees aren't aware of and involved with the changes.

THE EMPLOYEE CONNECTION
Regardless of the approach – internal or external – each ignores the most important element in delivering a memorable customer experience, creating loyalty and

improving financial performance: Employees. An organization's employees impact every aspect of the customer experience, which makes it imperative that employees are part of the process to plan, implement and sustain a successful customer experience.

To maximize the customer experience through employees, companies need to apply the same rigor and strategic thinking to employee engagement as they do to their customer and business strategies. Linking customer and employee engagement isn't an event or project, it's an ongoing strategic imperative. There are three steps involved in building an employee engagement strategy that translates into a positive, productive and profitable customer experience.

1. BUILD AN INTENTIONAL CULTURE
Build an "intentional" culture that links what employees do everyday to the principles and goals of the company. This is an often overlooked or missed step when defining the enterprise (i.e., employee, customer, channel partner, community, etc.) experience.

Revisiting the company's Vision and how the key elements of an operation all deliver on the Vision helps to align the organization and empower employees to make decisions based upon common principles and a thorough understanding of how their actions will deliver on the brand promise of a company.

2. INCORPORATE THE VOICE OF THE EMPLOYEE
Develop a consistent approach and strategy to identify the key drivers of your most engaged employees. The most efficient and cost effective way to establish a robust VOE program is to use an enterprise feedback management tool and platform.

Within many organizations, silos exist and surveys are conducted from multiple departments – marketing, HR, corporate communications, customer service – and rarely is data consolidated into a centralized database that can appropriately analyze and identify critical trends that impact engagement.

Adopt technology that will enable you to listen, collect, analyze and report on the key insights of engagement that most influence your customer experience and your business metrics. There are a number of methods for collecting feedback, including:

Voice. Essentially an online feedback submission form for collecting unsolicited employee questions, concerns and suggestions. This closed-loop channel is available 24/7/365. Each suggestion, complaint or compliment is categorized and managed within a centralized platform that tracks and aggregates the data.

This allows you to respond to employees, delegate responsibility to the person accountable and track the time to resolution or action. Along with submitting input, employees are also prompted to complete an employee engagement survey. This allows you to monitor the pulse of the company's culture and take intentional actions to positively shape and manage that culture. Most importantly, this step assigns an engagement score that allows you to track and correlate employee engagement to customer engagement.

Pulse. At least twice a year, conduct a more thorough engagement survey using driver and outcome questions, as well as customer questions relevant to your business. This type of survey ensures an accurate picture of your culture and engagement. Again, focusing on employees is a key factor in creating and maintaining a positive customer experience.

Involvement. This includes monthly roundtables with a cross-departmental representation of employees, daily leadership visibility, personal contact and involvement. In addition to collecting and analyzing data and feedback, infuse your program with direct relationships that are created with one-on-one, in-person interactions.

A great example of employee Involvement is the creation of an "Ambassador Team" whose members represent their peers. This team meets monthly with management and helps prioritize the suggestions and insights from VOE and VOC data. Consider holding a quarterly company-wide meeting to share employee engagement trends and discuss what actions or changes are needed to further support a positive customer experience. Share actual customer comments and experiences and role play how those scenarios could be improved.

The Employee-Customer-Profit Chain

A Compelling Place to Work	A Compelling Place to Shop	A Compelling Place to Invest
Attitude about the job → Employee Behavior ← Attitude about the company → Employee Retention	Service Helpfulness → Customer Referrals; Customer Impression; Merchandise Value → Customer Retention	Return on assets; Operating margin; Revenue growth

5 Unit increase in employee engagement → 1.3 Unit increase in customer engagement → 0.5 increase in revenue growth

3. LINK EMPLOYEE ACTIVITY TO BUSINESS OBJECTIVES

The final step in developing the customer/employee link is to identify metrics that connect employee activity to business objectives. There are several business outcomes that you can tie directly to employee engagement:

- productivity
- retention/turnover
- employee satisfaction
- quality
- sales

…which directly influence customer experience measures like NPS, customer satisfaction and revenue-per-customer, as well as the following business metrics:

- cost-per-sale
- cost-per-call or interaction
- sales conversion rate
- reduced operating costs
- margin
- CLV (Customer Lifetime Value)

Sustaining business performance requires a constant review of engagement drivers and metrics, as well as a constant review of processes. Without a thorough understanding of what employees do everyday and how it impacts the financial health of the business, you'll create an environment that may be a great place to work, but you'll find yourself quickly losing customers, efficiencies and money.

1. Enterprise Brand. This means defining the attributes of the brand so every department, division and employee has a clear understanding of who the company is and what it stands for. Understanding the attributes of the enterprise brand empowers employees to make sound decisions. Every employee is responsible for understanding how their actions and behaviors deliver on the brand attributes and principles of the company. Whether customer-facing or not, each person can influence how customers perceive the brand.

2. Communication. Communication plays a pivotal role in linking what employees do everyday to the impact they're having on customers and how they're contributing to the overall performance of the company. The purpose of communications is to be transparent in sharing information – the good, the bad and the ugly – as well as to provide customer, employee and personal examples of how to put values into action. This may include a discussion on one of your principles or values or an example of living your values. It should include the status on the key objectives for the year, how the metrics are tracking to meet goals and highlight employees and how they're making a positive difference with customers.

3. Training. Investing in your employees by providing training on new skills and capabilities shows you care about their success. It keeps everyone up-to-date on the knowledge, tools and skills they need to deliver your defined customer experience. Training is also a great resource for delivering leadership skills. One of the most important determinants of employee engagement is the relationship people have with their direct supervisor or manager. Providing leadership training and coaching skills is critical. Continuous leadership education has proven to help improve employee engagement, develop confident and successful customer interactions.

4. Innovation. Develop a process for employees to share new ideas and concepts. The process should capture and categorize ideas into three segments: Core, Extension and Innovative. By providing a structure and channel for employees to submit ideas, they'll begin to feel invested in the success of the business. As with any program, it's important to provide feedback on the status of ideas and where they are in the process.

5. Rewards & Recognition. This is an important factor in making employees feel valued and appreciated. Rewards and recognition should go beyond financial incentives and also focus on recognition by peers, company leadership and customers. See Chapter 18 for more on Rewards & Recognition

6. Measurement. Employee engagement is measured in several ways: employee loyalty scores, employee satisfaction, retention and productivity, just to name a few. It's important that these key metrics are communicated to employees so they understand the impact and the outcome of their behaviors, actions and decisions on the overall customer experience. See Chapters 21 and 22 for more on Measurement and Data

A CRITICAL FACTOR
Forward-thinking organizations now understand that employee engagement is a critical factor in delivering a positive and productive customer experience, in turn making it one of the leading indicators of sustained financial performance. This means employee engagement can't be developed in a vacuum. Linkages need to be examined and analyzed. Connections have to be nurtured and maintained. Remember: Customer engagement begins and ends with your employees.

Enterprise Engagement: The Textbook

Chapter 12

Case Study: American Airlines

By William Keenan Jr.

Sue Gordon has been with American Airlines for over 20 years. Starting as a flight attendant and working her way through a variety of roles, she spent a lot of time on the front lines of marketing, involved in customer communications, advertising, product development and employee communications. She has also worked in IT and had a hand in launching American's first employee portal in 2000-2001. She even did a stint in American's HR department, helping get a Human Resource Communications group off the ground. Most recently she has managed the company's Corporate Communications department.

As a result of that vast and varied experience, Gordon has not only gotten to know American Airlines and the American Way very well, she also understands very clearly how the company's internal communications and branding efforts work to promote employee engagement and employee retention, while at the same time contributing to a more positive customer experience. In other words, she's seen it all – what works and what doesn't.

"It's been kind of a meandering 20 years," says Gordon, "but every experience has built upon the last and has helped give me a very solid understanding, not only of communications fundamentals, but also of our employees and how they interact with our customers – how all of our different functions come together to create the products and services we offer."

A KEY LEVER
One of Gordon's – and American's – primary efforts in this regard is to engage employees in building and improving the customer experience. "Our customer experience efforts are a key employee involvement lever for us," Gordon explains. "From 2001 to today, our industry has essentially been in turmoil. But we found the most traction by involving employees in the business. This is where we've seen the greatest process improvements and the greatest cost savings. It's where we get our best ideas and the greatest amount of buy-in, by involving our employees from soup to nuts in the process."

For example, American introduced blogging on its employee portal as part of its mission to involve employees in the company's efforts to improve the customer experience. The blogs are written by managers and frontline employees, Gordon says, adding, "we've focused them almost exclusively around our customer experience efforts. We spend a lot of time on our blogs talking about the enhancements that various employees have come up with and how they're implemented, as well as gathering whatever other ideas employees have about how we can either improve on those efforts or get new ideas to improve other aspects of the customer experience."

She notes that one of the great things the blogs have generated is a feeling of company-wide participation – "our management team and executives also join the conversation to weigh in on a particular topic."

And to make sure that management is listening and attentive to what's going on in the blogs, Gordon's group creates a summary for each of the weekly blog topics and shares those with experts in each of the relevant departments, "so they understand what's being suggested most frequently and what trends we're seeing, so they have an inventory of the different ideas they can either add to initiatives that are under consideration or evaluate for future use."

PEOPLE IN THE PROCESS
American is involving its employees in an ongoing conversation about other aspects of the business as well. "[The airline industry] has been a very tough environment," says Gordon, "and a big question for us is, how do we communicate with employees in that environment – in particular, how do we continue that constant stream of communication when things aren't going so well? It's no secret that American – like other airlines – has made capacity cuts, and we've laid off employees. So we're working to realign the airline and our employees with the current economic realities. It's really more than a mission statement. We know our employees have to buy into that process."

And what better way to get employee buy-in than by making them an integral part of the process? "We understand that our employees have to work together to implement change – and that we really need their buy-in," says Gordon.

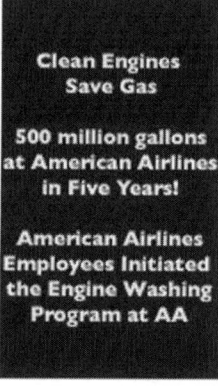

Clean Engines Save Gas

500 million gallons at American Airlines in Five Years!

American Airlines Employees Initiated the Engine Washing Program at AA

One example of this philosophy in action is American's Maintenance & Engineering (M&E) organization. Gordon explains: "Essentially, each of our M&E locations has something like a Town Hall meeting. It's difficult to describe, but we put up a whiteboard and people gather together to share their ideas and their challenges. We talk about our objectives and how we're meeting those objectives – and it really flows into every aspect of our M&E organization, because employees are informed, they understand our objectives, they understand how we're doing, where we're meeting or exceeding our objectives, and where we're falling short."

At the same time, Gordon says, the management team can see where employees may be lacking the tools they need to be able to achieve those objectives, where there are other resource challenges, or where the organization might be bumping up against other ideas and opportunities it's not taking full advantage of.

And this isn't an isolated case. "We have a joint leadership team out in our airports and in our reservation offices whose job it is to go out and facilitate employee involvement," says Gordon. "They're working with our local union leaders, local management team leaders and many of our frontline employees to identify local issues and problems that need to be addressed. They then create task teams to develop and implement solutions for those issues and problems."

SURVIVAL TO SUCCESS
The challenges American and other airlines have faced in the last decade still remain, of course, but Gordon suggests that, "We're moving from a survival decade to what we see as a success decade. Obviously, we still have a highly competitive industry, an extremely regulated workplace and a very unionized workplace – so how do you take all of those factors and get employees' support in helping fight to survive and win?"

Gordon says it all comes back around to getting employee buy-in, and that means a heavy emphasis on internal communications. "It's about engaging and creating employee advocates," she says, "and empowering our employees – particularly when it comes to communication – to help make a difference, both in terms of the service we're delivering and how we're satisfying our customers."

Another example of how employees got involved in helping improve American's business comes out of St. Louis: "We had a lot of older ground equipment there that was basically on its last legs," Gordon notes, "but we didn't have the resources to be able to go out and buy new equipment. We also had a circumstance where we had laid off a number of employees."

A no-win situation? Not if you have a motivated and committed workforce. Gordon says the employees in St. Louis came up with a solution: "Their idea essentially was, 'Give us a handful of resources that we can allocate toward this project and we'll take whatever steps are necessary to rebuild this equipment.' And that's what they did."

They even moved on to refurbishing equipment for other stations that were in similar positions, and eventually American was able to recall employees who had been laid off because they created such a successful model.

"It was just a matter of giving them the latitude to take their ideas and put them into action," says Gordon, "instead of just sitting around and complaining about how we had really old equipment that doesn't work and we didn't have any money."

A MOVING TARGET
Gordon is the first to admit that maintaining a high level of employee involvement and commitment isn't easy in an industry as volatile as this one. "The airline industry offers constant challenges – fuel prices, competitor pricing, the weather – there are so many factors that keep it in flux," she says. But that keeps it exciting, too. "It forces shifts in our corporate thinking – in our targets and priorities – that require constant reengagement with our employees."

To support and reinforce its efforts to involve employees on its many business fronts, American has also launched numerous initiatives to designed to enhance engagement. Some examples:

- The FuelSmart fuel conservation program. This program, which American launched a number of years ago, has been a huge success. "And most of that success comes from employee suggestions and different employee groups working together in light of the dramatic effect that fuel prices can have on the airline industry," says Gordon.
- The "green" movement. "The green movement has been very important for a lot of people globally, and our employees are no different," Gordon notes. "They're a subset of that population, and they care about the environment. So we work with employees to bring in that environmental focus so that it's not just about what we can do to save money, but also how we can do the right thing for our environment."
- Breast cancer awareness. "We've done tremendous things with Susan G. Koman and breast cancer awareness," Gordon says. "They're a big partner for American, and many of our employees feel very strongly about these and other causes."
- Military veterans. "A large percentage of our employee population is veterans or people who come from military families," explains Gordon, "so we also have a focus on veterans' causes."

TIES THAT BIND
And that, in the final analysis, is what makes engagement work for a huge, widely-dispersed company like American. Creating those small "communities" of employees that can put a face on a giant, faceless corporation. And maybe even a soul.

"We have a very big focus at American on our common causes," says Gordon. "These are the ties that bind us, so we look at how we can go out and support these causes, and get our employees involved in that process, so we're not seen as just a corporate façade, but as real people – regardless of whether we're management employees or frontline employees. To show that we care about the same things and we want to work towards supporting those causes together."

Part III
Tools of Engagement

Enterprise Engagement: The Textbook

Intro: Tools and Tactics

Never underestimate the power of organizational silos to thwart abilities to improve efficiency, especially when it comes to engagement. It has already been explained how silos affect the alignment of audience engagement. Similarly, the silos between the multitude of engagement tactics leads to needless competition for resources and strategies, when the best solution often involves a carefully planned combination of multiple tools and tactics. Depending on the engagement solution, and based on one's particular perspective, you would think that engagement is only about employee retention or social media or smart phone usage or gamification, when all of the above and more are essential to achieving engagement objectives.

The following section doesn't attempt to make readers an expert in any particular area of Enterprise Engagement, no more than the previous section would make you an expert in all audiences. If you're an expert in any one subject, you'll probably know everything about the chapter that corresponds to it. That said, most people aren't experts in most areas of engagement.

This section of the Enterprise Engagement textbook focuses on the various tools and tactics that comprise this field and demonstrate how they work together, so that people in any area of engagement – from executive coaching, assessment and communication to learning, innovation, rewards, recognition and measurement – can start to think about how they can leverage other engagement efforts across the organization to improve impact and results. The need for integration will never eliminate the need for expertise in specific areas and disciplines, it simply recognizes that a better understanding and utilization of multiple tactics maximizes impact and creates an open-mindedness toward connecting with people.

Promoting integration is no easy task. For decades, leaders in marketing – including the prestigious Medill School of Integrated Marketing Communications – toiled to make integration a reality. Today it's safe to say that despite the continued battle for marketing dollars among multiple marketing options, organizations are generally doing a better job of coordinating numerous marketing strategies – advertising, PR, social media, events and promotions – than was the case two decades ago. In other words, it can be done.

The now measurable financial benefits of Enterprise Engagement promise to drive the same evolution in terms of better aligning and coordinating organizational engagement and connecting it to results.

Enterprise Engagement: The Textbook

Chapter 13

Employee Assessment

By Kevin Sheridan

If there was ever a debate around the linkage between employee engagement and organizational success, that debate has long since ceased. The correlation is so well-established and so universally accepted that it requires no further documentation here.

The focus in organizations today must now be on action – how to drive better employee engagement rather than whether employee engagement is worth measuring and encouraging. Once an organization believes that a more engaged workforce is better for customer loyalty, revenues and profits, the next logical step is in measuring current engagement to set a benchmark, and then regularly re-measuring engagement to chart progress.

The challenge lies in getting measurement right. Organizations must bear in mind that the tools they choose to assess engagement in year one will be the foundation upon which future data is set. If the data collected isn't right or is missing important elements, it will have to be revised or even discarded. Doing so is potentially time-consuming and expensive.

Choosing the right instruments is also important from a user perspective. Too many questions, for example, might lower participation rates, while too few questions could limit the usefulness of the data. An engagement assessment must be balanced against the other surveys employees are asked to complete. An organization that uses an employee satisfaction survey, for example, might consider discontinuing it once they begin assessing employee engagement.

For decades, good managers have intuitively understood that employee engagement generates powerful returns. More recently, research results that quantify those returns have become more readily available. Naturally, knowing that employee engagement is a strong determinant of organizational success, executives want to better understand the level of engagement of their employees. As such, employee engagement surveys have mushroomed to the point where today there are thousands to choose from.

But while many valid tools exist to measure employee engagement, the careful selection of the *right* tool for a particular organization is often bypassed. The fact is, all employee engagement instruments are not the same, nor should they all be administered and interpreted the same. Finally, organizations must start with the premise that they're going to analyze – and then do something with – the data an employee engagement such an assessment provides. Knowing resource limitations and objectives up-front will also aid in the selection of the right engagement assessment instrument.

KEY ELEMENTS
Organizations must first understand the foundational differences between employee satisfaction surveys and employee engagement surveys. Satisfaction surveys can tell an employer just that – how *satisfied* employees are. Employees are generally satisfied when their pay and benefits are competitive and their working conditions (hours, environment, etc.) are clean, fair and reasonable. However, this has very little bearing on their engagement.

Engaged employees are committed to the organization. They're invested in its success, they're proactive in sharing their ideas, in promoting the organization inside and out, and they exert discretionary effort – effort that's above and beyond what it takes to earn their pay and stay employed. In short, engaged employees "Say, Stay and Strive" – that is, they *say* good things about the organization, they *stay* with the organization and they *strive* to succeed personally and help the organization succeed. Given this, it isn't surprising that engaged workers outperform disengaged workers by a significant degree across every position and in every industry.

Survey construction is both art and science. There are literally thousands of unique questions in use throughout organizations to determine engagement levels. The best assessment instrument must be succinct, yet capture meaningful and reliable data upon which decisions can be made with confidence. The question is, which drivers have the biggest impact on employee engagement?

Assessment specialists, including I/O psychologists and statisticians conduct ongoing key-driver analysis, using statistical tools that determine which survey items are most closely linked to overall engagement (or any other survey topic), and they assist organizations in prioritizing their assessment and action-planning efforts. Researchers have uncovered the following five key drivers of engagement for North American workers:

1. **Recognition** – An employee's feelings about the recognition he/she receives accounts for 56% of the variance in his/her level of engagement. These results illuminate that even as adults, people still want to feel appreciated for a job well done.
2. **Career Development** – Career development opportunities are an essential part of employee engagement. If peoples' desire to advance in their own career isn't fulfilled, they'll begin looking for work elsewhere.
3. **Direct Supervisor/Manager Leadership Abilities** – Even though this is the third driver, it's essentially the most important, because supervisors/managers are in charge of coaching and recognizing people. They should be having regular discussions about career development with their direct reports.
4. **Strategy and Mission** – The freedom and autonomy to succeed and contribute to an organization's success – in addition to the need for employees to understand why their individual tasks are instrumental in the big picture – is essential for them to understand exactly what the big picture entails. Senior

leaders should not only develop this vision, they should also effectively communicate it to staff.
5. **Job Content** – The might be called "the ability to do what I do best." Job content is an area where many employees don't feel as though they have a say in their own experience. Since many tasks simply have to be done, there often isn't an option to remove those tasks that are less interesting or pleasant or detract from engagement. Although every organization is different, there should always be some leeway in regards to adjusting job content to make a more enjoyable situation for employees. As best-selling author and management scientist Jim Collins says, "It's not just about who's on the bus; it's about what seat they're in."

BENEFITS OF ASSESSMENT

There are numerous benefits to employee engagement surveys. They give employees a voice, uncover employee engagement levels and capitalize on opportunities for improvement. They identify organizational strengths, help retain high performers and prioritize workplace efforts. Surveys help discover and implement cost-saving opportunities, predict the potential for union activity and align employees with organizational strategy and mission. They also help benchmark results to national, regional, global, and industry-specific data, and they're a key leading indicator of future financial performance

Most engagement survey solutions available today take a one-size-fits-all approach. While they accommodate and measure elements of engagement that are part of a key-driver analysis, there's no carefully tailored prescription for the workforce in question.

Therefore, while the organization might be measuring engagement, it might not be measuring the things that are important to its own diverse populations.

> **Research has clearly and consistently proved the direct link between employee engagement, customer satisfaction and revenue growth.**
>
> **~ Harvard Business Review**

CHOOSE THE RIGHT SURVEY

For example, numerous studies have shown that 'Millennials' (those born between the early 1980s and the early 2000s – also known as Gen Y) like to be recognized frequently; even several times each day. To some tenured employees, including supervisors, managers and executives, such frequent, positive re-enforcement might be viewed as an indulgent and unrealistic expectation.

But American culture has shifted dramatically over the years, causing workforce culture to change as well. For instance, Millennials have grown up in an era where thirteenth-place ribbons actually exist. To attract and engage this new generation, company recognition efforts must keep up with the times. The first driver of engagement for Millennials is job content – the ability to do what I do best. The second driver of engagement for this generation is senior management's relationship with employees. The third driver for Millennials is working for a green, eco-friendly company, as well as for an organization that gives back to its community.

The variances between Millennials and the general workforce are real, as are the differences between other demographic cohorts and even between employees in one industry or geography versus another. Most employee engagement surveys aren't tailored to measure these variances.

THE IMPORTANCE OF AN ENTERPRISE APPROACH

Many organizations continue to ignore the need to empower both managers and employees, often failing to effectively drive engagement from both sides of the fence. Research has found that most organizations are focused on only one side of the engagement equation, while the other half – employee ownership – isn't being measured and therefore is not being managed. The responsibility for improving employee engagement shouldn't fall solely on management. Rather, the driving force of workplace engagement should be shared between managers and employees.

To address and correct this imbalance, measure employee engagement from an enterprise-wide perspective, but also from the individual perspective. Employees should know and understand the broad drivers of employee engagement, as well as their personal drivers. Those drivers may be the same, but they're likely to be prioritized differently. Choose survey and assessment tools that provide both types of reports and data. For the employee, a fully confidential report that highlights their level of engagement (Actively Engaged, Ambivalent, or Actively Disengaged) and also makes useful subject-specific suggestions on how they can enhance their own engagement in the workplace is recommended.

WHO SHOULD GATHER THE DATA?

Organizations should consider using a third-party vendor to administer their surveys. Third-party vendors are neutral and have no stake in the results, and their findings aren't likely to be influenced by organizational forces.

Vendors should be selected for their process rigor and survey construct validity – for example, the use of scientifically-structured surveying scales (e.g., a Likert scale) to retrieve accurate results. Construct validity refers to whether a scale measures or correlates with the theorized psychological scientific construct (e.g., "fluid intelligence") that it purports to measure. In other words, it is the extent to which what was *to be* measured actually *was* measured. Unfortunately, many organizations that administer their surveys in-house have never conducted a construct validity analysis, and as such are probably dealing with a fairly errant survey with statistical error rates that are above the norm.

Even where an organization has the in-house expertise to devise a valid survey, conduct, collect and analyze the data, it may not have external data against which to compare the results. Normative databases allow organizations to compare their survey results against companies in their industry, across industries and against best-in-class organizations. Third-party vendors are also likely to have up-to-date benchmarking data, and some may even offer online action planning systems that provide access to a comprehensive and continually-updated knowledge library of field-tested best practices for increasing engagement and retention.

WHICH METRICS TO TRACK

Since the concept of employee engagement took root more than a decade ago, researchers have conclusively shown that engagement is positively correlated to operational budget, revenue and even stock performance. In other words, organizations that maximize employee engagement outperform their competitors on the financial

> **Employee engagement should be a key component in an organization's talent management strategy. Given all the benefits of an engaged, productive and loyal workforce, organizations have a lot to gain by embracing the power of engagement. The careful choice of the right survey is a critical first step in the process of driving a more engaged workforce.**

metrics that matter; it is for this very reason that engagement has seized the attention of C-level executives.

Despite the available evidence, organizations should track the same performance metrics for their own efforts. This will make continuous improvement possible, including the ongoing adjustments and fine-tunings that are required to keep an engagement program relevant year after year.

The following metrics are readily available or obtainable in most organizations and can be linked closely to engagement. Bear in mind
that individual engagement survey results should be strictly confidential. However, that doesn't prevent organizations from tracking the following metrics:

- **Retention.** Map the retention rates of Actively Engaged, Ambivalent and Actively Disengaged employees to retention (or attrition) rates.
- **Performance.** Map the performance rates (based on performance reviews or actual performance in the case of sales and other employees) to Actively Engaged, Ambivalent, or Actively Disengaged employees.
- **Employee Referral Rates.** Engaged employees are more likely to recommend/speak positively of the organization to friends and family (i.e., referrals for job candidates and potential clients). Track employee referral rates against Actively Engaged, Ambivalent and Actively Disengaged employees.
- **Absenteeism.** Engaged employees are absent less often. Track rates of absenteeism against Actively Engaged, Ambivalent and Actively Disengaged employees.
- **Customer Engagement.** Engaged employees are linked to satisfied customers/patients at a correlation coefficient of 0.85 (i.e., customer/patient satisfaction). Chart organizational engagement scores against customer engagement scores (or satisfaction scores, as the case may be).
- **Financial Performance.** Engaged employees create engaged customers who drive revenue and profits. Track engagement scores against revenue and profit as well. Attempt to allow for outside factors and influences. Just as improvements in revenue that follow improvements in engagement should not be attributed entirely to engagement, the reverse is also true.

What to Assess

Recognition	Career Development	Supervisor Manager	Strategy & Mission	Job Content
Accountability	Investment in Learning	Coaching	Purpose	Autonomy
Recognition Culture	Self-Directed Opportunities	Feedback	Inclusion	Creative Time
Transparency Honesty	Learning Culture	SMART Goals	Alignment	Fit
Rewards & Incentives	Stretch Assignments	Flexible Workplace	Inspiration	Empowerment
Fairness	Learning Options	Care, Listening Respect	CSR	Mobility Career Path

TRANSLATE DATA INTO ACTION
Openly communicate the results of the engagement survey to highlight strengths and link areas in need of improvement with specific action plans. Encourage department

heads to meet with supervisors in their department to discuss/clarify the survey results and design a plan for action.

As the implementation process unfolds and changes take place, send periodic updates to employees regarding the status of the action plan items. Incorporate branded stamps on post-survey actions to demonstrate the organization's commitment to acting on employee feedback. Make managers accountable for action planning, and explain to employees that they play an active role in developing action plans.

Finally, measure the results of the action plan. No more than three months after the action plans have been implemented, the organization should measure the results, and then repeat at regular intervals

OTHER WAYS TO IMPROVE ENGAGEMENT

Organizations should promote the importance of confidentiality in their surveys so workers will feel comfortable about being open and honest with what they would like to see improved throughout the organization. This doesn't mean the data can't be used to gather important insights. Where results will be made generally available, organizations should report on the data at a high enough level that individuals cannot be identified or even guessed. Where individual engagement data is used by the organization (i.e., to map engagement to performance) it should be kept confidential. Also keep in mind that:

- feedback sessions hold the key in further uncovering why employees responded a certain way in their employee survey.
- regular action planning meetings between managers and their direct reports ensure that a clear, concise plan can be established for acting on the survey results and improving engagement levels. The crux of employee engagement is at the front-line, immediate supervisor level. Supervisors and front-line managers should be encouraged to drive employee engagement and be recognized and rewarded for improvements, or held accountable when engagement slips.

GETTING IT RIGHT

The reasons organizations should be concerned about employee engagement are clear. Given the stakes, it's not surprising that most organizations today attempt to measure engagement in some way. Yet, with the myriad employee engagement survey instruments and rating scales available, choosing the right tool can still be difficult.

No one engagement survey can fit the needs of all organizations. At the same time, survey tools that are so customized as to be one of a kind will yield little ability to benchmark against other organizations.

It is therefore vital that organizations get the first steps right in measuring employee engagement if they're to correctly diagnose their workforce and make positive changes. Selecting the right survey tool, administering it properly and then interpreting the results correctly are prerequisites to knowing what interventions to make in order to drive engagement, performance and profitability.

Enterprise Engagement: The Textbook

Chapter 14

Communication

By Paul Hebert, Kristen McGowan and Paul Kiewiet

Engagement, almost by definition, requires communication. There are many tools to assist in achieving engagement, but none so important – and in today's world so complicated – as communication.

Enterprise engagement takes the importance and need of communications several degrees further, both in scope and quality. At its heart, engagement is about relationships and connections. Leaders know that communication – conversations, feedback, recognition – is the fuel for relationship-building and trust.

For better or for worse, communication options have changed as well. We have tremendous choice today in the medium for our messages – email, phone, tweets, text, video, TV, radio, "snail mail," social media networks (both corporate sponsored and public), face-to-face and so on – which makes our choice of media not only more difficult, but also puts added pressure on what to communicate through each of those channels.

A DECADE OF CHANGE
It wasn't too long ago that there were only one or two channels for communication. For employee communication, interoffice memos and letters came in brown envelopes with string that wound around the two cardboard buttons. For consumers, it was direct mail or roadside signs, and for larger brands TV and radio advertising. For your channel partners and vendors, communications might have included a catalog or quarterly print newsletter.

It was simpler. It was easier. It was limited.

From an "engagement" point of view there was little you could do to differentiate yourself from your competitors when it came to communication. Most communications were print-focused, one-way and expensive. And in many cases you still weren't really sure communication was taking place.

That has changed dramatically. The past 10 years have seen a huge expansion in the number of communication channels, the way those channels work and a shift of power in the communication equation. Caution is still the watchword, however. How you communicate can be as powerful as what you say.

COMMUNICATIONS CHALLENGES
One could easily write a book on each of the challenges you'll face trying to communicate and engage with today's audiences. These include:

Finding Your Audience. It used to be that you could mail your employees, your channel partners and your vendors in their offices, and your customers at their homes. Not so any more. With the number of telecommuting and/or work-at-home employees expected to grow by 69% between now and 2016, employees and potential customers will be a more mobile and difficult target.[1] In addition, many positions aren't really "desk jobs" – field sales personnel, retail salespeople, restaurant employees, etc.

These people aren't always able to connect to what we now think of as "traditional" communications – email or other communication portals. While these jobs have always been a challenge when it comes to communication, the need for instantaneous and ongoing communication is more critical than it has been in the past.

The rise of mobile devices has happened simultaneously and is enabling the mobile worker to be even more mobile. Where it was once sufficient to connect with employees in the field in a weekly call or meeting, the pace of business and change has made it essential to connect with them daily, if not hourly.

Communication Overload. There's little need to cite statistics to prove the number of communications messages has increased – you experience it every day with your own email, social network updates, constant calls, texts and pings. If you're still not convinced, consider this: Worldwide, there are 2.9 billion email accounts that are responsible on any given day for sending out 188 billion messages.

Every Day ...

3,000,000,000+ email accounts

send 200,000,000,000+ messages.

600,000,000+ Twitter accounts send

250,000,000+ tweets.

**1,000,000,000+ Facebook accounts send
100,000,000+ status updates**

**And workers discard 91% of work information before
it is fully read.**

---

1 - WorldatWork estimates that 16 million employees work at home at least one day a month, a number that increased almost 62% between 2005 and 2010.

There are also 1.393 billion monthly active users on Facebook driving 25% of the web's traffic[3], and Twitter's 500 million accounts that sent out 340 million tweets each day.[2] A study done in 2010 by Lexis/Nexis reported that 91% of workers in the U.S. (including your customers) say they discard work information without fully reading it.

And it's no wonder, given that the average American sends and receives an average of 180 email messages per day and is exposed to as many as 20,000 advertisements (in all forms). And don't forget that your employees, your vendors and your channel partners are all feeling this pinch. Everyone is affected, and this in turn affects *all* of your communication challenges – not just one audience.

Demographic Changes. Many argue that demographic changes are driving the challenges of communicating with today's audiences. While there's no doubt that Millennials – like their parents and grandparents, the Baby Boomers – are a force to be reckoned with as they make their mark on the workforce, make up more of the buying population and become influential within the companies you seek to sell to and buy from, the real communication challenge isn't demographic. The actual percentage of the workforce in the Millennial category is decreasing as older workers stay engaged in the workforce.

This means that, as communicators, we need to be smart about which tools, which messages and which audience we communicate with and not just assume that "everyone" is on Facebook. In fact, recent data show a decline in Facebook usage. The message is that we need to be sure we know and understand our own specific channel demographics, not just demographics in general. Your audience may not match up to the trends many marketers are fond of pushing. Do your due diligence and make sure you have good data on your own audience.

The biggest communication challenge is that we have so many new channels available to us. Add to this the preferences and trends within and between age cohorts – and whether communication should to be tailored to each group – and things become even more complex.

CHANNEL CHOICES
So we know that the world of communication has changed dramatically over the past 10 years or so. No longer is there a single, dominant channel of communication. Today's marketer is faced with a huge variety of options. At a minimum, your communications strategy should include a discussion of the following:

Audience. Who is it you want to connect with? Is it a single group of homogenous members, or do you need to target different groups? Do any of your audiences overlap with respect to their communication? Millennials are very different than Boomers, yet they use similar communication channels. Do you need different messaging for each group even if you use the same channel? Does a Facebook post appeal to Gen Y's but not Boomers, even if both are on your page?

Consume vs. Interact. Identify the type of information and communications you'll be sending out. Some information is purely about consumption. Dates, times, processes – these are all consumption-based communication assets. They can be best served via email, a blog post, a document uploaded to the website, a tweet with a link to the information.

---

2 - http://socialmediaslant.com/social-media-stats-2-2015/

Of course, not all communication should be broadcast. Make room in your strategy for interactivity and engagement. Ask questions, run polls, allow your audience the opportunity to provide feedback, and then communicate how you used the feedback. At the very least, try to make 30% of your communication interactive in order to demonstrate that you truly desire and understand engagement with your audience.

Objectives. Almost concurrently to determining what kind of communication you'll be developing, ask yourself what your objectives are. If no plan is in place, then no strategy is going to be successful if you first don't ask yourself – "What do I want to happen if I do this?"

That simple question will guide the type of communication, the channel, how interactive it is, how often, etc. You can have multiple objectives. Examples include:

- Increase awareness of "x" program as measured by a poll or questionnaire
- Increase number of "likes" on our Facebook fan page
- Grow our opt-in mailing list
- Increase size of our social network footprint by choosing the right network and then increasing engagement/interaction through that channel

Each corporate objective should have corresponding communications objectives, and remember that a single goal could have multiple communication objectives. In today's world, with so many cost-effective options available, it's only practical to use as many as make sense.

Tactical Plan. Your tactical plan is the nuts-and-bolts document that informs your day-to-day activity as it relates to achieving your communication objectives. It should be specific. It should spell out the number, type and responsibility for each area of communication. In some companies they call it a communication calendar – detailing the dates and times for releasing communications. While that type of calendar is important, it's only half the equation. Today's communication plan needs to include a monitoring function where someone is responsible for reviewing the "chatter" on the various social media outlets.

Communication is no longer a controlled experience. Your audience has as much power – and in many cases more power – than you do when communicating with your audience. Through their individual social networks, good news and bad can go viral quickly if not addressed immediately. Therefore, monitoring mentions of your brand, company and products is critical in creating a true engagement process in your communications plan.

This part of the communications activity is much more ad hoc and free form. It's not driven by a schedule, but rather by what your audience wants and needs. If you see a post on twitter saying good things about your brand, thank the poster in that medium. If you see negative things, find a way to solve the problem. Don't ignore posts…social networks embolden everyone, and your lack of attention will likely be noted in multiple tweets and Facebook posts.

ELECTRONIC, DIGITAL & SOCIAL MEDIA
Electronic communications covers a broad swath of options for marketers interested in engagement. For our purposes, electronic communication includes (but is not limited to):

- Internet
- Mobile Phones
- Social Networks
- Tablets
- Digital Signage
- Web-based TV and Radio

In other words, "electronic" doesn't just mean the web. Electronic communication is more a category than a specific product or service. Think of electronic communication as a format that has two distinct elements:

1. The message disappears when you hit an "on/off" button
2. You have the potential for real-time interaction while your message is in front of your audience.

COMMUNICATION 'ASSETS'

These days, electronic communication is the key element in any communications discussion. The real value of electronic communication is the ability for the communication "asset" to be used in variety of ways. A podcast can be shared via social media, embedded on your blog, uploaded to another company's website and shared on Facebook. Each of those options target a potentially different audience using the investment made in one marketing asset.

One thing to get particularly familiar with is the advent of mobile access to information. The number of people who use mobile equipment to access information either from the web or some other internet-connected location is exploding. The time to think about mobile is now.

And mobile isn't just phones. Mobile includes tablets, laptops, phablets (large phones/small tablets) and a variety of electronic equipment that allow untethered access to the internet. The move toward a more mobile world has become a reality.[3]

> **Keep in mind the various ways people will access your information and provide them with an experience that is designed for the device.**

Over 20% of website visits are made on mobile devices. And that isn't counting app usage and other internet enabled information. What this means to you as a communicator is that you need to consider the constraints and the processes you ask your audience to participate in on the web. Fat fingers and small check boxes don't work well together. Keep in mind the various ways people will access your information and provide them with an experience that is designed for the device.

Long-winded documents don't fit a mobile application any more. The audience dictates how your communication asset will be consumed – be prepared to deliver that asset in multiple formats.

INTERACTIVE AND INTEGRATED

Before we discuss the various channels available it is important to understand two things...

1. Today's communication environment is **interactive**. Read that again and again. Almost every communication channel in today's world allows for some form of interactivity. Don't ignore that powerful option with your

---

3 - http://www.smartinsights.com/mobile-marketing/mobile-marketing-analytics/mobile-marketing-statistics/

communication planning. Regardless of channel used – and there are plenty – consider how you will use it to "interact" with your audience. Ask questions, pose challenges – encourage feedback.
2. Today's communication environment is about **integration**. No one single channel of communication is as effective as a portfolio of communication options. Regardless of audience, having multiple connection points across a wide variety of communication tools increases your chances that you will create engagement. While reviewing the following options always keep the idea of "integration" and leveraging multiple mediums to really drive your message home with your audience and meet them where they work and play.

CHANNELS TO CONSIDER
Given that the number and type of communication channels has exploded in recent years, there is no way we can provide you with an exhaustive list of options.

Despite all these options, in most situations you'll only need a handful of channels. Your job is to create a communication plan that uses the most common channels for your particular audience, not try to use all the channels available. Here are a few to consider:

YOUR WEBSITE OR PORTAL
From a communication standpoint, consider a website "home base" or portal where all relevant information lives. Regardless of the channel used, every engagement initiative needs a home base where your audience can access anything they need. Your website is the one constant for all audience members.

While the way in which information is received and/or broadcast can vary (and it should), you need to create and maintain a home base. Make sure you design the website with logical and clear navigation, easy-to-find customer service information, links to other communication channels such as Facebook pages, twitter accounts, etc. (see below for more on those options) and links to additional information that may help.

EMAIL
Email is and will continue to be a cost-effective and popular communication option. It allows for more lengthy discussions, can connect to other assets via links and has the ability to be tracked and measured.

Indeed, according to data from email marketing provider Informz, there has been an increase in the click-through rate of email from 19.5% to 21.1% between 2011 and 2012. Email is still a valuable tool. Emails are constant touchpoints that can be customized to personal preferences and ongoing communication to keep recognition and engagement "front and center" in any program. Thus, the use of email is still important in an overall program strategy.

TEXT MESSAGING
Although it's losing some energy recently, text messaging to phones can be an effective communication option. Simple to use, immediate and inexpensive, text or SMS may be an option if you have access to your audience's phone numbers and permission to text them (remember, some people still have to pay for each text message).

Keep in mind that this is a particularly audience-sensitive option and should only be used if other options don't provide the reach or immediacy your engagement initiative may require.

SOCIAL NETWORKS

The following is a very brief overview on some of the various social media options available for marketing to your audience. Though fast-growing tools such as Snapchat, Pinterest and Instagram aren't covered, they should not be overlooked. A complete graphic of the expanse of social networks available in 2014 can be found in the appendix (not sure if you have one but I put a big image in at the end of this so you can decide if you want to include it or not.)

Each social media option will require different techniques, so develop a unique communication plan tailored for each platform, rather than just duplicating what you say in one program with all the others. Each platform is focused on different outcomes.

Facebook. Depending on your audience and your program, Facebook may provide a simple and easy base for your communication needs. Facebook has the ability to create groups with limited sharing to members, as well as the ability to create brand pages where you can create events, provide links to relevant content and engage in two-way communication with people who are connected to your brand. Facebook is ideal when your audience is already engaging on the platform, when two-way interaction is valuable and when your potential audience is difficult to identify.

Google+. This is a relatively new Facebook competitor with strong membership growth numbers. Google+ provides a very robust set of engagement options within its platform, such as the ability to upload and share photos, videos, links and "blog" type posts. It also features "circles", which is an easy and intuitive way to segment followers into smaller groups, enabling you to share information with some followers while barring others. For example, you might try creating a Super Fan circle and share special discounts and exclusive offers only with that group. Google + also provides the ability for you to host video conversations through their Hangout function. These videos can be recorded and saved to Google+ via Youtube (another Google product.) Google+ is not as widespread as Facebook, of course, so engagement within the network may be limited. However, from a broader marketing discussion, Google+ content will increase your brand's search engine optimization (SEO), making it easier to find by Google search.

Twitter. This social media marketing tool lets you broadcast your updates across the web. Follow tweeters in your industry or related fields, and you should gain a steady stream of followers in return. Mix up your official-related tweets about specials, discounts and news updates with some fun and quirky tweets interspersed. Using Twitter as a social media marketing tool revolves around dialog and communication, so be sure to interact as much as possible. It can be used as a broadcast medium, pushing updates, and can also be used as an interactive medium, allowing a brand to hold "tweet chats" and interact with fans in real time.

LinkedIn. Considered a "professional social media marketing site" with a more formal tone and demeanor, LinkedIn includes a Groups service that allows you to create and invite participants to a segmented group of individuals. This is an effective way to engage in professional dialog with people in similar industries, and it provides a place to share content with like-minded individuals. These Groups can be built for consumers, employees or even a vendor community. LinkedIn can also be used as a broadcast medium by simply adding content to a LinkedIn Group or using a Group for two-way communication through polls or questions.

LOCATION-BASED SOCIAL MEDIA
Social media platforms like Yelp, FourSquare and Level Up are effective for bricks-and-mortar businesses looking to implement social media marketing. Register on these sites to claim your location spot, and then consider extra incentives such as check-in rewards or special discounts. Remember, these visitors will have their phones in hand, so they'll have access to providing reviews, which could significantly help (or hurt) your users.

Internal. Simple and quick text messaging is still a valuable communication option. Like Twitter, but confined within the walls of an organization, are tools like Yammer and Chatter (a salesforce.com option), which allow employees to quickly communicate across an organization. Think of these tools like "mini email" with limited shelf life and quick actionable content. Deploy these tools as a way to quickly tell your staff about websites.

Company Intranets. For employee programs, don't forget an obvious choice for communication – your company intranet. Many companies have a "portal" product where various programs and initiatives associated with engagement can be advertised and promoted. This applies to vendors and channel members as well. Many companies have similar portals for ecommerce. Don't neglect an existing channel for providing updates and information to all your various audiences.

Recognition Program Websites. These are also important platforms that offer multiple touchpoints in a recognition program. They allow administrators a variety of ways to reach participants, keeping the program top-of-mind.

PROMOTIONAL PRODUCTS
Promotional products – also known as premiums, logoed merchandise and advertising specialties – are a communications tool that engages all five senses. They're a creative way of both informing and interacting with an audience, providing a sensory experience.

> **88% of recipients recall the advertiser and 62% recalled the message on promotional products received in the past twelve months – a recall level that other communications media would surely envy.**

Unlike other advertising media that interrupt the recipient, promotional products engage an audience. They're the one communications medium where people say "thank you" when they receive it. Practitioners like to point out that promotional products are the original medium of engagement – in fact, the very beginnings of the industry support that sentiment.

While promotional products in America can be traced back to things like commemorative buttons for George Washington and advertising calendars, rulers and wooden items, it was a printer in Coshocton, OH by the name of Jasper Meeks who's considered the father of the industry. Meeks was able to convince a local shoe store to buy book bags imprinted with the store's message and give them out for free to the local school. A competitor picked up on that same idea, and soon Meeks was selling all kinds of items imprinted with the messages of local businesses.

RECALL AND RELATIONSHIPS
Each item imprinted with an organization's message stimulates basic human gratification factors. The act of giving and receiving is the basis of a relationship and engenders goodwill, trust and loyalty.

The law of reciprocity comes into play as the recipient desires to return the positive feelings to the giver. The high perceived value creates a high pass-along rate as well. The PPAI *Promotional Products Awareness and Usage Study* found that 88% of recipients recall the advertiser and 62% recalled the message on promotional products received in the past twelve months – a recall level that other communications media would surely envy.

Organizations wishing to build stronger bonds of engagement with their stakeholders often choose promotional products such as apparel, writing instruments, drinkware, bags, desk and business accessories, electronic devices, computer products health, safety and wellness items, among numerous others. Here are some specific uses of promotional products:

- Appreciation for extra effort, loyalty, patronage or donor support.
- Recognition of outstanding achievement and for reinforcement of positive behaviors.
- Marketing in a way that informs, influences and enables, turning strangers into friends, friends into customers and customers into advocates.
- Branding to create long-term awareness, engagement and action.
- Extending the organization's presence beyond a specific location, event or program with items that carry an implied endorsement by their recipient and that start conversations and create word-of-mouth continuity of message.
- Incentives, offering lifestyle enhancing products or products that serve as a reward for acting now – a huge variety of items that excite, engage and motivate people to pay attention and perform with enthusiasm.
- Training and teaching new skills, reinforcing key messages and communicating culture and values requires repetition and multiple exposures to a message. Placing key learning messages on items that are kept and used multiple times will do just that.

THE FIVE SENSES
Because promotional products are tangible, physical, multi-dimensional and customizable, they can be effective for engaging an audience via all five senses:

- Sight - reinforce the colors, branding cues and appeal to the visual senses with selections that have aesthetic appeal.
- Touch - products can be textured and shaped to reinforce attributes of the communication message such as hard, soft, furry, warm, round or unique.
- Taste - food is an extremely popular category and a strong sensory cue. From custom-shaped and debossed chocolate treats to custom-labeled bottled water and even fruit, candies and gourmet treats, taste can deliver your message in a way that creates positive associations with your brand.
- Sound - from the cracking of a chocolate bar to a noise maker at a sporting event to a sound chip embedded into the item, promotional products can reinforce and replay a message – from reinforcing notes of a jingle to a president's speech.
- Smell - the one sense that we can't turn off, but one that evokes memories. Scent is a part of food items and is something that can be added to pens, ink

and post-it pads. If a unique scent is a part of the communication, promotional products may be the right way to extend that messaging.

Promotional products are an effective communications tool because they "remain to be seen." Most recipients keep items for more than a year, and many items are used daily and kept on or with a person. Great communication should have three key factors to be a strong tool of engagement, and promotional products excel in all three:

Relevance: The message must relate to the lifestyle, needs, values or aspirations of the target audience. Promotional products are uniquely geared to relate. After all, these products are usually also sold at retail, where people spend their own money to buy them. Whether it's a beautiful writing instrument and journal book for taking notes at a conference, or a fishing lure with your message imprinted on it given to the avid anglers in your company, this communications medium is the most targeted of all. Almost any product you can imagine may be imprinted and customized.

Repetition: An audience must be exposed to the message multiple times for recipients to retain it. Promotional products have a long "shelf life," offering continuous repetition and exposure to the message. This exposure stimulates conversations and interaction and generates highly valuable reach, frequency and impressions, providing even more repetition of the message and the meaning behind it.

Reward: The message must promise to create pleasure or reduce pain, save money or increase income, or in some way reward the recipient. By their very nature, this medium is of useful value, providing a sense of reward to the recipient and in turn creating positive emotions towards the person or the brand delivering it.

KNOW YOUR OBJECTIVES
To be effective, engagement professionals need to thoughtfully select promotional products as a communications device. And selecting the right products means knowing your communication objectives. It's critical to know what message you're trying to deliver. Be specific. Focus on helping, enabling and informing your target audience.

When it comes to selecting promotional products, skip the Golden Rule and use the "Platinum Rule." Rather than doing unto others as you would have them do unto you, do unto others as *they* would have you do to *them*. In other words, choose items based on *their* interests, *their* values, *their* lifestyles. Don't select them based on your personal preferences or tastes. Also, select items for longevity of message. It's better to spend more for an item that the recipient will interact with for years rather than an item that will be used once and forgotten. Remember, it's not what a product does; it's what a product *means*.

Promotional products are easily delivered at seminars, events, in direct mail and from person to person. They're a communications tool that engages an audience through touch, taste, smell, sight and sound, creating feelings of goodwill toward the organization that delivered it to them.

CONCLUSION: IT'S AN ECOSYSTEM
In the "good ole days" communication was simple. Limited choices for how the message would be delivered. Limited choices on what the message would include. Limited choices on how the message would be formatted

"The single biggest problem with communication," as George Bernard Shaw so perceptively pointed out in his day, was "the illusion that it has taken place."

Not so any more.

Today, communication is less of a channel than it is an ecosystem. The most successful organizations will capitalize on the ability to take a small piece of information, make it accessible and interactive within their target audience, and drive higher levels of brand/company engagement.

There are multiple ways to send your message, format it, track who got it and know what they did with the information.

Communication is two-way, engaged and interactive. Taking the time to outline your communication needs, understand the various options available and how you might connect one, two or three different mediums together to create greater understanding and engagement with your message and your brand is the critical challenge in today's ever-more-crowded communications space.

Yes, it's more complicated…but it's also more important than ever to look at your communication strategy as a key linchpin in your engagement strategy rather than an afterthought. Remember: *How* you communicate will determine *if* you communicate.

Enterprise Engagement: The Textbook

Chapter 15

Preference Management

Eric Holtzclaw and Eric Tejeda

To remain competitive, businesses must continually look for better ways to engage with customers and prospects. Now that we're in the digital age and the era of Big Data, the opportunities grow exponentially for better customer engagement – as do the odds that a business crosses the line between relevant communications and being unsettling or invasive.

Consumers want to be in control of the conversation with a business. Unsolicited offers sent by mail, email, text message or phone might be welcome. Or, they could be viewed as not relevant or communicated via a channel that is deemed as disruptive. For instance, a consumer might want to hear about offers for carpet cleaning, but a text message that they essentially must pay for might be considered unwelcome. The same goes for a phone call that interrupts dinner.

Instead of putting the consumer in control of the conversation, the business is dictating how they will communicate. Businesses that go this route face the risk of opt-outs and unsubscribes. Instead of enhancing customer engagement, they find closed communication channels and the inability to market to these consumers.

ENABLING THE CUSTOMER
That's where preference management comes into play. Technology has enabled organizations to predict a consumer's behavior by collecting data on previous purchases or what consumers have viewed on a website. However, unless a company specifically asks for a consumer's particular product or service interests or their desired form of communication, they're not enabling the consumer to control the conversation, the communication method and the frequency of engagement.

Preference management is the term used to describe the active collection, maintenance and distribution of unique consumer characteristics, including product or service interest, desired communication channel and even the frequency of communication.

Combined with Big Data, the use of preference management gives organizations a powerful technology tool to further enhance and boost customer engagement. That's because the preferences are not derived from profile data or purchase history or what page they viewed on a website, but were expressly stated by the consumers themselves.

ENTERPRISE PREFERENCE MANAGEMENT

Enterprise Preference Management (EPM) goes beyond simple permission-based marketing. It's also more than a preference center, which allows customers to manage the data you maintain on them. Preference centers for single channels such as email can be deployed quickly and inexpensively. For small companies that use one communication channel, and if all departments share that channel, a single preference center is adequate.

The operative word in Enterprise Preference Management is "enterprise." An enterprise has the following characteristics:

- Multiple business units, brands and/or products or services
- Multiple communication channels, including email, call centers, social media, text messages and mobile devices
- Multiple departments (marketing, sales, customer service, support, etc.) within the organization that communicate with customers and prospects
- Multiple databases throughout the organization, including marketing databases, marketing automation systems, CRMs and third-party vendor databases such as those of an email service provider.

An Enterprise Preference Management solution provides the ability to: 1) Capture and maintain opt-ins via all customer touchpoints (web, mobile, social, email, etc.) for multiple campaigns and communications channels; 2) Capture the desired frequency of communications; 3) Centralize all customer and prospect preferences in one repository; and 4) Leverage API tools to status all databases across the enterprise with current opt-in preferences.

Unlike a preference center, Enterprise Preference Management incorporates the ability to obtain and maintain customer permissions and preferences across the whole organization. Its ability to track, archive and report on privacy preferences also satisfies any and all state, federal and industry requirements.

THE IMPORTANCE OF EPM

There is mounting evidence that the moment has arrived for Enterprise Preference Management. A recent Oracle survey[1] of more than 1,300 senior executives found that 97% agree that customer experience is critical to success, while 93% have made it one of their top three priorities for the next two years.

That's not surprising. According to Forrester Research,[2] consumers that engage via multiple channels spend two to three times more than average consumers. So the Customer Lifetime Value (CLV) for delivering on customer preferences is significant.

Still, the Oracle study points out that fewer than 40% of respondents have customer experience initiatives in progress, and only 20% of those that do would describe them as sophisticated.

---

1 - "The Year of Preference Management," DestinationCRM, March 29, 2013
2 - Unified Communication Industry Study, Forrester Research, February 2006

Forrester's *Interactive Marketing Predictions* study says that by the end of 2013 nearly half of online adults globally will be always addressable. This is fueled by the increased adoption and utility of tablets, smart phones and other devices. These customers demand personalized, relevant attention that is designed around their needs and wants, rather than around your marketing channels.

If you don't change the way you think about engaging these customers, you'll quickly lose relevance.

RULES AND REGS
Numerous regulations govern opt-outs or privacy, including Do Not Call laws, the CAN-SPAM Act and the Junk Fax Act. The latest change to the Telephone Consumer Protection Act (TCPA) requires prior express written consent (or opt-in) for soliciting consumers via an automated telephone dialing system (ATDS) for voice, text or recording on their mobile phones, effective October 16, 2013.

Canada and the European Union also have laws that require companies to obtain opt-ins before marketing to consumers. The regulatory environment continues to become more restrictive, not less.

MAKE IT RELEVANT
Consumer and customer preferences are relevant to organizations of all sizes (B2B and B2C) that want to remain relevant and engage their customers. However, small companies typically use preferences on a single channel such as email.

EPM that spans divisions, departments, brands and channels tends to be more relevant to large companies today. Early adopters include *Fortune* 1000 companies, but many mid-size companies can leverage preferences as well.

Compliance with multiple federal, state and international regulations makes EPM relevant to a wide range of organizations. Marketers face the tedious task of complying with a myriad of state and federal "do not contact" laws. Compliance is not an either/or proposition; companies that ignore these laws face the risk of significant fines, undesirable publicity and loss of consumer trust.
So in addition to building a technology infrastructure for preference management and gaining stakeholder buy-in, marketers must also have the ability to collect, manage and archive privacy choices for state, federal and industry regulations.

Additionally, regulatory compliance is an ongoing effort. Regulatory requirements change, so it's essential to have an infrastructure and processes in place to stay current. Beyond compliance, organizations profit from EPM through the increased engagement of customers and prospects, who feel more in control of the relationship and the content they receive. As such, they are more likely to read the content and less likely to opt out. This also results in less marketing waste by not sending communications to customers that don't want them.

Ultimately, better customer engagement leads to increased CLV, as well as loyalty and "share-of-wallet."

BEST PRACTICES
A key to driving authentic customer engagement is letting customers share ownership of the conversation based on their interests and preferences. This isn't a new idea, but to achieve it requires brands expand their collection of consumer preferences throughout all organizational customer touchpoints such as websites, call centers, email campaigns,

mobile devices and social media. In doing so, the following best practices (and the impact they have on development) should be considered:

- Preference centers should be optimized to collect just the right amount of data. For example, "customer typing" should be leveraged to present only the relevant options to a customer (e.g., don't offer Canadian customers services that are only available in the U.S.).
- Don't overwhelm consumers with too many questions, or they will abandon the process. Rather, ask questions that are pertinent to what they're doing at the time. Then progressively add to that information over time.
- Optimize the preference centers for the platform through which you'll be collecting the preferences. For example, preference centers for mobile devices should be developed specifically for mobile devices and should only ask a few questions.

SILOED DATA & TECHNOLOGY

Legacy systems and fragmented customer data remain key obstacles to advanced customer experience initiatives. In order to truly impact the customer experience, EPM must span all departments, business units, brands and third-party vendors.

Report your results to management team – demonstrating a successfully deployed solution, along with favorable results, can help build enthusiasm for the next phase and make it easier because of the experience you've gained

The EPM system must integrate with marketing databases, CRM systems and third-party vendors in order to empower organizations with preference data that can be used to improve campaign results, increase sales revenue and improve customer loyalty, with the added bonus of satisfying ever increasing privacy requirements.

A BEST PRACTICE CHECKLIST

- **Ensure your systems are designed to house and archive customer preference data**
- **Centralize your preference data**
- **Ensure your system is designed to easily set up new programs**
- **Develop an Application Programming Interface (API) toolset to share data across the organization**
- **Develop configurable reports so that you can see trends**
- **Develop a validation and alert process to ensure that processes are run correctly**
- **Ensure that your preference architecture is configurable**
- **Develop robust user management and security**
- **Develop a dynamic compliance rules engine**
- **Ensure that you have a defendable position if a regulatory compliance mistake is made**
- **Take a phased approach – start with a pilot such as a business unit or brand, or a customer segment that has a high potential of success**
- **Set success metrics – it's important that you set measurable goals so you know how to reach them and when they've been met**

When organizations can't effectively share or collectively interpret full-spectrum customer data, they can't implement customer experience programming with confidence.

Ensuring that every customer touchpoint can both collect preferences and act upon stated preferences provides the customer with the desired engagement across the organization.

Preference data is unique in that it's one of the few pieces of data provided directly by the consumer. It can be used as lens to unlock and better use data that has been collected by other systems and via other means.

Organizations should build their preference management solution with the goal of how they want to report and use the preference data after they collect it centrally and share it across the enterprise. A unified view of preferences across the organization allows it to interpret preferences correctly, honor preferences consistently and reduce risk by maintaining compliance.

Field agents, call center reps or checkout clerks that have preferences available to them via system lookup capabilities can quickly look up preferences before contacting a customer, which ensures that they honor existing preferences. They call also ask for additional preferences or changes to existing preferences and update the system in real time.

GAINING EXECUTIVE BUY-IN
Because Enterprise Preference Management affects each department or business unit differently, organizations must educate all of the stakeholders, including marketing, IT, legal and customer service, so that they understand the importance of this initiative and the benefits it will offer. Speak directly to the objectives and concerns of each department. For example:

- Marketing wants to improve campaign results and CLV
- Customer Service wants to improve satisfaction scores and cut support costs
- Legal wants to be in compliance in order to minimize risk
- IT wants to be on time and on budget.

CONSUMER CHOICE
According to Forrester Research, more than three-quarters (77%) of consumers say companies should let them decide how they can be contacted[3]. By offering opt-in marketing, IBM showed an 80% increase in sales, a 75% decrease in marketing waste, and a 6-point increase in customer satisfaction. [4]

The average conversion rate for opt-in marketing and advertising stands at 25.15%: considerably higher than the rate for mobile display ads (in the low single digits), more than twenty times the response rate for direct marketing (1.38%) and also much higher than web advertising (where a response rate of 0.08% is considered a successful campaign response rate).
According to a study by MyBuys, an e-tailing group, 40% of respondents stated that they buy more from retailers that personalize their shopping experience across channels. Additionally:

- 41% buy more from retailers that send them personalized emails
- 39% buy more from retailers that personalize Web recommendations.

The study noted that the practice of tailoring offers and promotions to consumers based on their past shopping or browsing experiences appears to increase buyer readiness, engagement and sales activity. These findings are reinforced by sales data from MyBuys' own database of some 250 million shoppers: Customer-centric marketing

---
3 - Source: Forrester Research: Marketers: Stop the Abuse! Adopt Preference Management. July 22, 2009
4 - *Opting In*, The Magazine of Direct Marketing Management, By Ernan Roman and Scott Hornstein

delivers a 25% increase in total online sales and a 300% improvement in customer lifetime value, according to the company.

COST CONSIDERATIONS
Third-party software solutions typically have implementation and ongoing monthly fees based on preference volumes. You should compare the cost of outsourcing with the cost of building an in-house solution.

If you build an in-house solution, keep in mind that Enterprise Preference Management isn't a one-time project; it's an ongoing activity. You must ask yourself if you have the internal resources to build and maintain an EPM solution. Initial development can take two to three years and may cost millions of dollars. Ongoing tasks include collecting, managing and sharing the preferences among departments and business units, and maintaining compliance with relevant state and federal consumer privacy legislation.

The number and range of disciplines involved in defining, building and maintaining an EPM solution include, but are not limited to, the following positions:

- Marketing Management
- Business Operations
- Project Managers
- Technical Operations
- Systems Architects & Developers
- Business Analysts
- Quality Assurance

BUILD IT FOR THE CUSTOMER
Providing access to preferences at every consumer touchpoint with a brand is critical. For example, consumers should have easy access to their preference on the website, in emails, on mobile devices and when they interact with staff in call centers. Additionally, interfaces should limit the choices they have to make – providing the ability to opt-out of a specific communication that isn't of interest to the consumer is an elegant and simple way to allow self-management, or to opt-in to specific topics of interest and preferred communications channels.

Providing visual clues and examples with the preference management center assures consumers understand the choice they're making when presented with a larger list of options or potential channels.

Ultimately, the organization needs to build the EPM solution from the perspective of the user – not the internal organization – to ensure it's both intuitive and simple to use. Remember to respect opt-outs and ensure they're processed across specific channels, or all channels, depending on the user's preference. Let consumers determine when, how often, through what channels and what they want to receive from you, and make sure that analysts and marketers have all of the preference data for customers available in one up-to-date place.

Enterprise Engagement: The Textbook

Chapter 16

Content Marketing

One of the more recent business services to arise out of engagement is Content Marketing, which refers to the use of informative, useful information, entertainment or games in communications with customers, distribution partners or other audiences rather than the traditional emphasis on using communications in business to sell, train or inform.

Content marketing arose during the pre-Internet era in the form of "advertorials" provided by media to sponsors who wanted the opportunity to address information specifically related to their area of business in the publication. Organizations also created videos and road shows to attract prospects by providing useful information or entertainment.

During the Internet era, the use of Content Marketing has grown exponentially because marketers have discovered that effective content can:

- Enhance website "stickiness" by providing useful, how-to information like you find on the websites of leading hardware retailers and other service-oriented organizations
- Improve organic search engine results by creating content relative to a specific brand
- Enhance the value of social media strategies by giving people more reasons to engage or share information
- Improve customer, distribution partner and employee engagement by giving people the opportunity to gain recognition by having their own content published
- Generate free exposure by creating a communication vehicle that goes "viral"

Content marketing is the use of any type of content to attract and build relationships with prospects and customers. Content can consist of news, features, how-to information, profiles, photos, videos, games, music, business theater, etc. It can include distribution through any type of media, including print, email, social media, video, live events, broadcast TV or radio, aimed at both customers and prospects.

Here are some of the critical steps to developing a Content Marketing strategy:

1. Vision. What are you specifically trying to accomplish with your content marketing? Is it to get people to opt in, respond to offers, optimize search engine results, become better informed, share information, visit your website more often, increase trust? What are the important performance measures?

2. Audience. Who are the people you need to target? In what formats are they most likely to consume content? What type of content will likely attract them? Chances are you'll come up with a combination based on different types of audiences.

3. Assessment. What is the current state of your content marketing strategy? What content do you have available? What types of content have proved effective in the past? What is the best media for your audience, given how they interact with your organization (computer, smart phone, etc.)? Who do you have on staff or via other resources that can create the content? Ideally, these resources have expertise in your field.

4. Type of content. What type of information will be of greatest use to your audiences? Is there news or how-to information you have from which they can benefit? Are there games, theater, music that will have a special impact on your customers? It's no easy task to identify content that will engage customers. What content do you want to make sure you *do not* include? A major fast food company got stung when a content provider posted on its website advice for holiday tipping precisely when the company was embroiled in minimum wage protests.

5. Which media make sense? Technology has significantly lowered the production costs of all media, but there is also a valuable time and resource component of one medium versus another and how best to combine media for different types of people. See Chapter 14 for more information on different options.

6. How will the content be marketed? How should the content be integrated with your website, social media, event strategies, etc.? How can you leverage other marketing to make people aware of this content?

7. Integration with other engagement strategies. How will your communication efforts support other parts of the organization that may wish to communicate with your audience? Can their needs create opportunities to make your communication more valuable? How can communications continually reinforce the key marketing proposition?

8. Measurement. The Internet and social media provide unparalleled ways of measuring engagement in terms of how many people visit sites, how long they stay, what they do, how often they come back, etc. Customer Relationship Management makes it ever more possible to measure participation in live events or telephone interactions.

CONTENT SKILL REQUIREMENTS
One of the obstacles to Content Marketing is the lack of experts who understand how to merge traditional content with marketing.

Traditional journalists think like reporters or how-to article writers and have to be reoriented towards understanding the audience of the organization and the specific goals of the effort. Traditional marketers often don't know how to stop selling – providing objective, useful information is not in their makeup or training.

These folks have to be reoriented toward providing useful information, engaging entertainment, games or user-submitted content that has a benefit to the consumer as well as to the sponsor.

> **Traditional marketers often don't know how to stop selling – providing objective, useful information is not in their makeup or training.**

Enterprise Engagement: The Textbook

Chapter 17

Learning and Training

Few engagement tactics are as powerful, motivating and beneficial to both engagement and organizational performance as learning. Year after year, in surveys by leading consulting firms and research groups, learning and career opportunities are rated at or near the top of the most motivating benefits provided by organizations to employees and channel partners. In BlessingWhite's *2013 Employee Engagement Research Update*, for example, the lead reason employees gave for leaving organizations was "… don't have opportunities to grow or advance here." Learning was also the fourth most critical driver of engagement among survey takers in the research.[1]

Organizations often overlook the importance of engagement in developing and disseminating their training or learning materials. At the same time, they overlook the impact of training and learning as a tactic when implementing any type of engagement effort for customers, retailers, distributors and vendors.

THE CHALLENGES
Despite all the benefits of learning, many of us avoid typical training because it's often slow-paced, uninspiring and time-consuming – in other words, it fails to engage us. While learning in general is a powerful engagement and performance driver, it's much more effective when the learning activities themselves are engaging. Moreover, as the urgency to convey knowledge quickly, flexibly and inexpensively grows, traditional learning continues to cede more and more territory to e-learning and its subsets (e.g., mobile learning). Yet the challenge to make e-learning compelling and engaging for the learner is perhaps even steeper than for traditional, classroom learning.

Of course, learning that can be termed "formal" – whether in a classroom or online – represents only the tip of the iceberg. Various forms of informal learning continue to grow in importance. In addition to learning by doing, we learn by reading and seeing.

Today, tremendous volumes of "thought leadership" produced by academics, consultants, think tanks and companies are available live at conferences and on webinars, radio and TV. Even more is accessible online in the form of articles, books, essays, presentations, videos and other media. The extent to which any of the above is

---
1 - BlessingWhite, Employee Engagement Research Update, January 2013, p.10

engaging is the often the largest determinant of whether it gets used and passed on, and whether it makes any sort of impact.

While formal training and informal on-the-job learning might dominate educational efforts for employees and channel partners, thought leadership is the primary vehicle organizations use to "teach" customers, suppliers and the community or larger society about themselves, their ideas and their offerings. White papers, presentations, PR, videos, conferences and the like are use by well over 80% of U.S. organizations[2] to inform consumers, corporate buyers, the community and other stakeholders by introducing new ideas, educating consumers or buyers about trends and products or services, and shaping public opinion around social, environmental and other issues. Organizations use thought leadership to educate, build reputation and, if done correctly, to tangentially increase market share and revenue.

> **While most learning may be intrinsically engaging at some level, the mountains of material available make it difficult for organizations to find audiences for their thought leadership, and even attentive students for their training.**

The challenge is to rise above the information glut to bring attention to ideas. While most learning may be intrinsically engaging at some level, the mountains of material available (combined with greater pressures on most people's time) make it difficult for organizations to find audiences for their thought leadership, and even attentive students for their training. Employee engagement during training and courses cannot be taken for granted, nor can it be assumed that investment in employees' development will necessarily translate into higher levels of engagement and commitment afterward.

New techniques and old, including interactive learning, scenario-based training and so-called "gamification" techniques, to name a few, are being updated, digitized and deployed to capture the attention of learners, keep them coming back and help them retain what they've learned. Whatever the technique, it's critical to gain and hold participants' interest by tapping into their intrinsic motivators like autonomy, mastery, social interaction, progress and purpose.

Learning should be explored in the context of its usefulness as an engagement tactic and the degree to which it can be made more engaging itself. Learning is a powerful instrument in engagement, but it encompasses a vast range of activities and tools, making it ubiquitous – available constantly and in unlimited supply. Thus learning itself must be engaging in order to stand out and be utilized by intended audiences. And while training and development is a critical component of internal talent management for organizations, it's also used extensively with other key stakeholders.

LEARNING & TALENT
In its 2013 survey of C-Suite executives from around the world, the Conference Board found that "human capital" remains the number one global challenge among organizations.[3] Rounding out the top four are "operational excellence," "innovation" and "customer relationships." Few would argue that talent is the key ingredient to overcoming these challenges. The extent to which people are engaged determines whether they innovate, lead effectively, treat customers well and execute in their daily activities.

---

2 - Laurie Young, *Thought Leadership*, Kogan Page, 2013
3 - See: http://www.aon.com/human-capital-consulting/thought-leadership/talent_mgmt/2013_Trends_in_Global_Employee_Engagement.jsp

Organizations must also think beyond employees where engagement is concerned. Engaged customers, partners and even volunteers can make an enormous difference to innovation, operational excellence and most human capital challenges. Fortunately, many of the same engagement tactics that drive employee engagement also propel other stakeholder engagement.

In driving engagement, there are myriad important factors and tactics, but among them, learning and career-enhancement opportunities are possibly the most powerful. In its *2012 Global Engagement* report, Aon Hewitt reported that "career opportunities" – including learning & development – top the list of engagement drivers for employees around the world, as well as most employee subsets, all generations of workers and most types of employees, including sales, operations, management and technical disciplines.

Employees expect their organizations to invest in them and to provide opportunities for them to further their careers. Likewise, channel partners become more engaged and productive when the organizations they represent invest in their product knowledge. But learning as a driver of engagement isn't limited to employees or channel partners. Customers and communities frequently engage with organizations and their missions through learning and education as well.

It can be argued that for many business-to-business customers, learning and the career opportunities learning affords are among the most important drivers of engagement. Executives, buyers and others in organizations of all sizes consume white papers, books, articles and other thought leadership materials at an astounding rate, such that corporate spending on thought leadership today roughly equals what is spent on advertising.[4] According to research by ITSMA (Information Technology Services Marketing Association) in 2013, 88% of U.S. business buyers said thought leadership is important to get onto their shortlists for sales opportunities.[5]

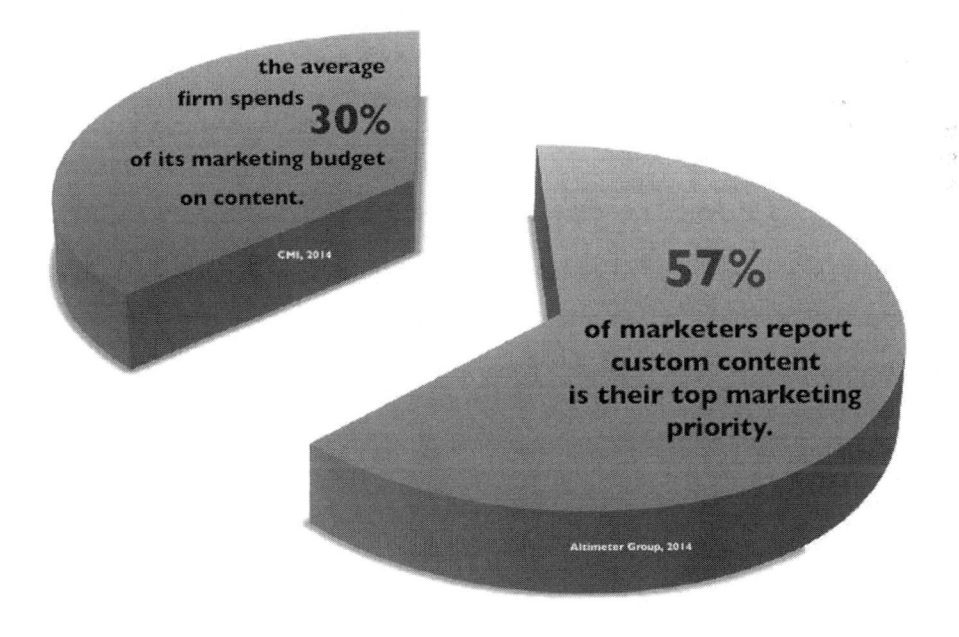

---

4 - Laurie Young, Thought Leadership: Prompting Businesses to Think and Learn, 2013, Kogan Page
5 - ITSMA, 2013: How Buyers Consume Content, Knowledge, and Wisdom, see: www.itsma.com

For consumers and communities, learning is also gaining an increasing share of marketing and PR efforts. Consumers are more likely to trust and "engage" with a brand or product if they know more about it (obviously excluding organizations that engage in nefarious practices they wish to hide). Organizations undertake tremendous efforts through websites, commercials, articles – and, increasingly, games and reward-based learning programs – to educate communities about their mission, social responsibility initiatives and their care for such things as the environment, health and human development. Leading professional services organizations and others also use learning to shape the public discourse and engage citizens around ideas or concepts they seek to promote or introduce.

LEARNING & PERFORMANCE

As Nobel Prize-winning economist Paul Krugman puts it: *"It is a truth, universally acknowledged, that education is the key to economic success."*[6] Investments in learning and development pay enormous dividends, whether considering individuals (college graduates earn about 35% more per annum than high school graduates)[7]; nations (there's a near perfect correlation between national standards of living and average per-capita level of education)[8]; and organizations.

For at least the past decade, researchers – Dr. Laurie Bassi foremost among them – have shown that by every measure, organizations that spend more on training perform better.[10] And while companies should plan their learning budgets carefully, even blind spending on training often results in remarkable gains, driving home the message that investments in learning generate more highly engaged employees and stakeholders.

> '...of 1,500 classrooms visited, 85% of them had engaged less than 50% of the students. In other words, only 15% of the classrooms had more than half of the class at least paying attention to the lesson.'
>
> ~ Dr. Michael Schmoker, Results Now[9]

Research conducted by Bassi and Dan McMurrer reveals that firms residing in the 3rd and 4th quartile of spending on training outperform those in the bottom two quartiles significantly and across all standard measures of business success.

Thus learning forms a central pillar in any organization's efforts to engage employees, partners, customers, communities and other stakeholders. But learning is a broad term, encompassing formal and informal methods and including far more information on most topics than any human could wade through in a lifetime of effort.

Today, ubiquitous information threatens organizations' ability to gain even the most fleeting attention of stakeholders, let alone engage and inform them. And so the focus must widen from the use of learning and education to engage to the deployment of educational techniques that capture the attention and the imaginations of learners.

ENGAGING LEARNERS

Organizational efforts at learning and education are rarely confined to employees. Channel partners who represent partner organizations – often their main sales forces – must be educated too.

Once the right channel partners are onboard, you should change your focus to reducing the time it takes them to become productive on your behalf. In the spirit of engagement and building a partner engagement

---

6 - See: http://www.nytimes.com/2011/03/07/opinion/07krugman.html?_r=0
7 - See: http://www.pewsocialtrends.org/2014/02/11/the-rising-cost-of-not-going-to-college/sdt-higher-education-02-11-2014-0-01/
8 - See: http://hdr.undp.org/en/statistics/hdi
9 - See: http://www.amazon.com/Results-Now-Unprecedented-Improvements-Teaching/dp/1416603581
10 - See: http://home.uchicago.edu/~ludwigj/papers/BassiEtal-Singapore-2002.pdf

culture, think less about their obligations and more about how you can offer support to get them up and running with minimal effort on their part. A great deal of this will be accomplished through training and other forms of learning.

Similarly, suppliers should understand the end products and overall goals of their customers and, in most non-commodity businesses today, customers themselves should be educated about ideas, markets, products and services. And while superficial customer/consumer education might be possible through traditional advertising, true learning is only accomplished through the creation and dissemination of thought leadership in all its forms.

The point, again, is that learning and education are powerful drivers of stakeholder engagement. For some, learning opens new career opportunities. For others, it helps them understand a product or idea and how it might further their professional and/or business interests. But the flood of articles and white papers, magazines, journals from consulting firms, videos and slide presentations – not to mention the tens of thousands of business, technology, science and other professional books published each year – make it difficult to capture audience attention for the period of time necessary to actually educate or inform them. The volume of information today makes it necessary for educators to seek ways to engage audiences, both through superior content and valuable information, and by using techniques that connect with learners at an emotional level.

Accurate and valuable content is a must, and many, if not most, organizations are capable of producing good content in their areas of expertise or practice. Creating an emotional connection with the learner is normally far more difficult and often completely overlooked. Yet lessons and best practices can be learned from other industries – perhaps most directly, the entertainment industry,

THE LURE OF STORYTELLING
Despite information overload, American adults spend about 4 hours or more watching TV programming every day[11] [12]. They may be watching TV instead of taking online courses or reading white papers and business books because they engage with TV's stories and characters at an emotional level, whether movies, sports, sitcoms or game shows.

The lure of storytelling allows even mediocre movies and TV programs to dwarf the attention paid to the most important business books and research papers. Organizations must strive to make their content creative and captivating, and usually with nowhere near the budget of even the least expensive television productions.

Storytelling is an important and credible tactic used in even the most rigorous academic work where general audiences are sought. Case studies featuring real challenges – especially those that employ the proven components of antagonists and protagonists overcoming conflict – work well.

Based on research for his 2012 bestseller *Drive*, author Dan Pink recommends a simple formula he calls the "Pixar Pitch" for storytelling. Entertainment giant Pixar uses this approach consistently to engage and "move" audiences:

"*Once upon a time* there was a widowed fish named Marlin who was extremely protective of his only son, Nemo. *Every day* Marlin warned Nemo of the ocean's dangers

---
11 - http://www.bls.gov/news.release/atus.nr0.htm
12 - http://www.huffingtonpost.com/2013/08/01/tv-digital-devices_n_3691196.html

and implored him not to swim far away. *One day*, in an act of defiance, Nemo ignores his father's warning and swims into the open water. *Because of that*, he is captured by a diver and ends up as a pet in a fish tank of a dentist in Sydney. *Because of that*, Marlin sets off on a journey recover Nemo, enlisting the help of other sea creatures along the way. *Until finally* Marlin and Nemo find each other, reunite and learn that love depends on trust."[13]

In communicating their ideas through thought leadership or formal courses, authors might engage their audiences using these same techniques. Obviously, they'll drop "once upon a time" from their narratives, but consider variations of the passage below and how it might be used to introduce a technical paper about advances in chemical compounds:

"*Once upon a time* a junior researcher named Pat discovered that by adding a chemical to jet fuel, most commercial aircraft could travel 25% further. *Every day* Pat tried to convince her leaders and customers that her process should be adopted. *One day*, without telling her bosses, Pat applied to present at a national aviation conference. *Because of that*, she was able to share her findings and convince a large portion of the audience of the merits of her discovery. *Because of that*, her company began to receive enquiries and requests for the product. *Until finally* Pat's bosses realized the importance of her breakthrough and turned it into a blockbuster product."

Other tactics include the use of scenarios and games to capture and hold learners' attention. The next chapter offers an examination of "gamification" tactics in engagement that are highly relevant to the design of training and learning.

SUMMARY
Few would argue that learning is a critical component of engagement at all levels and for all stakeholders. It's possibly the most important element in employee engagement, and it's becoming essential in customer engagement wherever sophisticated products or services are offered. Learning can generate interest in organizations' latest ideas and/or offerings and can be used to shape corporate reputations at the community, national and international levels. But learning is broad and learning opportunities surround everyone during every waking hour.

To compete, you must make your learning and information content compelling. Not only must it be good in the traditional sense – accurate, valuable, expert – it must engage learners emotionally. Unfortunately, even the most brilliant ideas and concepts can be lost if they fail to engage. Use techniques perfected by storytellers, gamers and other creative disciplines to powerfully tap the emotions of your target audiences and engage them in your material.

---

13 - Dan Pink, *To Sell is Human*, Riverhead Books, 2012, p.171

Enterprise Engagement: The Textbook

Chapter 18

Gamification

By Rajat Paharia and Bruce Bolger

Not long after the turn of the millennium, gamification burst onto the scene with great fanfare and considerable media attention. But like many new business technologies, the true potential of the gamification solution remains largely misunderstood years later. Gamification is not just a marketing strategy or a learning tool – it's both of those things, and more.

Today's gamification solutions provide a means for organizations to more deeply involve their core audiences in virtually any interaction, for almost any purpose. Gamification applies the same data-driven techniques used by game designers to engage players, and these techniques have been shown to motivate specific actions in a variety of business scenarios important to an organization. Results are not simply measured by the time spent interacting with the experience, but on the improved quality of interactions between customers, employees, distribution partners, and others, that can drive additional sales, stronger collaboration, deeper loyalty, increased customer satisfaction, higher "net-promoter" scores, increased learning and significantly more knowledge sharing.

It's useful to note the difference between games and gamification: Games are self-contained experiences the sole purpose of which is to entertain. Gamification refers specifically to the process of enhancing or further "activating" an existing online experience through the use of motivational techniques found in video games, strengthened by leveraging the data gained from users as they interact with the system. But it is important to note that gamification is far more than one-size-fits-all game mechanics. In fact, real gamification programs combine human motivation, digital strategy, and analytics to architect and deliver a scalable data-driven motivation program within each enterprise. It's equal parts art and science, big data and analytics.

This is not about "tricking" a user into activities based on a points, badges or leaderboards. Rather, the overall goal of gamification is to more deeply connect with existing and potential customers, employees, partners and other audiences, and inspire them to participate, collaborate, share and interact in ways that are simultaneously rewarding at the individual level and positively impactful to the enterprise. By integrating a gamification strategy and analytics into a website, business service, online community, content portal, marketing campaign or even internal business process, enterprises can measure and motivate increased participation and engagement by a target audience.

What makes gamification so compelling? It starts with the addictive nature of online games – which leverage behavioral science strategically to motivate behavior. Consider that as of 2013, 58% of Americans spent an average of 13 hours each week and over $15 billion dollars each year playing video games.[1] Games attract and retain the attention of players by tapping into their intrinsic need for autonomy, mastery, relatedness, purpose and progress -- rewarding them as they advance through a set of increasingly difficult levels, while promoting competition or collaboration (or both) and creating a community with whom to connect. At the most simplistic level, gamification replaces "meaningless games" with meaningful business or consumer behaviors – those that drive meaningful personal or professional success, while also driving positive enterprise results.

CUSTOMER APPLICATIONS
In the U.S. today, there are more than 2.6 billion loyalty program memberships. The average household belongs to 21 loyalty programs but actively participates in fewer than half. Clearly, rewards alone are not sufficient to deeply engage people, especially when many companies offer strikingly similar incentives. The resulting loyalty is not to the brand or the company, but to the best current offer.

Moreover, as these loyalty programs remain squarely focused on discounts and monetary rewards, they fail to take advantage of the valuable data generated as businesses interact with their core audiences. While some businesses do leverage *transactional* data, this is only a one-dimensional view of what motivates the individual customer. Gamification allows businesses to leverage multi-dimensional data to tailor the online experience in a way that motivates the target audience and rewards them in a manner that is meaningful to them.

The USA Network television program *Psych* created a gamified loyalty and fan engagement program called Club Psych that tapped into viewers' appetites for access, reward, recognition and power. It enabled fans to obtain related content online, watch and share videos, play games, take quizzes, interact with promotions, chat with other fans, and redeem points for a space on the site where they could share their creativity and demonstrate their community status. The company gained a three-dimensional view of their audience and measured success in terms of viewership, frequency and time spent on the website.

Gamification impacts B2B communities similarly, but here the drivers are focused on professional status and contributions. By example, business software giant SAP uses gamification to enhance its community portal for developers, partners and business clients. Members in the network earn points for their contributions in content, code samples, and demonstration videos. They earn additional points and reach elevated status tiers as community members recognize the value of their contributions. Top performers are recognized at the company's annual conference and an established reputation within the community has become a valuable and recognized measurement of expertise beyond the SAP Community Network.

---

[1] See: http://en.wikipedia.org/wiki/Video_gaming_in_the_United_States

While they'd been using gamification elements since 2004, implementation of a comprehensive platform and program delivered a rapid 1,113% uptick in activity and collaboration, and a 250% increase in community feedback. SAP has transformed its community portal into a powerful innovation and collaboration tool measuring over two million unique visitors in 2012 and over 200,000 total contributors.

EMPLOYEE ENGAGEMENT

Gamification can be an effective cure for the epidemic of employee *dis*engagement many companies struggle with today. All too often, employees cannot easily identify how their specific activities impact the company's bottom line. Gamification provides the clarification necessary to focus teams and individuals on key business priorities by aligning individual and team goals with key corporate objectives. Real-time feedback on performance lends greater visibility into their impact on the business and provides a deeper sense of accomplishment. And the ability to gain status and build reputation increases interest across the organization.

> **Gamification provides the clarification necessary to focus teams and individuals on key business priorities by aligning individual and team goals with key corporate objectives.**

By incorporating the daily activities of employees into the program, encouraging collaboration and a healthy sense of competition while including business metrics specific to each role such as quota achievement, issue resolution, product ideation and process alignment, individual goals feed directly into key business drivers. The end result is often measurable increases in revenue per employee.

In an effort to drive exceptional customer service, T-Mobile redesigned its "T-Community" social business environment — a peer-to-peer collaboration tool that helps customer service and in-store reps quickly and efficiently respond to customer queries. To promote adoption and usage of its new platform, T-Mobile integrated gamification into the environment, allowing it to reward users when they search for information, post new questions, answer peer questions, and "like" content they find valuable.

Today, more than 30,000 T-Mobile customer service call centers and store employees are using the T-Community to its fullest potential. As a result, they've experienced a 96% increase in participation, a 583% increase in contributions, and a 783% increase in responses. Customer satisfaction scores improved by 31% and call center costs decreased due to a 40% improvement in call deflection rates.

Employee recruitment, development and retention are additional areas that can be positively impacted by gamification. With greater visibility into what motivates different employee groups, businesses can more effectively target and attract recruits, accelerate their onboarding, ensure participation and effectiveness of their training programs, improve self-driven and collaborative learning, accelerate ongoing usage of enterprise systems, and increase overall engagement.

INTEGRATING AUDIENCES

Gamification is frequently used to help break down silos and encourage collaboration and knowledge sharing across departments, partners, between customers and employees, and perhaps the entire organization. It can turn a traditional "suggestion" program into a community of self-reinforcing innovation that creates task value for everyone in the organization. Gamification can create deeper visibility into employees' and partners' experiences and expertise so that it may be leveraged outside of their immediate department or daily responsibilities.

As part of an initiative to leverage unrealized potential across its half-a-million member global partner network, a leading global virtualization company uses a gamification platform to motivate partners to build their product expertise and drive sales. The platform encourages members to quickly develop expertise around the company's product offerings and motivates them to improve their skills by completing a series of challenges. Participants pick up recognition badges as they achieve progressive levels of proficiency, and real-time feedback lets them know where they stand against both their own goals and other partner organizations.

As members engage, they generate information about what interests and motivates them. And the company draws on that data to create a highly customized gamification experience that speaks to those individual motivations.

POINTS
1:49AM JANUARY 14, 2014

1	Ted Alspach	5300
2	Sam Yoder	2670
3	Judith Coyn	2333
4	Jeffrey Gonzales	1946
5	Ronny Runfield	1862
6	Marina Esterlis	1850
7	John Garner	1559
8	Rob Mullany	950
9	Brian Perasso	900
10	Rajhat Paharia	600

Judith Coyn
2333

The company's gamified environment threads through its partner portal and learning community. As they ascend through the programs, partners gain knowledge, certifications, accreditations and experience that will help to attract larger deals, achieve better close rates and generate more revenue, resulting in a shared business imperative that benefits everyone's bottom line. The company's 60,000 partner organizations accounted for most of the company's multiple billions in revenue last year.

MEASUREMENT AND ANALYSIS
One of the great advantages of gamification is the ability to attribute and measure behaviors for a deeper understanding of your employee, partner or customer. In some cases, motivating specific behaviors drives faster or bigger ROI, other times it delivers business insights. For example, gamification has been proven to motivate the consumption of training materials – that can be a key behavioral goal. But what if the new behavior doesn't equate to a better business result? What if there is not a meaningful impact on sales or service in the form of ROI? In those cases, the enterprise has a new insight – and adjustments can be made to the training. This is a new approach to management – one based on measurement and insights, not just hunches. The old model of relying on surveys, or purely on quantitative data is now transcended by the ability to correlate not only surveys and sales data, but also behavioral data -- the number or duration of site visits, content consumed, information and recognition

shared, behaviors rewarded, levels of accomplishment, community response, referral activity, and more.

ESSENTIAL ELEMENTS OF ENGAGEMENT PROGRAM DESIGN

According to a 2012 Gartner study on gamification, by 2014 80% of all programs will fail to meet business objectives because of poor planning. Following a few basic principles can help ensure success:

1. Design programs that support your corporate strategy. A corporate strategy is *supported* by gamification, not *driven* by it. Successful gamification is layered on top of existing programs and platforms such enterprise applications, portals, mobile apps, websites and intranets that have value in and of themselves. Gamification *augments* the experience to motivate desired behaviors and results.

2. Create a formal business plan to aid buy-in and keep you on track. Include meticulously defined business goals, a clear understanding of target users and what drives them, a set of prioritized actions you want your users to take, and pre-defined success metrics.

3. Design a comprehensive digital strategy. Determine which combination of gamification mechanics makes sense, and then define a long-term engagement map. Examine and select your appropriate methods of continuous measurement and adjustment. Have a plan to launch, monitor, and optimize--plan on fine-tuning your programs frequently for maximum success.

4. Select appropriate tools and technology. Consider the maturity, scalability, flexibility, robust functionality, customization options, and ease of use and administration of the technology platform you are evaluating. An established track record of successful similar engagements and a list of client references will go a long way in helping you to ensure that the provider has the ability to deliver proven, innovative software and service solutions, can provide consultative services to improve the envisioned program, and can execute a sound implementation, maintenance and support strategy.

5. Measure and optimize. It is imperative to measure the success of your initiatives in order to respond to the preferences of your users and ensure their ongoing engagement. What motivates early users may not be what motivates those who have been interacting with your business long-term. Common metrics may include:

- Sales: Pipeline growth and revenue achievement; time to onboard new sales representatives; lead, call and deal conversion volumes; and (in CRM) improved data integrity.
- Service & Support: Customer satisfaction and support performance metrics including first call resolution, average handle time, and cost per contact.
- HR: Employee engagement and retention rates, collaboration or learning platform activity levels, annual attrition rates, and time required to onboard.
- Customer engagement: Return visits, duration on site, purchase value and volume, community activity levels and social media amplification.

A smart, thorough program design will go a long way towards ensuring the success of any gamification program, but perhaps the most important key to success is in the understanding that gamification is much more than game mechanics and badges.

Don't get caught up in the game aspects of the solution when the focus should be squarely on using gamification's data-driven motivation techniques to align with corporate objectives and deliver business value in a sustained and scalable way.

At the end of the day, businesses simply need to understand that successful implementations occur when gamification is used to drive behaviors that drive business.

Enterprise Engagement: The Textbook

Chapter 19

Collaboration and Innovation

By Ira M. Ozer

Companies with a culture of collaboration and innovation enjoy significant benefits, including improved productivity and efficiencies, new product and process development, increasing revenues/profits and reduced costs. Although most companies have "innovation" listed in their mission statement and advertising, they don't actually have an effective culture of collaboration or innovation, or the systems and processes to support it. This chapter explains why this is so and how companies can build such a culture by learning from the knowledge and best practices of innovation consultants, trainers, research and technology companies and leaders of corporate centers of innovation.

OPEN AND TRUSTING
To be effective, people must work together in an open way, with trust and understanding of each other's intentions to share and create improved solutions. People who work in collaborative teams usually achieve better and faster results than people who work separately, as long as the task is aligned with the objectives of the organization. If not, time and energy can be wasted and people can become frustrated.

Wikipedia is an excellent example of an "open" online collaboration platform that allows people to work together to improve definitions of words and topics for the greater good. There are many examples of collaboration platforms that allow corporations to have their own "closed" collaborative communities as well, such as Lithium and Jive. Each of these systems allows employees to communicate to share their thoughts, opinions and success stories across their functional areas, business units and sometimes across the entire enterprise. This creates a more open environment of understanding and engagement through social communities, but generally doesn't provide the tools and processes necessary to move from collaboration to innovation.

INVESTING IN INNOVATION
Innovation is the process of generating creative ideas that when acted upon can improve experiences, products or services. In a business sense, innovation improves revenues and profits and/or reduces costs. The investment necessary to support a

culture of innovation should provide a return-on-investment because, if properly designed and implemented, innovation is a trainable, repeatable process.

Having a culture of collaboration and innovation has always been important for companies, but with today's fast-paced technological changes – data processing power, speed, storage and search capabilities, Big Data, expanding knowledge, service levels, social media, etc. – it's even more critical. We have seen many examples of companies that were leaders in their fields for many years, such as Sears, J.C. Penny and many others in retailing, leapfrogged by more recently established firms like Amazon and Overstock. This trend is most pronounced in the world of technology, where companies like Blackberry, which was recognized as one of the most progressive and profitable a few years ago, are now on the verge of bankruptcy. Companies must collaborate and innovate or, literally, die.

> **Companies that are ranked as having high employee engagement scores are also usually leaders in collaboration and innovation.**

The primary reasons for building a culture of collaboration and innovation are to improve products, processes and to reduce costs. Related secondary benefits to employee productivity, engagement, retention and advocacy are also important. Companies that are ranked as having high employee engagement scores are also usually leaders in collaboration and innovation. Increases in revenues and profits are much higher for companies that have formalized cultures of collaboration and innovation – Apple, Google, Zappos, JetBlue and others.

People are using collaborative shared services to reduce costs, eliminate waste, improve convenience and in some cases earn income. Start-up businesses such as AirBnB, which allows people to rent an extra bedroom in their house to travelers, has grown so fast that within five years it has become one of the biggest booking site for rooms, even greater than many of the big hotel chains. Sarah DaVano, Chief Strategy and Cultural Officer of Sparks & Honey, an agency that syncs brands with culture, calls this the "Collaborative Economy" and sites many examples of collaborative shared services, not just from start-ups, but from major corporations as well, such as Citibank's sponsorship and payment system for the Citi Bike bike-sharing program recently launched in New York City.

SOME CHALLENGES

If the benefits and critical need to have a culture of innovation are so easily understood, why don't all companies have one? The simple answer is that they're not led and managed with methods and behaviors that can support such a culture. Sirota Survey Intelligence, a leading employee engagement research company, recently published a report citing 33 myths about work and workers that are basically the opposite of how employees should be treated to maximize engagement and collaboration. These myths include:

- People who feel secure in their jobs become complacent
- It is useless – even counterproductive – for employees doing routine, highly standardized work to be involved in decisions about the work.
- People who have too much to do are more unhappy than people who have too little to do
- Companies that are loyal to their employees are less successful as businesses
- Whether a company is ethical and a good corporate citizen is of little concern to most of its employees
- Professionals are much more concerned about doing a quality job than are nonprofessionals

Another major challenge to launching an effective system that will support and sustain a culture of innovation is that the majority of companies are managed based on hierarchical structures with ingrained bureaucracies and policies. Conversely, openness, creativity and recognizing the accomplishments of others are the cornerstones of collaboration and innovation, rather than covering your back, keeping your head down and taking the conventional route, so that risk-taking and mistakes are minimized.

A STRATEGY, NOT A PROGRAM

Having a culture of collaboration and innovation isn't something that should be implemented periodically; it should be part of the culture on a day-to-day basis. It is something that can be learned, with processes that can be tracked and measured, rewarded and recognized.

John Bidwell, Chief Innovation Officer at Chubb Insurance, explains that "innovation is an enterprise business process that can and should be better understood, redesigned, improved and measured to improve performance." Most innovations aren't based on big breakthrough ideas or inventions, but on small incremental changes that can have a huge cumulative effect over time. Chubb has been using an idea management system for several years, and more than 1,500 new ideas have been developed, with many business cases funded and more in process. "The Chubb Idea Management system has allowed us to successfully shift the 'center of gravity' of innovation to line employees and out to agents, thereby embedding innovation deep into our day-to-day operations," says Bidwell.

> **Most innovations aren't based on big breakthrough ideas or inventions, but on small incremental changes that can have a huge cumulative effect over time.**

KEY COMPONENTS

To have an effective innovation system that supports a company's culture and turns the dream into a reality, there are many interrelated components, processes and support mechanisms that have to be in place and working properly:

Strategic Plan. The first step is to develop a strategic plan for the company's culture of innovation, based on the mission, vision and values of the CEO and leadership team, company history, competitive environment and other factors. As part of this planning process, it's important to determine which stakeholders should be involved and to what extent. Participation can range from specific groups like technical engineers or product development teams all the way up to a company-wide approach that even adds channel partners, dealers, distributors and even customers and suppliers.

Another major part of the plan is to determine the types of ideas that are valuable to the company and can/should be acted upon, otherwise a funnel can be created to just gather a broad selection of ideas with no parameters and little practical value. In his book *Sidestep and Twist*, author James Gardner points out that companies can avoid commoditization and create entirely new market opportunities for their products if they think and act innovatively. An example of a "sidestep" for an airline would be if it enters into a more lucrative and less competitive charter contract than its normal commoditized consumer ticketing business and then add a "twist" by packaging all of the hotel and ground services that travelers will need during their trip.

According to a May 2013 report by Accenture entitled *Why Low Risk Innovation is Costly*, 93% of executives believe their company's long-term success will be due to innovation, but only 18% believe their own innovation strategy is delivering a competitive advantage.

There are hundreds if not thousands of innovation consulting companies, as well as internal experts who can help create a strategic plan and ensure participation, engagement and results.

Assessment. The current innovation environment should be assessed by conducting employee, partner and customer engagement surveys to determine which groups believe the company has a genuine culture of innovation with a feeling of openness and interest in gathering ideas, collaborating and innovating, as well as the processes and tools to support an effective innovation system.

It can be valuable to benchmark other companies that have cultures of innovation in order to set reasonable goals and have an understanding of the communications campaign and other support that will be necessary.

Methodology. There are many methods and processes by which an innovation system can be created and administered, such as TRIZ or TIPS (the Theory of Inventive Problem Solving), originally conceived in the 1940s for creative problem solving.

Stephen Shapiro, author of the best-selling book, *Best Practices are Stupid: 40 Ways to Out-Innovate the Competition*, and former leader of Accenture's 20,000-person process and innovation practice, outlines the process for accelerating collaboration and innovation as: 1) Ask the right challenge, which plays to the company's existing strengths; 2) Ask the challenge in a way that isn't too abstract, yet not too specific; 3) Pose the challenge to the right people, which shouldn't be limited to subject matter experts who may think too narrowly about it; and 4) Motivate people through rewards and recognition for going beyond their jobs.

There are almost as many innovation methods as there are consultants, and the correct one for a company must fit its culture, work processes and the tools it will be using.

Communications. Once the commitment has been made to implement a culture of innovation, it's important to create and launch a communications campaign, just like any other marketing or advertising endeavor, although with a focus on internal audiences. This campaign starts with an initial announcement and should then be used to continuously communicate the collaborative culture and innovation system throughout the launch period and, ideally, on an ongoing basis.

> **Having a culture of innovation isn't a 'program,' it must be reinforced to become a way of life ingrained in the company DNA.**

As noted previously, having a culture of innovation isn't a "program," it must be reinforced to become a way of life ingrained in the company DNA. The communications campaign should include an impactful, multi-media approach – an interactive innovation website, collaborative tools, in-person innovation meetings, etc.

Training. Training is necessary on many levels, starting with cultural awareness, then moving into creativity, behavioral styles, work competencies, team dynamics, collaboration, innovation methods and processes, coaching, authentic recognition and more. Gerald "Solutionman" Haman, a leading creativity and innovation trainer and facilitator, whose company SolutionPeople, trains corporate teams around the world and at their "Thinkubator" facility in Chicago, has created tools and processes to train company leaders and managers to become innovation champions. His "KnowBrainer" tool helps people solve problems by utilizing all four quadrants of their brain in an inspirational and innovative way to think outside of the box.

California-based Root Learning helps CEOs translate their cultural vision into reality by working with company leadership and employee teams to create "mind maps" – graphic illustrations of where the company's been and where it's going. This can be especially helpful to show how a company's traditional marketplace has transformed into a more complex and competitive environment. This helps people understand emotionally the need for change and to move away from complacency.

Platform. Once the commitment has been made to launch and support a culture of innovation through a sustainable innovation system, the message has been communicated to all of the stakeholders about the types of ideas needed, and some training has been initiated to power creativity and collaboration, a platform must be selected and implemented to support the system.

For the last 30 years or so, software has been used to manage "suggestion systems," which were basically database programs to manage the input of ideas for improvement and cost reduction. With the advent of more powerful software, the internet and many years of innovation knowledge and experience, innovation platforms have been introduced with many enhanced functions beyond being the central repository for ideas, including:

- Challenges...problems or situations that can be improved or solved through collaboration and innovation and are put forth because they're in alignment with the company's objectives.
- Collaboration...where teams are often comprised of people from different disciplines, geographies and business units to help break down the "silos" of corporate divisions that generally don't work together and sometimes compete for resources.
- Evaluation...of solutions using ranking algorithms and "gamification" techniques (such as points, badges and leaderboards) to vote on which ideas have the most application and merit for the company.
- Social Recognition...as a means to recognize participants directly and/or through their ranking score in "points," which can have tangible value or just serve as a social currency.
- Idea Submissions...for new products, services and processes; generally not free-form.
- Project Management...using integrated tools to shepherd the best ideas from development through implementation.
- Archiving...ideas so they can be referenced in the database for later use, if not appropriate to implement immediately.
- Rewards...so participants can redeem their points for tangible rewards such as innovative merchandise and gift cards, or experiences such as lunch with the CEO.

Coaching. Like anything else, there's an art as well as a science to creating a culture of collaboration and innovation. It starts with the CEO, but it should be supported by immediate supervisors and local managers. To be effective, these leaders have to be trained to be coaches, and there should be tracking systems in place to assure this happens on an ongoing basis. According to Keith Rosen, President of ProfitBuilders a leading coaching training company, most managers aren't properly trained to be coaches; they need to develop skills such as empathy and listening and focus on leading the innovation initiative.

Rewards & Recognition. It's essential to have a recognition system integrated with your innovation strategy, or it is doomed to fail. In general, most innovation experts believe that the "intrinsic motivation" of allowing people to participate in and be recognized by their company's innovation program is important. Motivation professionals will tell you that offering cash isn't as effective (and can sometimes be counterproductive or even harmful) as tangible awards such as innovative merchandise, gift cards, travel and/or experiences to thank people for their contributions and going "above and beyond" their normal work.

Implementation. Once the best ideas have been selected and vetted and management has approved and budgeted for them, they must be implemented or the whole innovation system becomes just a meaningless exercise. In addition, if ideas aren't successfully implemented, there can be no return-on-investment of the system and management will be hesitant to undertake similar initiatives in the future.

> It's important to track the leading indicators of success (such as participation rates) rather than just the final results, because these are lagging indicators that won't occur for some time into the future.

Measurement. The entire innovation system should be measured, from front-end idea submissions and challenge participation, to collaboration to solve the challenges, straight through to the back-end of implementation. It's important to track the leading indicators of success (such as participation rates) rather than just the final results, because these are lagging indicators that won't occur for some time into the future. And keep n mind that there are many ideas that can't be effectively measured, even though they have an impact on the quality of the workplace, customer service and other key areas.

CENTERS OF INNOVATION

Best practice companies are creating "Centers of Innovation" – cross-functional business units that lead and promote a culture of innovation across enterprises. This allows the company's innovation strategy to break down divisional, functional and business unit "silos."

John Geyer, VP of Innovation at the MetLife, describes his office as a "catalyst that works with the different business units to create process improvements that strengthen our culture of innovation." Using their innovation platform, MetLife launched seven challenge campaigns in 12 months to over 8,000 associates, received more than 2,600 qualified ideas and implemented 24 of them, for a return of more than $10 million.

Companies with cultures of collaboration and innovation have revenues and profits significantly greater than those that do not, as well as employees who are intrinsically motivated and engaged. The key is to design and implement a system that combines these integrated components in the proper balance.

Enterprise Engagement: The Textbook

Chapter 20

Rewards & Recognition

Managers responsible for attracting, retaining and motivating employees must identify the right combination of compensation, benefits, training, rewards and recognition to optimize the organization's efforts. The mix of such tools impacts employee behavior and beliefs, and consequently their output. Much like a chef who needs to use the right ingredients to bring their well-crafted recipes to life, managers must understand the crucial importance of each "ingredient." Too much or too little of any one element can be detrimental to the company's attraction, retention and engagement objectives.

The inevitable question, therefore, relates to the "how" of the matter. How do managers determine the right mix of these ingredients for their respective businesses?

The immediate answer is…it depends. Years ago, the correct mix was a simple formula: start with six parts compensation, then add in two parts benefits (an ingredient that only became part of the mix in the mid-20th century), followed by one part recognition and one part incentive. An employer acted as a kind of patriarch, while the employee "did as he was told."

Today's workers are different. They're more intelligent, diverse, informed, internet-savvy and connected. The current formula is dynamic and depends on what the organization is trying to accomplish, as well as the makeup of the people the organization is trying to influence. Generally speaking, all the same elements play a role in the mix, but there's no one recipe.

This chapter explores how each of the elements referenced above play a part in enhancing a company's total rewards strategy for its employees and, by extension, the engagement of all stakeholders. It will also provide guidance on how to best determine which elements will be of greatest value to your own organization's goals.

UNDERSTANDING THE ENVIRONMENT
Significant progress has been made in recent years in terms of how managers can better understand the environment in which they operate, and thereby better interpret the most powerfully motivating strategies for their organizations.

For example, a survey conducted by the Forum for People Performance Management and Measurement shares details on the most popular motivational tactics used in a rewards and recognition context. Among the many compelling findings:

- Non-cash motivators are viewed as superior to cash for "less tangible, morale-improving outcomes such as creating positive internal 'buzz' and improving teamwork." In fact, non-cash programs are viewed as more effective for 9 of the 10 organizational objectives that were studied.
- Cash, conversely, is typically more effective when short-term sales gains are the primary objective.
- Employee surveys are the most common of the measurement tools used to evaluate the impact of rewards and recognition programs. The key point here is that measurement is critical to ensuring that the organization is succeeding in its motivation efforts.

Other researchers echo these findings. Todd Manas and Michael Graham, the authors of *Creating a Total Rewards Strategy*, studied the eight chief causes of employee turnover. The top seven of these involved the lack of application in such areas as learning new skills, coaching, feedback and satisfying work. Actual compensation ranked eighth.

In evaluating these outcomes further, the authors determined that non-cash rewards are the only real way to differentiate your employment offerings. Cash will always be a commodity; it's the intangibles that will distinguish your company from the competition.

NOT 'ONE-SIZE-FITS-ALL'
At the same time, we're gaining a better understanding of the relative strengths of individual motivational tools and the need to understand shifts in the environment in which those tools are being applied. We have clearly evolved from the days of "one-size-fits-all" workplace strategies to a place where customization and individualized rewards programs are both philosophically and statistically linked with people, productivity and profits.

For example, there is a fairly dramatic shift occurring in the workplace that can be attributed in large part to generational composition. The younger generations (GenX, Millennials) are adding a new set of motivators to the list, including training and development, the opportunity to be mentored, corporate social responsibility and an employer's willingness to be flexible in how, where and when they do their job.

Given this, demographics and generational preferences become critical indicators in assessing what's most likely to influence engagement among employees, customers, vendors and other constituencies. Organizations whose "mix" still reflects the biases and preferences of Baby Boomers – a generation moving rapidly towards retirement – are at serious risk of becoming dinosaurs in the realm of engagement.

TALENT WARS
With ever-changing world economies, there has been a dramatic shift in the way companies recruit people, resulting in battles for key talent versus a simple "fight for bodies." Companies are also finding that new concerns are on the minds of today's employees. Some of these concerns revolve around the lingering fear of terrorism and crime, resulting in a higher value being placed on "rewards" such as expanded security, employee assistance programs and flexibility in time off during personal crisis and/or emergencies.

The CANE Model of Motivation

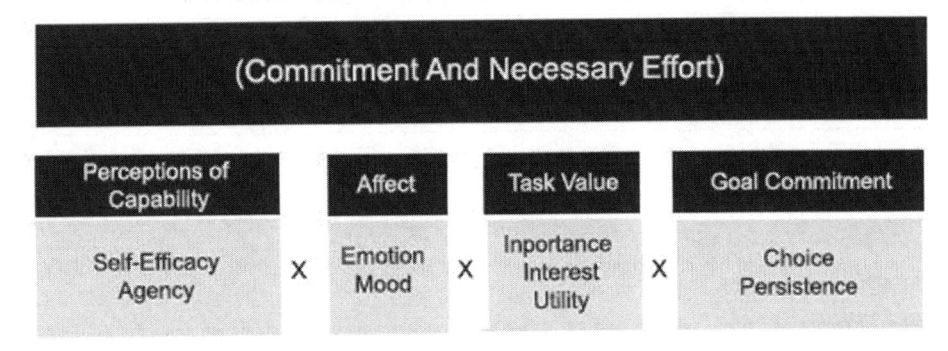

(Commitment And Necessary Effort)

Perceptions of Capability		Affect		Task Value		Goal Commitment
Self-Efficacy Agency	X	Emotion Mood	X	Inportance Interest Utility	X	Choice Persistence

Despite high unemployment numbers, many organizations face shortages of skilled labor. And this problem will grow more acute as demographic changes reduce the number of young people entering the workforce in the next few years. While the labor shortage may be lessened somewhat by the possibility that Baby Boomers will delay their retirement, many of today's high-tech jobs rely on younger workers for whom technology is second nature.

As noted above, these younger workers tend to look at more than just money when evaluating the desirability of a particular job. An organization's rewards and recognition strategy can serve not only as a motivation and engagement tool, but also as a means of recruiting and retaining employees who seek a work environment that supports their practical, emotional and lifestyle needs. As a result, many cutting-edge employers now tout their benefits, rewards and recognition strategies in their recruitment efforts – the so-called "invisible paycheck" that can make them an employer of choice.

Younger workers tend to value lifestyle issues and support from their management almost as much as they do compensation. They will be intrigued if you have a rewards and recognition system that honors performance and longevity with the organization. These employees are pragmatic and see a balance in life and work as critical to their existence. They seek the finer things in life, but to be shared with their contemporaries – self-gratification as a gateway to shared-gratification. Compensation and benefits are a means of expressing a lifestyle match, while recognition and rewards are a means of expressing a "workstyle" match.

FOUR RESPONSE MECHANISMS
Research on motivation indicates that rewards and recognition address several of the critical psychological factors related to motivation and engagement.

According to the study *Rewards, Incentives and Workforce Motivation* conducted by the International Society for Performance Improvement and funded by the Incentive Research Foundation, employees generally respond positively to the following workplace factors:

- **Support.** Do employees feel that the organization values their work? Do they feel that their actions will be noticed and that management cares about their accomplishments? Properly structured rewards and recognition systems specifically convey organizational support for employee initiatives.
- **Task value.** Employees will work more productively when they understand that the labor they perform has a value to the organization. This is often more

difficult to convey when more lower-level jobs are involved. A program recognizing performance of employees at all level often makes work feel more meaningful to them.

- **Capability.** Most companies understand that employees will work more effectively if they feel able to do a task. Rewards and recognition programs often work in conjunction with training by rewarding people for completing training or demonstrating their knowledge. This helps to enhance the learning process and reinforce the value of knowledge within the organization.
- **Communication.** People work more productively when they have a clear sense of their organization's mission and how their function relates to overall business objectives. Rewards and recognition programs help communicate the actions valued by the organization and increase the chances that people will perform those actions that have an impact on achieving the organization's goals.

Once you've gotten a fix on the environment, demographics and "triggers" of your various constituencies, you can then determine the right mix for a specific organization or situation. Here are some of the most common of tools and techniques that directly influence engagement.

COMPENSATION

For all of the talk about non-cash motivation tools, it would be all too easy to dismiss the perceived importance of compensation. But remember that the key is to consider a *total rewards* system that influences at every stage of employee interaction.

Compensation has historically played (and continues to play) a critical role in the acquisition of talent. Therefore, an appropriate compensation scheme is essential to secure the employee talent you need to achieve your organizational goals.

Compensation and benefits are used to satisfy the basic needs for sufficiency and security laid out in Maslow's Hierarchy. Although compensation and benefits are considered entitlements, they are the basis for the employee experience. To maximize compensation's role in the mix, ask:

> **Benefits represent an investment in a company's 'human capital.' Such investments and offerings are meant to convey the personality and commitment of a company – a reflection of the value it places on its people.**

- Is your compensation competitive, enabling you to secure the best talent?
- Do you regularly audit your compensation levels against similar organizations in your industry?
- Do you compensate through straight salary, variable pay, or a combination of the two? This will greatly influence the personality and attributes of the people you attract to your company.
- Do you provide performance-based compensation (bonuses)? These should be used to help sustain employment and share company success.

BENEFITS

Benefits represent an investment in a company's "human capital." Healthcare, wellness, personal care, day care, retirement planning and gain-sharing are but a few of the areas devoted to "holistic" employee benefits. Such investments and offerings are meant to convey the personality and commitment of a company – a reflection of the value it places on caring for its people beyond offering money.

An organization needs to determine its own beliefs and create/position benefits programs accordingly. Strong, fixed benefits that are evergreen will assist in your employee acquisition efforts; variable benefits that can shift over the course of employment based on performance are more likely to support retention and motivation. To maximize the role of benefits in the mix, ask:

- Does your menu of benefits speak to the practical, emotional and lifestyle needs of the different generations, genders, demographic cohorts and socioeconomic groups that make up your workforce?
- Do you conduct periodic "reality checks" to determine what kinds of benefits are most meaningful to your current or desired employee population? Benefits that were of greatest value five years ago might no longer have the same cache.
- Do people know the dollar value of their "hidden paycheck" – the portion of their total rewards package above and beyond their base salary?

TRAINING

In his book, *The Four Elements of Successful Management*, Don Marshall wisely points out that "We equip employees in the business world through training and experience," and that it's training which truly enables employees to "translate knowledge into action."

The abovementioned study conducted by the Forum for People Performance Management and Measurement found that slightly fewer than half of all organizations have training programs in place. This will need to increase as a new generation replaces the older one. A changing world requires continuous improvement and refinement of skills. Workers know this intuitively and will demand continuous training and education. Since the lack of opportunity to learn new skills is one of the chief reasons employees leave a job, strong training options become a key retention mechanism. To maximize training's role in the mix, ask:

- What does your employee mix look like now? While generalizations are dangerous, if your employee population is getting younger, there is a strong chance that training will help you keep them longer and motivate them as well.
- Do you encourage training across the board? Be sure to strike the right balance. Training is a positive for young, highly motivated individuals who are looking to advance their careers, but it can be demeaning to experienced managers who may find it too rudimentary or irrelevant.
- How do you communicate and position training? Based on what we've described above, semantics are important. Once you've decided what training to offer, make sure you're calling it the right thing based on your employee demographics and that you're promoting it to the right people within your company.

NON-CASH REWARDS

Decades of research have made a very strong case for non-cash rewards and recognition programs. Rewards and recognition should be used to reinforce specific behaviors that are both measurable and subjective. This is a skill that should be taught to all managers and is vital to employee engagement.

A meta-analysis of dozens of research studies on non-cash rewards published by the Incentive Research Foundation[1], Aberdeen and others, indicates that non-cash rewards have the greatest impact when they focus on reinforcing communication, creating

---

[1] www.theIRF.org

positive emotions, recognizing the role of significant others in the lives of people, encouraging fun and strategically differentiating rewards from compensation or discounts and rebates in a way that addresses intrinsic and not just extrinsic motivators.

On this basis, non-cash rewards such as travel, merchandise and gift cards work best when they:

- Reflect the organization's appreciation culture through careful selection or choice
- Possess high perceived value
- Come with some kind of personal thanks from management; the more personal the better
- Get delivered in person or to the home with a personal, meaningful note customized to support the organization's brand
- Create the opportunity for lasting memories and emotions associated with the organization
- Provide experiences with their significant others either on their own or with others in the organization to created shared memories
- Are available to people at all levels in the organization or tiers of customers based on transparent opportunities.

MORE THAN THE SUM OF ITS PARTS

So what is the right mix? What is the right formula? It's not linear, nor is it simple addition like it used to be…five parts this, two parts that. This is a new machine with an infinite number of moving parts. Today the mix is different for each employee, each organization, each department, each objective. And the correct mix is now determined on a one-to-one basis.

This individualized total reward offering starts with understanding the total reward "portfolio" for each level of employees. What are the "ingredients" that are available? And are they reviewed and updated periodically as the needs and preferences of the workforce changes? Then there is a need to understand which "ingredients" are "standard" or fixed, and which ones are "flexible" and offer the employee choices.

This Total Reward framework, its on-going review, communication, and continual management ensures that the most effective reward offering is being deployed, and employees will feel personally rewarded.

Enterprise Engagement: The Textbook

Chapter 21

Loyalty

Of all of the traditional tactics undergoing major change in the new world of engagement, traditional loyalty programs are among the most notable. Reinvigorated in the 1980s by the travel industry after the near death of trading stamps in the early 1970s – and given a further shot in the arm by the advent of gift cards, the Internet and social media – many loyalty programs remain built on the traditional "do-this, get-that" model that fails to address all of the issues research shows are related to engagement and performance.

In truth, many traditional loyalty programs are based on the premise of providing people rewards for specific behaviors and then making it either difficult for people to redeem those rewards or deliberately playing down the ways to redeem rewards in order to create "breakage" – the cost savings or extra profit margin that comes from people not actually using the rewards. Breakage is the same model that underlies many traditional rebates. The issuers hope that people will be motivated enough by the incentives to buy, but not sufficiently motivated to redeem. This is a model well-suited to process-oriented, rather than people-focused, management.

The breakage model makes sense in the context that loyalty programs primarily have evolved into database-marketing tools in which organizations induce people to opt-in to receive information and/or have their purchases tracked. So organizations win even if the person isn't particularly loyal by at least getting permission to communicate or the ability to gather valuable purchase data.

DRIVERS OF LOYALTY
Supported by extensive research and increasingly reaffirmed by big data, Enterprise Engagement takes a longer view of customer relationships and therefore builds loyalty based not only on promoting rewards and encouraging people to use them, but also by addressing all of the other aspects that research tells us engages people – emotional connection, trust, a sense of feeling valued, fun, capability (the ability to do what is being asked of us) and the consistent fulfillment (or even exceeding) of expectations.

Over the years, research has remained inconclusive related to the long-range impact of loyalty programs that focus primarily on rewards. According to a 2012 Hanover Research report on consumer loyalty programs, "an analysis of overall research shows that the connection between participation and enduring loyalty is unclear...the data do not indicate that all companies benefit from having a consumer loyalty program."

In a 2011 Gallup Report, *Making Loyalty Programs Work*, Jordan Katz, a managing consultant at Gallup, noted that "Across all industries, companies spend two billion dollars each year on loyalty programs. That's a significant amount. What isn't significant, though, is the positive effect most companies receive through these programs. Most of these programs leave a lot of money on the table." The report also found that:

- Roughly half of respondents (49%) said they flew on a primary airline in the past year, but only 52% participate in a loyalty program with the airline.
- Fully 80% of respondents said they had a primary department store where they shopped during the past 12 months, but only 30% participate in that store's loyalty or rewards program.
- About three-quarters of respondents (74%) said they have a primary credit card, but only 66% said they participate in a loyalty program with that provider.

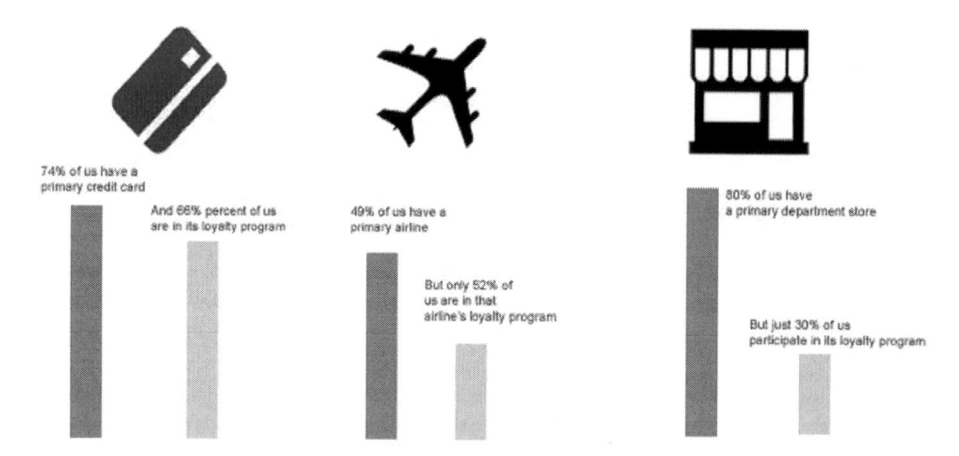

That said, there's no question that people sign up for loyalty programs, and many track and redeem their points, if nothing else providing invaluable behavioral tracking data for companies. The underlying question is to what extent can these programs generate long-term results and encourage what loyalty expert Fred Reichheld calls the "net-promoter" effect – the willingness of people to refer a brand or company to others. As with any traditional incentive program, the research suggests that the most enduring results come from programs that address all of the factors that drive loyalty, and that the opportunity derives from the ability to better integrate all the traditional tactics that turn customers into advocates.

THE BENEFITS OF SUCCESS
The journey is worth it, because loyalty and referrals provide both short- and long-term benefits that translate into more sustainable growth, cost efficiency (lower marketing costs), higher profitability and a better chance of surviving economic downturns. The Whole Foods grocery chain fared remarkably well during the recent recession, arguably because of customer loyalty – it's certainly not a company well positioned when it comes to pricing.

The big opportunity is to connect the dots...breaking down silos between the database marketers, brand managers, salespeople and even the behind-the-scenes employees responsible for delivering organizational promises. This creates the overall positive experience that leads to what Gallup calls the "wow factor" – the level of positive emotion required beyond being merely satisfied to become a true brand advocate.

The ultimate goal with loyalty programs is to go beyond collecting data and build an emotional bond with people that can dramatically reduce the waste of traditional adverting and other marketing by funneling the results of those activities into an enduring, self-sustaining relationship.

Think of the organizations you feel most fondly about. Loyalty program rewards might very well be a part of that affection, but it's more likely that it's the products and services – the way you're treated – that have the most bearing on that relationship.

Gallup's Jordan Katz: "We looked deeper into the data and found that activating participants is not an end game in itself. There is a way to create more value, and it comes from fully engaging these activated customers by building an emotional connection with your program, brand, or product…If you're not doing that – if you're not measuring, tracking and acting to create a strong relationship between your customers and your company's program, brand or product – your program is falling short."

DEFINING LOYALTY
According to a 2006 Conference Board report, customer engagement is "a heightened emotional connection that a customer feels for his/her brand that influences him/her to exert greater discretionary effort to buy or promote." In the simplest sense, loyalty is the willingness of people to repeatedly buy from the same source, and can theoretically be measured by the organization's share of the customer's use of that product or service category.

Beyond that, one can look at the willingness of an individual to promote that organization, product or service to others. Even deeper, we can understand the emotional connection that turns customers into "fans" or advocates of a brand – the ultimate goal. This creates an audience of people willing to spend their time thinking up new ideas to benefit the organization – new products, ventures or a better way to accomplish a goal. Organizations cannot achieve that level of advocacy by focusing exclusively on rewards or by using rewards in a way to promote breakage.

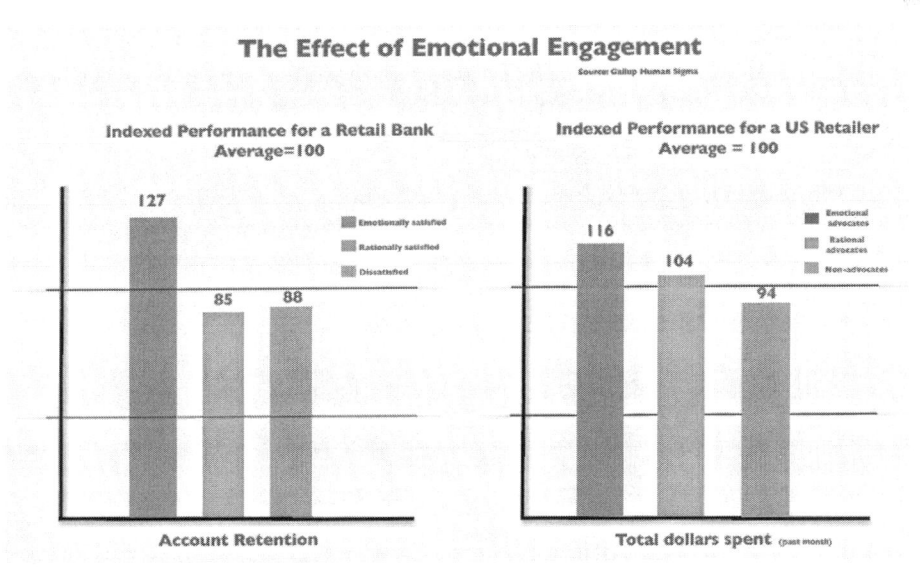

The Effect of Emotional Engagement
Source: Gallup Human Sigma

Indexed Performance for a Retail Bank
Average=100

- Emotionally satisfied: 127
- Rationally satisfied: 85
- Dissatisfied: 88

Account Retention

Indexed Performance for a US Retailer
Average = 100

- Emotional advocates: 116
- Rational advocates: 104
- Non-advocates: 94

Total dollars spent (past month)

John Wanamaker once famously said, "Half the money I spend on advertising is wasted; the trouble is I don't know which half." Couple that with the fact that every unhappy customer tells nine others of his dissatisfaction, while only 1% tell others when they're satisfied, and organizations can see more clearly than ever the impact of advertising that creates unfulfilled expectations. Today companies spend millions to track social media, but the bigger issue isn't how to profit from social media, it's how to create loyalty.

THE NEW LOYALTY ROADMAP
The roadmap below follows a framework that starts at the top of your organization. That's not to say that a tactical loyalty program manager can't profit from these steps as well, but you'll get the greatest benefit when you address all of the elements of engagement at all levels of the organization.

1. Have a clear definition of the "enterprise brand." What are the promises an organization is making to all of its constituencies in terms of what they can expect as customers, retailers, distribution partners, agents, employees, vendors, shareholders and even the communities where you operate? What is the thread that holds that community together? Your brand is the essence of your organization's culture; what does that culture mean to the people who are part of it. Brand alignment across the organization is critical so that brand promises get delivered. See Chapter 3 for more on the enterprise brand.

2. Define how that brand applies specifically to your customers. What really drives the passion of your customers? Is it price, service, product features, convenience, availability, the loyalty program, uniqueness of your offering or some combination? What is the personality of your brand? How can you enrich your customer's experience or relationship with your brand through content, events, experiences, etc.? Numerous engagement tools and technologies are available to dissect various customer drivers. The best combine qualitative and behavioral data and provide benchmarks comparing similar organizations for further insight.

3. What is the plan? What specifically are you trying to accomplish with your loyalty program? Is it primarily to obtain data, or does your organizational seek to build a true relationship and increase "net-promoter" scores? How can you measure the results in terms of repeat sales, willingness to refer or provide ideas and suggestions to improve your business? What specific strategies and tactics are most suitable given your organization's particular circumstances? Ideally, a loyalty program is based on a business plan that includes all of the elements outlined in this chapter.

4. Who can affect results? Most loyalty programs start and end with the customer, but who is the customer? Should that include distributors, retailers or agents through whom your organization sells? What about the connection with the employees who have to deliver the brand promise and help create the "wow" effect? How can your employees directly promote loyalty, and what can be done to encourage those actions?

5. Inform the right people. The challenge of breaking through the clutter has never been greater. The key is to focus on the essential benefits of your brand and loyalty program proposition to customers; communicating it concisely over time; mixing it up with useful information, fun and promotions when appropriate to get attention; enabling people to interact and share through social media; and measuring communication consumption.

A good communications strategy begins with a loyalty portal where all customers can easily interact. It might start with a Facebook or LinkedIn page or Twitter community, but a loyalty portal, where people can presumably redeem rewards, provides an incomparable opportunity to cement relationships through useful or entertaining content – precisely when people are most receptive. The portal can include news about the program, winners and what they did to win, games, or even what people did with their rewards.

6. Make sure people are fully able to do what is asked. So many customers use only a portion of the features we sell them, because most people hesitate to invest time to learn something unless they see a clear benefit. A key to long-term engagement is to encourage people to explore all of your benefits so they don't take for granted a key feature when ready to make a change. Many people have a loyalty to a product without even knowing why – the more they know about your products and services, the better they become as net-promoters.

7. Commit to innovation. More organizations are beginning to use crowd-sourcing to develop new ideas. Loyalty becomes particularly valuable when people are willing to invest their time to brainstorm ideas to help your organization. Coming up with ways for customers to provide ideas is easy if your organization can benefit, but it requires the commitment of qualified people to evaluate them and respond appropriately with the proper appreciation. Soliciting and rewarding ideas is another way of telling people you value them. Companies from General Electric to Clorox have reported generating significant innovations from customers – a sure sign of engagement.

8. Don't forget rewards and recognition. When loyalty is viewed holistically, rewards and recognition become even more important. Rather than being used to simply get attention or in the hope that people won't redeem them, rewards can become an invaluable part of the relationship your organization builds with people. A research study by Scott Jeffrey, Associate Professor at the University of Wisconsin, Waterloo, *The Benefits of Tangible Non-Cash Rewards*, indicates that when properly designed, rewards strike a personal, memorable chord, especially with significant others, that reinforces values long after the reward has been used or consumed.

> **When properly designed, rewards strike a personal, memorable chord, especially with significant others, that reinforces values long after the reward has been used or consumed.**

Unfortunately, companies think nothing of sending out non-personalized rewards or cash-equivalent rewards while overlooking research that suggests that it's the way rewards are delivered and the emotions and memories they generate that have the greatest residual value in terms of building brand relationships. If your rewards strategy isn't designed to reinforce your brand over time and to build emotions and relationships with significant others, it's time to rethink your strategy.

It is also important to consider having tiers based on levels of purchases or other activities, with a "closed-end" or predefined top level and more "open-ended" opportunities for middle-level customers. Instant rewards are useful to promote signups, but the idea is to reward reasonable tiers of loyalty or other behaviors critical to hitting certain goals. The program should also include a way for people to track their performance. You can also use your portal to house engagement surveys.

9. Measurement is critical. Today, with data analytics capabilities, some organizations already have more data than they can use. The Holy Grail is to obtain data that connect as much as possible how people have heard about your organization to the specific communications, offers, people or other touchpoints that drive particular actions. The ultimate goal is increased sales with lower traditional marketing costs.

The good news is that research suggests that if organizations focus specifically on all of the drivers that create loyal, engaged customers who are willing to promote the organization and submit ideas, you won't need the measurement to show the benefits, only to make sure you're continually identifying new ways to tap the inherent willingness of people to become fans.

Remember, one of America's best known brands, Mary Kay Cosmetics, has almost no advertising budget.

Enterprise Engagement: The Textbook

Chapter 22

Social Recognition

By Brad Callahan

Praise, recognition and appreciation have long been recognized by philosophers and psychologists as critical to human happiness. Effective teachers, managers and parents also know that recognition and praise are among the most powerful motivational tools at their disposal. Consistent findings from research provide indisputable evidence of the near causal link between recognition, engagement, performance and profit.

Indeed, almost a decade ago Gallup analyzed data from interviews and surveys involving more than 10 million workers to conclude that variations in recognition and praise account for 10%-20% differences in productivity among employees and revenue, as well as in customer engagement.[1]

The debate, if there ever was one, is not whether recognition, praise and appreciation are important to productivity, but rather, how can organizations accelerate the incidence of recognition and develop it into their culture – their DNA, so to speak? In the past, the process could take years, and only then when executive management was deeply, consistently and publicly committed to it. Today, the promise of social media and peer-to-peer recognition stands to turn this paradigm on its head. Social Recognition tools and technology are helping early adopters increase the frequency and meaningfulness of recognition, integrate recognition with corporate goals and, ultimately, to build enduring "cultures of recognition" quickly.

WHAT 'SOCIAL RECOGNITION' IS
Today the word "social" is less likely to conjure thoughts of companionship and society than have people thinking media, networking, blogging, tweeting and gaming. According to research from Bersin & Associates, social is the dominant form of Internet communication on the planet.

---

1 - Rodd Wagner and James Harter, *"12: The Elements of Great Managing"*, Gallup, 2006

Tellingly, 39% of those aged 18-24 would consider leaving a job if they weren't allowed to access sites like YouTube and Facebook from work.[2]

In the world of talent management, social networks have been used successfully in knowledge sharing, the identification of skills, construction of teams, recruiting, onboarding and certainly learning. "Social Recognition" is a relative newcomer to the party, yet successful public social networks such as Facebook and LinkedIn have featured recognition as a mainstay from the beginning. It is arguable that among the chief drivers of the popularity of social networks (Facebook has recently passed an astonishing one billion users) is the ability of people to recognize and be recognized – "likes," "thumbs up" and other icons, alone or combined with messages, proliferate. There can be little doubt that people use social networking sites, at least in part, to fulfill a deep-seated need for recognition.

Perhaps even more than in our private lives, we crave recognition at work. The unfortunate reality, however, is that most organizations do a poor job of recognition. For example, U.S. Department of Labor research has found that 64% of working Americans leave their jobs because they don't feel appreciated.

In many organizations, recognition occurs only annually during the performance review. Indeed, recent research reveals that 40% of employees believe their peers are recognized just once per year or never – and 58% say they themselves are recognized only once per year or never.[3]

As Harvard psychologist and author William James said more than 150 years ago, "The deepest principle of human nature is the craving to be appreciated." In the workplace, however, recognition isn't important for its own sake. Most leaders acknowledge that satisfying employees' needs – at least their fundamental needs – is essential to driving engagement and performance.

Consequently, experts and consultants advise organizations to develop a "culture of recognition." Many emphasize the need to better select and hire leaders and/or develop them so they know how and when to recognize employees. Recognition from the boss is undoubtedly important, but a true culture of recognition – one in which appreciation is frequent and meaningful – cannot be strictly a top-down exercise.

Social Recognition, which uses software and online systems to allow people to recognize one another, is a relatively new entrant into the pantheon of talent management technology. Yet it draws on practices from some of the world's most popular Internet applications.

In connecting peers to peers – in this case employees to employees and employees to customers, partners, suppliers and others (the extended enterprise) – it creates another dimension in recognition that has the potential to generate powerful cultural changes within remarkably short timeframes. In others words, social recognition systems can be transformative. They can fill a recognition gap quickly and extend recognition beyond the organization to help engage customers and other constituents.

SOCIAL RECOGNITION ON THE WEB
In the broadest sense, social recognition has been part of the community fabric ever since man gathered into collaborative groups to benefit in ways that would not otherwise be possible on an individual basis. Public displays, ceremonies, the sharing of

---

2 - New Talent Technologies: Managing People Better, Bersin & Associates, 2012
3 - The State of Employee Recognition in 2012. Bersin & Associates. P11

stories, recognition events, acknowledgements of a person's status and/or merits (achievements, virtues, service, contribution etc.) were, and still are, common occurrences performed in social settings. Hence recognition, by its very nature in the physical world, is inherently social.

However, the notion of social recognition from today's connected business perspective has evolved, and will continue to evolve, into something quite different as the lines between the physical and virtual worlds are being blurred by advances in social networking concepts, practices, applications and technologies. Utilizing online networking models for communities of people to recognize and reward the contributions of others is a natural extension of existing on-demand recognition and reward systems in use today.

More organizations are realizing that a connected workplace isn't just about implementing new technologies – it's also about adopting organizational design changes that focus on an open workplace environment where employees are encouraged to share, recognize, collaborate and innovate virtually. Online social recognition provides the foundation for this transformation and can be instrumental in spurring vital value-creating shifts in an organization's direction.

The online world is rife with peer-to-peer recognition. Most social media, including blogs, discussion boards, magazines and news outlets, invite ratings – "likes" and other feedback from users. The most popular social networking sites encourage recognition as well.

A typical Facebook or LinkedIn page provides numerous examples. Popular social media sites have also morphed to become social referral and recruiting tools used to make introductions, recruit members and even for match-making.

They've also become tools for recruiters, both to promote positions and connect with prospective employees. Many recruiters also use these sites to "investigate" and screen applicants based on the appropriateness of some of their social media activity.

As Facebook passes the billion-subscriber mark, social media is already the number one activity of the web (Socialnomics, 2011). According to Neilson in 2009, "In the U.S. alone, total minutes spent on social networking sites increased 83% year-over-year." Incredibly, total daily minutes spent on Facebook have increased from 1.7 billion in April 2008 to 10.5 billion in January 2012 – and that figure doesn't include minutes accessed via mobile devices.[4]

> **Total daily minutes spent on Facebook have increased from 1.7 billion in April 2008 to 10.5 billion in January 2012 – and that figure doesn't include minutes accessed via mobile devices.**

The use of social networking technology has grown incredibly inside organizations as well. By many estimates, the adoption rates of corporate social networking applications have surpassed even that of email inside organizations. To many a college student or Millennial, email is already akin to cursive writing – an anachronism. Given all this, it's difficult to argue against social media and social networking as a "fad" or an insignificant development as far as business is concerned. Increasingly, corporate social platforms are becoming the medium of choice.

---

[4] - "10.5 billion minutes spend on Facebook daily, excluding mobile", Emil Protalinkski, ZDNet, March 28, 2012

Inside organizations, social media is used in an "intranet" environment to disseminate information, encourage knowledge-sharing and connect the workforce for collaborative purposes. Given the fundamental recognition-related elements of popular public social networks, it's somewhat surprising that recognition is late to the game inside organizations. Nevertheless, the gap has closed quickly; there are numerous technology providers now offering services that enable online social recognition.

The fundamental advantage online social recognition brings to organizations – even those with formal recognition programs – is that appreciation and recognition become ongoing, daily activities driven predominantly by employees recognizing other employees, as opposed to an annual, formal evaluation driven by management. Consequently, organizations stand a much better chance of building a culture of recognition and do so relatively quickly.

Beyond employee-to-employee recognition, corporate social recognition can also connect employees to customers, partners, suppliers and other key constituents in order to give and receive recognition. Where employees can reach out to recognize colleagues' contributions (and those of the broader, external community), broad, enterprise-wide engagement is more likely to occur and productivity is more likely to increase.

Experts agree on one thing: the social recognition world isn't a trend that will fade away. It's really the next-generation evolution of the rewards & recognition systems most organizations already have in place.

Today's social recognition platforms will prove to be the first layer or entry point into the powerful collaborative systems and social-strategy tools of tomorrow. When one thinks about successful companies, it all comes down to people and the quality of their conversations and interactions. Hence, social recognition and the use of social media are vital elements in well-designed rewards & recognition programs.

THE NETWORK AS COMPETITIVE ADVANTAGE
Sharing stories, comments, opinions and insights online is second nature for many people. But until recently this bore little resemblance to the way we work. Traditionally, businesses operated in silos, with little done to encourage collaboration or the sharing of ideas and information – even within individual departments. Corporate knowledge, people, processes and vital information remained hidden and closely guarded.

In today's business environment, competition is no longer a contest between companies; it's now a competition between networks – the sum of connectivity, communications, collaboration and rewards & recognition systems used to empower a collective value chain. Having the ability to bring together thoughts and ideas from team members scattered across the country – or even across the globe – and being able to find information, people and expertise faster can only help businesses grow and remain competitive.

Today, people are more social than ever before. The global village has shrunk to the size of a smart phone. And the tools that make it easy to connect and work together online are starting to disrupt traditional working practices in ways we're only just beginning to realize. There's a growing understanding that, rather than being a distraction or a time drain, social tools could actually hold the key to a more productive way of doing business and provide an engaging "virtual forum" for showcasing achievements, recognizing people and identifying pockets of expertise within the organization.

THE RECOGNITION GAP

Peer-to-peer recognition can be a powerful force in driving a sustainable recognition culture in organizations. Yet the majority of organizations – even those with formal recognition programs – don't always incorporate the notion of employees recognizing other employees. According to Bersin & Associate's *State of Employee Recognition* research, the top reason employees don't recognize each other is simply because there's no established way to provide recognition in most firms. In other words, there's no barrier to peer-to-peer recognition from a willingness or attitudinal perspective – employees *want* to recognize each other, they just don't have the tools to do so.

Bersin & Associates Survey: Reasons Employees Don't Recognize Each Other (2012)

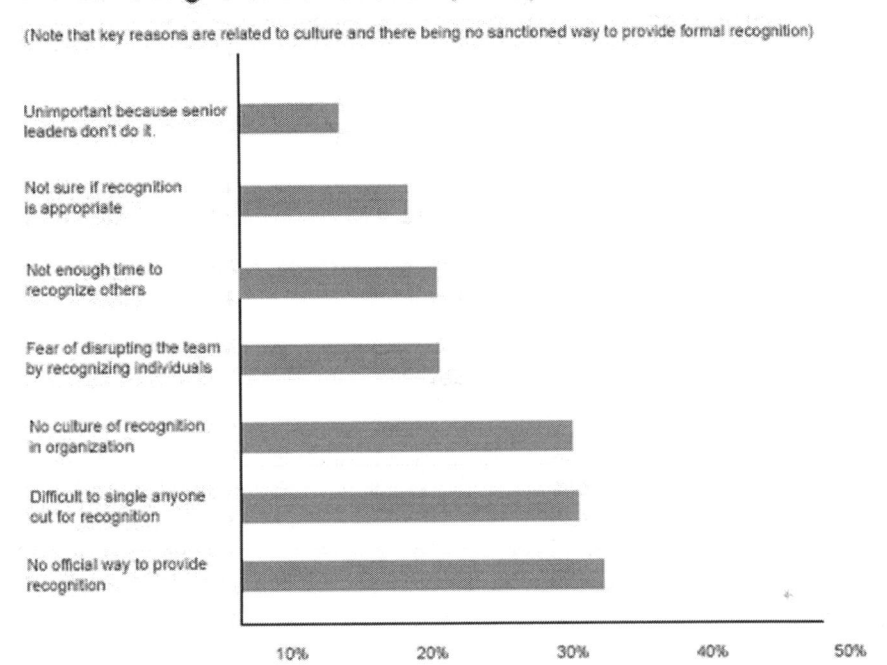

(Note that key reasons are related to culture and there being no sanctioned way to provide formal recognition)

Reason	Percentage
Unimportant because senior leaders don't do it	~13%
Not sure if recognition is appropriate	~18%
Not enough time to recognize others	~20%
Fear of disrupting the team by recognizing individuals	~20%
No culture of recognition in organization	~30%
Difficult to single anyone out for recognition	~30%
No official way to provide recognition	~32%

Organizations can overcome this barrier by implementing simple systems that allow employees to recognize colleagues' work and contributions. Corporate Social Network (CSN) platforms, social recognition technologies or add-ons to intranets are relatively simple tools that enable recognition through short statements, the awarding of points and/or by telling stories about what a colleague did that merits recognition. Over time, these statements, awards and stories grow to become part of the foundation and legacy of a recognition culture

Social Recognition software can increase the frequency of appreciation and also provide guidelines to employees on when recognition is appropriate. These tools can allow for varying levels of sharing, so that some recognition can remain private, some can be limited to a team and some shared enterprise-wide, even out to (and in from) customers, partners and other constituents of the extended enterprise. Combined with a cascading or SMART goals program, the software may be equipped to align recognition with performance management. Most software will also include useful analytics and reporting tools to help organizations gauge progress and make adjustments.

As traditional job roles are increasingly being reframed around enabling a more modern, collaborative work culture that reflects the way people function in their interconnected, networked world, next-generation solutions need to support a combination of social recognition, media and collaborative tools that allow professionals to:

- Recognize contributions
- Inspire performance and drive value-adding activities
- Reinforce behaviors and organizational culture
- Showcase achievements and provide public validation
- Foster collaboration, conversation and recognition
- Find people, information or expertise more quickly
- Foster knowledge sharing
- Widen personal networks, build relationships, and raise individual visibility
- Identify subject matter experts (SMEs)
- Build meaningful relationships across a widely distributed workforce
- Support Communities of Practice (groups of people with domain expertise)
- Extend corporate knowledge
- Invite peers into a personalized group

In essence, a social recognition solution should function as an enabler and an accelerator of existing core capabilities, values, attributes and strategic plans.

EXTENDING SOCIAL RECOGNITION

As soon as we acknowledge the increasingly important role of social media and social networking in corporate communications, the path forward is clear. Organizations should support and foster the growth of internal social networking to encourage collaboration, idea-sharing, innovation and knowledge transfer. Equally, the tools should include components – like social recognition – that will accelerate team-building, employee engagement and productivity.

Given the state of volatility, uncertainty, complexity, ambiguity and information overload in today's business environment, organizations must learn to leverage collaborative networks and nodes to aggressively sense and respond to the marketplace and remain competitive.

Corporate transparency and knowledge-sharing will become the harbingers of success. A key element of any social platform is the ability for individuals to provide feedback, insights and positive reinforcement. Social recognition will be an integral part of these systems, designed to bolster connectivity and the flow of information and creative conversation. Employees who can share and access information with their colleagues – the contextual knowledge that's so valuable to awareness – are increasingly vital in a competitive global business landscape.

Even beyond today's social recognition tools that focus on employees, there are additional competitive advantages for organizations that extend recognition to other critical stakeholders. Customers, partners (including resellers), suppliers and even volunteers (where applicable) are crucial to an organization's success and should not be overlooked.

A social recognition strategy should include a means for recognition to and from the extended enterprise to be captured and shared. In the same way that employee recognition drives employee engagement, recognition (to and from) stakeholders will drive Enterprise Engagement. Foundational transformation around the culture and people of the organization – including its customers, partners and suppliers – is essential to sustained success. As the pace of business change accelerates and the world becomes more interconnected, the agility and responsiveness of the extended enterprise will be its most critical competitive advantage. Social networks and their recognition components are key pieces in the integrity of the *connected* extended enterprise.

SUMMARY

By internet standards, social media took its time getting to recognition in the workplace. Yet a better application of corporate social networking would be difficult to find. The age-old problems of finding and/or developing managers and supervisors talented and aware enough to build and sustain a culture of recognition is, in part, solved through peer-to-peer and extended enterprise social recognition. Moreover, the disadvantage of recognition taking place (if at all) during annual, formal performance reviews can be replaced with ongoing feedback and recognition from peers, managers, subordinates and even to and from the extended enterprise.

That a culture of recognition is a prime advantage in driving engagement is taken for granted by most leaders today and is nothing new. The hurdle has always been achieving that culture within a broader workforce culture that has long emphasized bottom-line results, short-term goals and rewards for individual achievement. Managers and supervisors are constantly told about the importance of recognition and engagement, yet they're rarely held accountable or rewarded for it directly. The lessons from successful public social networks are there for all to see. They have succeeded, in part, based on people's willingness and enthusiasm for recognizing each other.

The same lessons apply inside organizations. Today, the power of recognition is opening up and is in fact being driven by employees. However, as the research indicates, the main obstacle to social recognition is the lack of an official means for employees to recognize each other in the great majority of organizations. Social recognition software and tools offer a simple, affordable solution.

Organizations are in a constant state of organic flux and need to constantly adapt to accommodate performance objectives. Social recognition and its further evolution will bring a new layer of sophistication to employee and "extended enterprise" interactions that will transcend the one-dimensional approach of many existing rewards& recognition programs.

Enterprise Engagement: The Textbook

Chapter 23

Wellness

By Amy Kramer and Paula Godar

Wellness goes beyond the obvious benefits of lowering healthcare claims, cutting lost time due to illness, or worse. Wellness strategies provide organizations a unique opportunity to help promote better health practices, prevent disease and better the lives of their employees – and that's good for everyone.

The new approach to wellness is holistic: it considers the whole person – both their mental and physical well-being. It places emphasis and responsibility on individuals to take ownership of their health. Wellness becomes tied into your organization's value systems and can influence outcomes at your organization and improve the quality of life for your people. Wellness programs provide a so-called "virtuous circle" because they're good for people and for business.

According to a 2010 study by Harvard Business School professors Katherine Baicker, David Cutler and Zurui Song entitled *Workplace Wellness Programs Can Generate Savings*, properly designed wellness programs can yield healthcare cost savings of $3.27 for every dollar invested, as well as $2.37 in reduced absenteeism costs. The study also noted that in 2006 only 19% of companies with 500 or more workers offered wellness programs, while a 2008 survey of large manufacturing companies revealed 77% offered some kind of formal health and wellness program – and the percentage is likely even higher today. The most common interventions at the time of the HBS study included: 1) health risk assessments, in which each person's condition is tracked; 2) providing self-help information; and 3) offering health-related incentives.

IT'S A PROCESS
Promoting wellness isn't simply a "do-this, get-that" proposition. It's a process that addresses all of the issues required for humans to change behavior. Based on a study conducted by Maritz Research in 2011, wellness programs should focus on four specific drivers that contribute to good health:

- physical activity
- mental well-being

- prevention
- nutrition

Start by understanding that improving health is one of the greatest challenges most individuals face. Improvement comes incrementally, one human being at a time, and any progress is worthy of celebration. Effective wellness strategies utilize engagement elements, connecting goals with strategies that shape people's behavior and choice in "owning" wellness and participating in the activities aimed at health promotion and prevention. Effective wellness program tactics incorporate attention, goal commitment, feedback and reward mechanics as a means of gaining and maintaining engagement to take people through the progression of change. Programs must also be fair and fun to create the mindset that living healthier is a positive experience and not a burden.

THE SHIFT IN EMPHASIS

In the past, most organizations implemented wellness strategies to manage costs related to healthcare claims, productivity and absenteeism – and there's ample research to support that investment. Today, however, a shift is taking place in workplace wellness related to the concept of Enterprise Engagement – i.e., the linking of wellness strategies to an organization's culture, retention, productivity, performance and even customer and employee satisfaction. These elements can lead to long-term growth within an organization, and as a result not only create healthier employees, lower healthcare claims and decrease in absenteeism, but also increased productivity and a sense of purpose.

> **Making wellness part of the culture helps foster engagement and a level of healthy behavior that can lower absenteeism, improve employee retention and satisfaction, and increase productivity.**

Wellness programs are also a unique way to increase levels of "task value" that research has demonstrated is important to long-term engagement. The fact is that many jobs are boring and repetitive, so aside from doing everything possible to address this, organizations can counteract drudgery by giving people a sense of purpose – not only through the contribution they're making to the organization and their livelihood, but also to their personal well-being.

IDEAL OUTCOMES

The best outcomes of wellness strategies include:

- Personal ownership and accountability in a person's own health.
- Preventative care – more doctor checkups, less acute care and emergencies, which can be tracked and accounted for in healthcare claims. It's not minimizing claims, so to speak, but shifting from a higher number of incident claims to more preventative claims.
- Improved health conditions through physical activity and better nutrition.
- Improved mental well-being, with reduced stress and happier employees.

From an organization-wide perspective, the opportunity is to make wellness part of the culture and to shift thinking from short-term to long-term healthy behavior among employees. This shift in culture helps foster engagement and a level of wellness that can lower absenteeism, improve employee retention and satisfaction, and increase productivity. Wellness strategies create better lives for employees and produce better business outcomes as a result.

Summary of Employee Wellness Studies Analyzed

Study Focus	Number of Studies	Average Sample Size - Treatment	Average Sample Size - Comparison	Average Duration (years)	Average Savings	Average Costs	Average ROI
Health care costs	22	3,201	4,547	3.0	$358	$144	3.27
Absenteeism	22	2,683	4,782	2.0	$294	$132	2.73

Katherine Baicker, David Cutler, and Zirui Song, *Workplace Wellness Programs Can Generate Savings*, Health Affairs, February, 2010

DRIVING COMMITMENT

Leveraging mission, vision and values and tying wellness strategies in with an organization's culture are key to maximizing the benefits of wellness programs. But the existence of wellness programs alone isn't enough to drive commitment and engagement in employee wellness, especially given the average individual's natural resistance to the dietary and exercise changes they need to make to optimize their health.

Organizations can provide the reinforcement and support necessary to get people to engage by helping them set realistic goals, giving them the tools and feedback to they need to progress, providing meaningful rewards, social and cultural support, and feedback. Just having a program won't create a sustainable return on investment. Promoting healthy behaviors and helping individuals weave wellness into the fabric of their personal and professional lives provides the best results.

THE FOUNDATION OF SUCCESS

A successful wellness program can include many components, but any wellness strategy should address the four key areas mentioned earlier – prevention, nutrition, physical activity and mental well-being. A one-size-fits-all approach to wellness is the sure way to failure. People should have the right to choose which area of wellness they want to focus on.

For prevention, people tend to align with behaviors aimed at lowering healthcare costs – preventative exams, coaching, disease management, regular check-ups with their physicians, etc. Programs might also offer health risk assessments in which individual's biggest issues are documented. These aren't enough to drive long-term change, but they're a great start to helping promote long-term health by identifying priorities.

> A successful wellness program can include many components, but any wellness strategy should address four key areas: prevention, nutrition, physical activity and mental well-being.

For nutrition, people should have an opportunity to learn about healthier eating, how to change eating habits, coaching to promote long-term change and even changes in the choice of food available on company premises. Physical activity is the easiest to engage in, but it often requires social support and accountability to encourage adoption and sustained behaviors. Finally, mental well-being and stress management are key to holistic wellness. The effort should include components that maximize mental health, which can start with a regular exercise program and outdoor activities.

STEP BY STEP
Here is a quick step-by-step guide to developing an effective wellness program:

1. Goals and Objectives. Establish clear goals and objectives for your effort in terms of quantitative and qualitative results, including general employee engagement. You don't want to set goals that would encourage people to forgo health treatment. Your wellness program should have a business plan just like any major initiative. A key issue to address is how people can select a specific health initiative they can focus on rather than giving them more goals than they could possibly achieve.

Each person can set their own goals, but you may wish to give them several related goals so as to provide satisfaction along the way. For example, if a goal is to get to a certain weight, people might be able to earn points and/or recognition for passing knowledge tests about good dieting or achieving some interim milestones. In other words, your program should include both a specific goal but also steps needed to achieve that goal, such as exercise and health education.

Part of business plan development involves establishing a budget and return-on-investment measures. The National Institutes of Health website publishes information on the cost savings resulting from smoking cessation and other health improvements that can be used to establish goals and the percentage of those anticipated savings your organization is willing to invest in the program.

2. Assessment and Coaching. How will you be able to assess engagement in the effort in terms of active participation by managers and employees? What types of coaching resources can you make available to individuals to support their individual efforts? What type of long-term assessment can you implement? Can it be included in general employee engagement assessment?

3. Communication. What strategies make sense to reach your particular audience? Can your company provide a wellness portal featuring news about the program and success stories; how-to information; social media features for mutual encouragement; and manager-to-employee and even peer-to-peer recognition?

4. Learning. Making information quickly available related to a person's specific goal or any goal – preferably on your wellness portal so everything is in one place – is critical. The wellness portal can provide tests where people can receive points for getting a passing grade. Games can be worked into your program to help people encourage one another.

5. Collaboration and Innovation. Can you create opportunities for people to work together, such as with lunchtime walks, exercise groups, or other activities? How can you make sure that people are continually encouraged to come up with ways to improve the program? Make it easy for people to submit case studies of their success stories, and even reward people who do. Your wellness portal can include news feeds and conversations between employees on how they're addressing their goals.

6. Rewards and Recognition. How can you add to the fun and satisfaction by enabling people to reap the rewards of their efforts in ways that won't get lost in their monthly bills – some sort of experience or tangible reward that can be enjoyed by significant others and that evokes memories or long-term satisfaction. Make sure it's commensurate with the level of achievement and that it has a personal touch.

Weaving wellness into existing recognition platforms is an opportunity to leverage peer-to-peer reinforcement and manager support for people seeking to hit certain health goals.

7. Measurement and ROI. Based on the goals and objectives in your business plan, what is occurring over time? What is the level of usage of the wellness portal? What are people accessing in terms of information? Are they responding to the engagement surveys? What are those surveys telling you? What is happening to your claims activity over time? What is happening to your lost time due to sickness numbers?

As noted above, properly structured wellness programs have been shown over time to have more than a 3:1 return on investment in terms of the cost-savings versus the cost.

BEHAVIOR CHANGES
A study of employees participating in a wellness program conducted by Emily Falk, a University of Michigan neuroscientist, for Maritz Motivation Solutions, found that:

- People who were rewarded walked an average of one mile more per day than those who didn't receive rewards
- People who were rewarded for keeping a health journal completed their tasks 25% more often
- People who chose their wellness activity had higher goal completion
- People who had social support had an increase in average daily steps over those who didn't
- One in three participants reported weight loss, one in two reported having more energy and more than 50% reported having a more positive mindset
- People with pedometers were more likely to discuss the wellness program; share success stories and compare activity.

WELLNESS TRACKING APPS
There are a number of smart phone apps in Android, Apple, and Microsoft platforms that can help people become more involved in wellness. The most popular are those that 1) track the number of steps each day; 2) track calories consumed; and 3) monitor heart rate.

Some of these apps require little more than remembering to bring along your smart phone or attach a sensor to your body; others require you to manually enter food consumption.

AFFORDABLE CARE ACT BENEFITS
The Affordable Care Act increases the maximum permissible reward under a qualified wellness program from 20% to 30% of the cost of health coverage and allows a maximum reward of as much as 50% for programs designed to prevent or reduce tobacco use. According to a Labor Department report, *The Affordable Care Act and Wellness Programs*, companies can deduct the cost of rewards for "participatory wellness programs" in which people in any health condition can participate. These can include programs that reimburse the cost of fitness center memberships, provide rewards to employees for attending regular free health education seminars, or that provides a reward to employees who have their health risks assessed even if they don't take further action.

There are a number of restrictions: programs must be designed to promote health or prevent disease. They must be available to all similarly located individuals, and all participants need to be notified that the program is available. The proposed rules for implementation of the Affordable Care Act wellness incentives don't specify the types of wellness programs employers can offer. No decisions should be made related to tax treatment of a wellness program based on this chapter. The information is intended to provide guidelines for confirmation by qualified tax accountants.

Enterprise Engagement: The Textbook

Chapter 24

Meetings and Motivational Events

Most people would consider motivational events such as meetings, corporate retreats and incentive travel to fall under the rewards and recognition category, and they certainly do to a certain extent. On the other hand, carefully designed motivational events can have a high impact on communications, learning, productivity and relationships that endures long after the program ends, which puts them in a separate category in terms of engagement.

Among the most common and effective of motivational events is the offsite business meeting or corporate retreat. Another form of motivational event is incentive travel, in which high performing employees, partners, vendors, even loyal customers are rewarded with travel to destinations that are meaningful to them. Increasingly, incentive travel and offsite business meetings/events are being merged to take advantages of logistical and cross-functional opportunities.

This chapter examines the use of incentive travel, offsite business meetings and events, in combination and individually, as an engagement strategy. We will draw extensively on research conducted by the Incentive Research Foundation (IRF) in its 2013 study, *Striking the Balance: The Integration of Offsite Business Meetings and Incentive Group Travel*. Wherever "the research" is cited in this chapter, it refers to this paper. Note also that survey respondents were broken into three groups: "Corporate" (managers, leaders and meeting or incentive travel planners/designers from across the organization); "Practitioners" (the large subset of incentive travel or meeting designers and planners among those who completed the corporate survey); and "Participants" (employees or channel partners who completed a separate survey).

REWARD, RECOGNIZE, MOTIVATE
According to the aforementioned research, most organizations (60%) offer travel rewards to top performers, and nearly all (90%) conduct offsite business meetings and events. In organizations of 100 or more employees, the numbers jump to 67% and 96%, respectively.[1]

---

[1] - Allan Schweyer, Lynn Randall, *"Striking the Balance: The Integration of Offsite Business Meetings and Incentive Group Travel."* Incentive Research Foundation, May 2013 (see: http://theirf.org/Striking-the-Balance.6109669.html)

Where incentive travel is concerned, the purpose is almost entirely to reward, recognize, motivate and engage high performers – mainly by sending them to luxury locations or nearby special escapes – and, increasingly, to boost their expertise, grow their networks and accelerate their careers.

Meetings and events that don't involve incentive travel, on the other hand, usually have a more immediate business purpose. Still, when they're held offsite – often in attractive locales – they also serve a purpose closer to that of incentive travel. Those invited often feel recognized and rewarded, and being out of the office environment provides a sense of "getting away." Increasingly, offsite business meetings aim to conduct serious business *and* reward those in attendance. The combination has numerous advantages, one of which is that if participants spend the majority of their days in business meetings or sessions at the events, the organizational expense incurred can have a favorable tax treatment.

A POWERFUL VEHICLE
As we mentioned, incentive travel (which was once all about the reward) and offsite business meetings and events are starting to morph and combine. While the practice of including business meetings in incentive group travel programs is nothing new, interest has accelerated of late.

The severe economic environment of 2007-2009 in the United States (aka, the Great Recession) and the accompanying government bailout of large financial institutions brought intense scrutiny on those companies that received assistance. Specifically, the "AIG Effect"[2] shined a negative spotlight on incentive travel and its perceived extravagances – especially for organizations with government ties or contracts.

Yet, while it's widely believed that most organizations currently combining travel rewards and offsite meetings are doing so in response to the negative perception of incentive travel brought on by the AIG effect and/or for tax reasons, the research suggests otherwise.

While the trend is real, it's occurring largely for reasons that have little to do with PR or taxes. The research shows that the combination of meetings and incentive events has been adopted by about half of U.S. organizations as of late 2012, and their chief reasons are surprising: Only 10% percent say they do so to save money, reap tax benefits or address the criticism surrounding incentive group travel.

By contrast, more than four times as many (42%) do so in order to maximize their investment in meetings and travel rewards and/or take advantage of having high performers in the same place at the same time as top executives, thereby increasing face-to-face communication between key constituencies.

The question is whether adding meetings or mandatory business events to incentive travel diminishes the "reward value" and associated benefits for the high performers that earn such trips. Interestingly, the research reveals that when done correctly, incentive travel recipients and those selected for offsite meetings and events are coming to view the business and learning elements of the trips as at least equal in attractiveness to the leisure components. This is a potential boon to organizations that do it well, because engaging high performers in serious business and learning will generate greater value for the business than pure leisure, even counting the rest and relaxation benefits of the latter.

---

2 - *The AIG Effect*, Mark Lewis, Forbes.com. February 16, 2010 (http://www.forbes.com/2010/02/16/aig-business-travel-leadership-meetings-10-corporate-conferences.html)

Incentive travel and offsite meetings/events with serious business and learning components can be powerful engagement vehicles if they're designed well and strike the right balance between business and pleasure. Essentially, the serious business or learning must be meaningful and beneficial for the high performers' careers. If it is, they'll often rate the meeting and learning components even higher than the scenery, leisure and amenities.

INCENTIVE TRAVEL ROI

In a 2013 brief, Aberdeen Research found that 100% of organizations that it defined as "best in class" use incentive travel rewards.[3] In research for this chapter, 260 of 278 combined participant and practitioner respondents (about 94%) stated that incentive group travel impacts performance positively. Indeed, an average return on investment (ROI) of $4 to every $1 spent is a commonly cited outcome of incentive travel programs.[4]

The ROI from incentive travel comes from analysis of past and future sales, performance, engagement levels, retention, absenteeism and other factors. As noted above, few dispute the impact of incentive travel and its value as a tool to drive better communication, performance and engagement, so why fix something that isn't broken?

The fact is, in many organizations pure incentive travel is held inviolate. In those companies, the gains are so significant and the "buzz" around the incentive travel program so energizing, that leaders won't consider risking the program and the engagement it generates in the workplace or among partners and customers for the sake of adding a meetings component. Nonetheless, most of the experts we interviewed told us that pure incentive travel rewards are a thing of the past in their organizations and/or those they provide services to.

Reasons For Combining Offsite Business Meetings with Incentive Group Travel

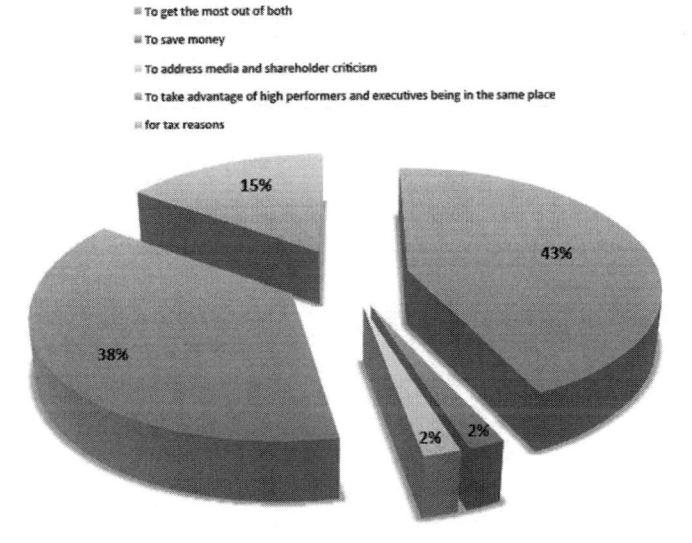

- To get the most out of both: 43%
- To save money: 38%
- To address media and shareholder criticism: 15%
- To take advantage of high performers and executives being in the same place: 2%
- For tax reasons: 2%

Striking the Balance: The Integration of Offsite Business Meetings and Incentive Group Travel, Incentive Research Foundation, May, 2014

---

3 - Non-Cash Incentives: Best Practices to Optimize Sales Effectiveness, Aberdeen Group, February, 2013
4 - http://www.ustravel.org/sites/default/files/09-10-09_Oxford%20Economics.pdf

And even among organizations that don't believe in the combination of incentive travel and meetings, social gatherings and informal networking between fellow high performers and with senior executives are almost always on the agenda or facilitated in some way. The temptation to take advantage of the convergence of the organization's top performers and senior leaders in one place at the same time is valued and hard to resist.

MAKE THE WORK THE REWARD
Imagine you've worked hard all year to reach and surpass your goals. You've done so well, in fact, that you're recognized as among your organization's very best performers, earning you an incentive trip with 49 other people – the best from across your company – to celebrate your accomplishments with the top executives in a beautiful tropical resort. You'll be there for a week with your partner, and there's plenty to do – everything from snorkeling and sailing to hiking, beachcombing and fine dining. There are even business meetings planned so that you can talk strategy with the CEO and other senior executives. On Tuesday and Thursday mornings, half-day business meetings are scheduled, and you're strongly "encouraged" to attend. Sound like fun? Would you feel rewarded or punished?

Your answer likely depends on the culture of your organization, your perspective and what you value, but even more so on how those business meetings are presented and organized. From the organization's perspective, having dozens of the company's top performers all in one place at one time is an opportunity not to be missed. Why not get senior leadership in the room with top performers to talk about the organization's customers, its strategies and its future?

While good for the company's leaders, isn't this also good for top performers? Wouldn't you rather spend at least some time building relationships, getting to know senior leaders and boosting your career than simply relaxing and having fun? Most highly motivated, driven employees would say yes, because they see real value in those opportunities. The goal is to use the travel experience to network and convey the productivity goals of the program while engaging the hearts and minds of participants.

CORPORATE INTERESTS
Corporate interest in conducting meetings during incentive travel programs isn't surprising, yet many organizations resist because, as noted above, they fear that high performers who earn the travel award will resent having to attend business meetings during their trips.

Indeed, "Practitioner" respondents to the corporate survey were consistent in rating participant outcomes as among the most important business benefits for the combined programs. For example, trip earners returning to work "feeling more engaged and motivated" and leaving the event "with a tangible sense that their individual contributions are critical to the organization's success" were the highest and second-highest rated outcomes of seven options provided.

Where management is concerned, their priorities are a little different. The most important reason for combining business meetings with incentive travel is illustrated by the 54% of "Corporate" respondents whose main purpose for combining the two is to have a productive meeting in which high performers and executives discuss the organization's business issues.

It's also interesting that 31% combine them in order to reward high performers. This suggests that managers in these organizations either view the meetings as a true reward, or possibly that they approach it from the standpoint of meeting first and incentive travel second (the reward is to have the meeting in a nice location).

Among all corporate respondents, 15% claim the main reason for the combination is to gain insights into how to better drive their incentive and reward strategy. This implies that at least part of the business meeting is focused on gaining feedback from top performers about incentives and rewards.

From the organization's perspective, combining offsite business meetings with incentive travel would seem to offer only advantages. However, planners should remember that from the reward-earner's perspective it could be disappointing and demotivating to attend business meetings during a highly anticipated trip they've earned. The good news for businesses is that it's possible to achieve their goals and priorities while still making the incentive travel experience highly rewarding and engaging for reward earners.

IRF research suggests that participants' don't view business components of their trip as a universally bad idea – indeed, far from it. When asked how earning an incentive travel reward impacts their performance, the appreciation and recognition of being selected and rewarded ranks first by a fair margin. Again, the key to a successful combined program is in designing an agenda that communicates appreciation and recognition throughout, including the business components.

It's also important to note that most corporate respondents to the survey approach the combination strategically and attempt to make the business meeting(s) part of the actual reward. Similarly, when deciding whether or not to combine a meeting or meetings with a group incentive reward, a full 50%t of corporate respondents decide based on an integrated strategy to achieve specific business goals. The remainder base their decisions on less far-sighted factors such as the cost and scope of the travel reward trip; the need for an offsite business meeting at that particular time; the types of people on the reward trip; and the likely ROI of doing them separately versus together.

BEST PRACTICES
Respondents to the corporate survey and the experts who participated in focus groups and interviews for IRF research were consistent in their view of the key best practices and principles surrounding the combination of offsite business meetings and incentive group travel.

The overarching sentiment among experts, practitioners and participants is that when business meetings are made part of an incentive travel program, they must be so important, useful and compelling that they become part of the reward itself. In other words, if a top performer has worked all year to earn a five-star trip, the meeting should be at least as compelling as spending that time with his/her partner doing something fun. It's a very high standard, but one that many of the organizational respondents and experts have attained through proper planning and, before everything, by seeing the meeting from the participant's perspective.

In the corporate survey, respondents were asked to select the top two drivers that optimize the impact of the combined event. The most commonly selected response was that planners must ensure that the incentive reward earners feel recognized and special (23.5%), followed by making sure that the content is meaningful and relevant (22%). These considerations, along with thorough planning and top-notch destinations and amenities, help make the combination work.

ENGAGEMENT TACTICS

To be clear, organizations can benefit immediately and significantly from business meetings in which their high performers and executives participate during incentive travel programs. The communication, feedback and learning that take place are valuable and often measurable. The networking and relationships formed between high performers (who might otherwise be off in many different directions) and executives is also valuable and possible to measure, and the learning and inspiration that results typically pays off in even higher performance when the reward earner returns to work, which is also directly measurable.

That said, the research confirms that reward earners continue to value all the things that incentive travel is known for – exotic destinations, five-star resorts, great food, fun and the opportunity to bring the family along. Even the fundamental fact of being recognized is among the most motivating aspects of earning the reward. Participants rate fun, the destination and the quality of the resort as the top three most important aspects of a travel reward. Surprisingly, having executives on the trip is ranked second-to-last. It's informative that the opportunity to network with other high performers and with senior executives ranks only above "time away from the office" in terms of motivation for earning the reward.

Yet despite participants' low ranking of networking and time spent with executives compared to other elements of a reward trip, most approve of at least one business meeting during their travel. Fully one-third of "Participant" respondents believe that "a meeting during their trip would make the experience better for them and the organization." Some are less welcoming of business meetings (23%) but still agree that it's a good idea, if mainly for the company. Only about 20% believe the combination is a bad idea for both the company and the reward earners.

By all accounts, a significant majority of high achievers welcome a balanced, structured opportunity to network with their peers and executives and to participate in meaningful discussions about the business with peers and senior executives. The better aligned the meetings are to the expectations and wants of the earners, and the better explained they are, the more receptive and engaged participants will be.

And organizations that actively follow up on the ideas and suggestions made during meetings – and then communicate subsequent actions and decisions back to the participants – can expect that business meetings combined with incentive travel will be better received.

GOING OFFSITE

The trend toward adding business meetings to incentive group travel exists in the opposite direction as well. As noted above, 90% of organizations surveyed – and 100% of organizations of more than 50,000 employees – conduct offsite business meetings.

And while it's three times more common for organizations to add business meetings to incentive travel than the other way around, many organizations are leveraging their offsite meetings by adding a reward element.[5]

An important business meeting that might have taken place in the home office in Oakland, for example, might now be conducted in Napa where a half-day meeting might be followed by dining, wine tastings and other evening activities. The entire trip

---

5 - Please note that the focus of the IRF paper is on incentive travel programs to which business meetings are added. Findings and recommendations do not necessarily apply to the reverse combination.

may qualify for a favorable tax treatment and the meeting can be used, in part, to reward and recognize high performers.

Where offsite business meetings are concerned, Participant survey respondents were asked the same questions about impact on their performance and behavior. In this case, sharing best practices with peers, collaborating with peers to solve business problems and acquiring skills and training are the top three drivers of performance.

Though higher than for incentive travel, only 20% indicated doubt as to whether offsite business meetings have a positive impact on their job performance.

In terms of behaviors and attitudes, 77% cited good information and being better informed and focused as outcomes of offsite business meetings; whereas only 23% said that offsite business meetings have either no impact on their behavior or a negative impact. When asked what they like best about offsite business meetings, respondents chose "getting good information" significantly more than anything else.

Clearly, participant expectations of business meetings and events – even those held offsite in "destination" hotels and resorts – are different than expectations from incentive travel. The first purpose of these meetings and events is perceived to be business, whereas the first purpose of incentive travel, rightly so, is recognition and reward. Yet as the two converge, it's clear that fun, leisure and serious business can combine to form the reward, whether in offsite meetings or incentive travel.

Simply being selected for either constitutes recognition and shows appreciation, which is one of the most effective drivers of engagement.

CHANNEL PARTNERS AND CUSTOMERS

Offsite meetings, events and incentive travel have long been important tactics in driving employee, channel partner and customer engagement. For channel partners who earn incentive travel, business meetings are a more risky and far trickier proposition.

Channel partners have less to gain in terms of career trajectory by attending strategy and brainstorming meetings or even in networking with executives during the incentive travel they earn. Meetings, if inserted at all, should be short, highly relevant to the participants, and very restricted. Instead, planners should use dinners, appreciation ceremonies and other less formal tactics to bring channel partner high performers together with executives.

Similarly, the use of incentive travel and offsite business meetings and events to reward and appreciate customers is often very effective – even where customers have to pay to attend, as is the case in many user conferences. In these instances, business meetings should focus on customer feedback and needs. Content should be designed to educate the customer about technology, services, processes or the industry and be genuinely educational. The participants generally evaluate the content on the basis of how it will improve their business or them personally. Informal dinners and events in the evenings are good tactics to bring customers together with managers and executives.

SUMMARY

Organizations should consider leveraging their incentive travel programs and offsite meetings and events with tactics designed to engage employees, partners or customers. But they should proceed cautiously.

It's extremely important to remember that every participant is different. Some will thrive on an agenda full of commitments for meetings and social occasions with senior executives. Others will desire fewer of those interactions and more time to relax and recharge with their partner and/or family.

Only rarely does it appear that reward earners reject business meetings and networking entirely. It boils down to quality and personal preference – how compelling and valuable are the meetings and networking to the individual reward earner? How much is too much for one participant versus another?

The key to a successful combination is in the design of the program. Careful thought and exceptional content can turn skeptics into eager participants. Planners must always place themselves in the shoes of the reward earner and put participants' needs ahead of the organization's desires.

No matter whether you're using a trip as pure incentive travel or in combination with meetings or events, it's important to consider how you can leverage that experience to reinforce values, messages, or behaviors linked to your overall engagement efforts.

It takes a specific skill set for a meeting planner or an incentive travel planner to manage both. The right person will have a combination of the most important skills of each, including the logistics and venue expertise of a meeting planner and the knowledge of rewards, recognition and motivation of an incentive planner.

Enterprise Engagement: The Textbook

Chapter 25

The Role of Travel in Engagement

By Patty Pae, Sandi Daniel and Allan Schweyer

Organizations' use of travel rewards to incentivize key stakeholders – employees, partners, resellers and customers – is a tried and true practice stretching back decades. Despite the costs, incentive travel has long been considered among the reward tactics that yield the highest return on investment with the longest-term impact on recipient performance and engagement.[1]

This chapter explores the directions incentive and business travel are taking today, including incentive travel, offsite business meetings, business travel and the use of holiday travel time. In keeping with the theme of the textbook, less emphasis is placed on reward aspects and more on how organizations can create lasting engagement among stakeholders through travel.

INCREASING IMPACT
The impact of well-designed incentive travel on reward-earner engagement – as compared to cash and merchandise incentives – is increasing as both consumers and high performers seek tailored experiences over commodity goods aimed at the mass market. Travel itself, whether for reward, to attend meetings, even to conduct business such as sales calls, can be rewarding and memorable.

Unlike cash and merchandise, reward travel has the potential to make lasting, even profound, impressions through positive memories and shared experiences. Well designed incentive travel reinforces organizational values and fosters recognition. At its best, it makes work, partnerships and even consumer relationships more meaningful by demonstrating to reward-earners that their contributions are truly valued.

> "Incentive travel programs will require increasingly personalized experiences."
>
> ~ Incentive Research Foundation, 2014

---

1 - At Last, A Real Way to Measure ROI, Incentive Research Foundation; Determining the Return on Investment of Incentive Travel Programs, Incentive Research Foundation, 2001; and ROI Incentive Programs: Driving People, Driving Profits, Donna Oldenburg, Incentive Marketing Association, 2002.

Incentive travel is just one part of the picture. High performers and others – whether employees, customers or partners – can be engaged through travel even when the main purpose is work and business rather than holiday or adventure. Business travel to desirable destinations to attend offsite meetings may not be an earned reward per se, yet such travel often confers recognition on those invited to attend and is often seen as a reward.

Even business travel to meet with clients or conduct other business can be rewarding and incentivizing in many circumstances. For younger workers especially, the opportunity to travel for work is often highly prized, especially where their organizations allow them to combine business travel with holidays – a growing trend, especially for Millennials and younger generations in the workforce.

Finally, corporate attention to "business" travel should extend to employee holiday time as well. In the U.S., workers leave millions of paid vacation days on the table each year. The cult of hard, continuous work – while admirable in some ways – may bring with it negative consequences for workers and employers in terms of health, productivity and creativity. Savvy employers have started to encourage employees to not only use their vacation time to disconnect from work, but to use it to travel. Travel takes people out of their routine and forces them to deal with the unfamiliar. It's often a renewing and revitalizing experience that can reduce stress, increase creativity, improve productivity and boost engagement for weeks or months to follow.

> 'After devoting days to selecting the perfect hardwood floor to install in a new condo, home buyers find their once beloved Brazilian cherry floors quickly become nothing more than the unnoticed ground beneath their feet. In contrast, their memory of seeing a baby cheetah at dawn on an African safari continues to provide delight.'
>
> – Elizabeth Dunn, Daniel Gilbert, Timothy Wilson, 2011

As always, the key to engaging stakeholders through incentives and rewards is in the design. Organizations must avoid a one-size-fits-all approach to any business travel. A reward that one employee, customer or partner finds rewarding and engaging, another might find inconvenient and annoying.

Again, demographics play an increasingly important role in incentive and reward design as lifestyles, tastes and opinions change. A week at the beach or several days of golf no longer appeal to the masses as they once did. Organizations must explore the experience and meaning of travel, including elements of wellness and volunteerism, to create bespoke experiences and lasting memories. Suffice to say that extracting the greatest impact and ROI from their investments in business travel requires more imagination and creativity than ever before.

THE 'EXPERIENTIAL' ASPECT

The bar on incentive travel programs has risen. Participants are no longer as satisfied with the one-size-fits-all luxury resort vacation with beach and golf. And from the perspective of sponsoring organizations, return on investment (ROI) and the measurement of the impact of investment in travel has become more important since the most recent financial crisis and recession.

Incentive travel is among the most expensive rewards organizations offer. Dittman Incentive Marketing, a leading advisor to organizations on reward travel programs, suggests that a good experience costs at least $5,000 per reward earner,[2] more than enough for the latest big

---

2 - EEA interview with Susan Adams, Dittman Incentive Marketing, November 2014

screen high definition TV, and certainly adequate enough to make an impression using cash.

Yet many organizations prefer incentive travel to cash and merchandise rewards because travel is widely thought to have a greater impact on engagement and performance. Indeed, a good deal of research over the past two decades has demonstrated the link between incentive travel and performance (Severt et al, 2010; Peltier et al, 2011; Xiang & Formica, 2007; Cho, Woods, Jang, & Erdem, 2006; Shinew & Backman, 1995; Witt et al, 1992). This holds true for all stakeholders, including channel partners, in which over 90% cite incentive travel programs as driving more sales.[3]

Harvard Psychologist Daniel Gilbert attributes the ROI on incentive travel to its emotional impact. He believes that heightened engagement (leading to higher performance) derives from the "experiential" elements of travel and other, similar "purchases." In a 2011 study by Gilbert and his colleagues, two-thirds of the more than 1,000 Americans surveyed equated an experiential purchase with increased happiness. Comparatively, only about one-third of those who made material purchases felt the same way.[4] In other words, a big screen TV might make a strong initial impression on a reward earner, but it won't have as lasting an impression as a great travel experience.

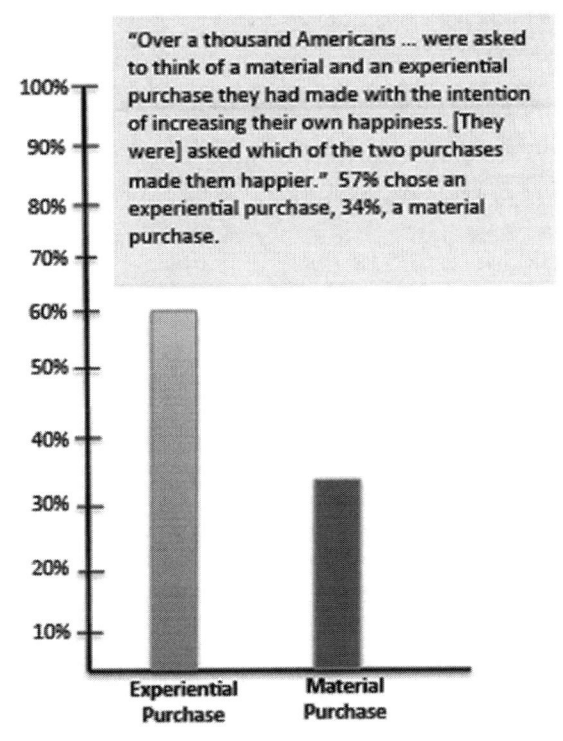

"Over a thousand Americans ... were asked to think of a material and an experiential purchase they had made with the intention of increasing their own happiness. [They were] asked which of the two purchases made them happier." 57% chose an experiential purchase, 34%, a material purchase.

Elizabeth W. Dunn, Daniel T. Gilbert b,1, Timothy D. Wilson, Journal of Consumer Psychology, July, 2011

INDIVIDUALIZED TRAVEL
Incentive travel offers benefits to organizations before, during and after the event itself. As employees, customers or partners strive to earn the reward, their productivity and

---
[3] - *Channel Incentive Travel: A Case Study*, Kimberly Severt, Tom Rutkowski, Incentive Research Foundation, October 2011
[4] - *If money doesn't make you happy, then you probably aren't spending it right*, Elizabeth Dunn, Daniel Gilbert, Timothy Wilson, Science Direct, March 2011.

engagement increases, and this can last the entire year. Recent SITE Foundation research determined that of those who earned an incentive travel reward, 95.5% said they were motivated to earn the reward, and 90.7% of non-earners were similarly motivated.[5]

To achieve this effect, design is paramount. The program should not be exclusive or too difficult to attain. The more stakeholders that can see a realistic chance of earning the reward, the more the organization will benefit from their extra efforts and engagement.

Design is important in creating programs that appeal to as many people as possible. This is more attainable in individual reward travel than with group travel and should be taken advantage of as much as possible. Offer flexible travel options. Many, perhaps most, will continue to opt for the dream beach or golf destination. For others, a significant health & wellness component is essential. Some will want an "extreme" experience. Others may be motivated by the opportunity to give back in some form through volunteerism (for example, paid time off to build houses with Habitat for Humanity in Central America). For most, individual travel must include their spouse or "significant other" to be rewarding.

Finally, in most cases (volunteerism and extreme travel being possible exceptions), programs should pamper reward earners. Make the experience as positive as possible by removing as many of the inconveniences and hassles of travel as possible. This might include fast passes at airports, preferred boarding and seating on planes, pre-arranged concierge services and local transportation at the destination, welcome packages and thoughtfully planned agendas, etc.

GROUP TRAVEL

Group reward travel offers greater potential benefits to organizations than individual travel, and when done exceptionally well it can be a more rewarding and memorable experience for reward earners as well. Group travel is usually designed to bring high performers together with the organization's best customers, partners and top executives. Getting the "best of the best" together in one place without the distractions of the office can unleash a bonanza of networking, idea-sharing and bonding. The results, though often long-term and not always easy to measure, can provide near limitless returns.

But group travel shouldn't focus too much on meetings, group dinners and networking events. Organizations must balance the benefits to the business with an agenda that truly rewards the individuals who earned the trip. From memorable, exciting experiences to relaxing spa and beach time, the program should cater to as many tastes as possible.

According to IRF research from 2013, the niceties still matter a great deal: "Reward earners rated the location, 'exotic and nice' as the most motivating aspect of an incentive travel program, and by a fairly wide margin. This was followed by 'food' and 'activities.' The fact that they had been recognized and rewarded was also rated as very important, as was the time they got to spend away with their spouse or partner."[6]

So as long as reward earners' needs are addressed, organizations can carefully weave business meetings into the agenda. Indeed, if those meetings are substantive, and high

---

[5] - Incentive Travel: The Participant's Viewpoint Part 1: Incentive Travel as a Meaningful Motivator (see: file:///Users/allanschweyer/Downloads/Participant%20Viewpoint_Meaningful.pdf)

[6] - Striking the Balance: The Integration of Offsite Business Meetings and Incentive Group Travel. Allan Schweyer and Lynn Randall, Incentive Research Foundation, May 2013

performers or top customers are really heard by senior executives, the meetings might even rate as the best part of the trip by some participants.[7] Nonetheless, most reward earners believe that no matter how good and career-enhancing the meetings aspects of the incentive group travel, those components should constitute no more than 20% of their time. Reward earners also strongly emphasize the need for significant others to be included in the reward travel.[8]

Program designers who wish to engage participants and hopefuls before, during and after the event should strike the right balance between free time and time spent in business meetings or networking activities. Take care to properly recognize reward earners. Offer varied leisure, sports, adventure, health & wellness and other activities to cater to a group that is bound to have diverse interests. Make every effort to exceed participants' expectations – after all, the buzz generated back at the office after the event starts a new cycle of engagement toward the program the following year.

Whether for group or individual incentive travel, the experience is the key to a long-lasting impact on engagement. Personalize it and make memories, try to create emotional experiences, as those create the longest and highest impact memories.

One sign of the times is the trend to incorporate Corporate Social Responsibility (CSR) into travel programs. The *2014 Incentive Travel Survey* conducted by the IRF found that a whopping 47% of organizations already integrate CSR components into their programs. Wellness experiences are also trending upward. The same survey found that 62% of respondents have either implemented health and wellness components into their programs or are planning to.[9]

DEMOGRAPHICS

To some degree, the trends above are driven by demographics. A recent Wharton study argues that, depending upon their age, people differ in what they find motivating (in terms of experiences, including travel). The report found that people under age 35, for example, are more engaged by exciting and/or unusual and even extreme activities, while those over 45 prefer quiet times with friends and colleagues while traveling.[10] While these generalizations can be useful guideposts for designers, participants should never be pigeonholed into programs based on their age or other demographic factors.

Incentive travel is shown to deliver a range of long-term benefits beyond lasting engagement. Better teamwork, longer retention among participants, higher sales, better customer service and a recruiting tool to attract new employees into the organization are among them.[11] Beyond incentive reward travel, other forms of business travel prove to impact stakeholder engagement as well.

MOTIVATIONAL EVENTS/OFFSITE MEETINGS

As of 2013, Incentive Research Foundation surveys of meeting and

> 'Meetings are a crucial element to solidifying and forming new relationships, sharing best practices and ensuring industries are forging ahead.'
>
> – Roger Dow, President and CEO, U.S. Travel Association

---

7 - Ibid
8 - Ibid
9 - 2014 Trends in Engagement, Incentives and Recognition, Incentive Research Foundation, 2014
10 - *10 Trends Shaping The Future*, IRF, 2010
11 - *Behavioral Economics of Incentive Travel*, Incentive Travel Council (see:
http://c.ymcdn.com/sites/www.incentivemarketing.org/resource/resmgr/imported/Behavorial%20Economics%20of%20Incentive%20Travel%20w%20Members%20Listings.pdf)

reward planners found that at least 90% of organizations conduct offsite business meetings.[12] In contrast to pure incentive travel programs, offsite business meetings that combine at least four hours of meetings with other activities (dinners, wine-tastings, etc.) qualify as business expenses and incur no tax implications for participants. However, according to 2013 research by the IRF, organizations often conduct offsite business meetings not because of the tax advantages, but to recognize, reward and bring key people together.[13]

Offsite business meetings in attractive locations where real business is discussed can, in a way, constitute recognition for those invited. Such gatherings offer a chance to connect with colleagues and leaders in a neutral, more intimate setting. For some employees or partners, just being invited can be an engaging experience. But many organizations are also adding clear reward elements to their offsite meetings. An offsite meeting that might have taken place at a windowless, local hotel, for example, might instead be conducted in a "destination" location, like Las Vegas or Miami's South Beach. Fine dining, entertainment or other evening activities might follow several hours of meetings during the day. Though much more expensive than typical meetings, motivational meetings of these sorts can be used, in part, to reward and recognize high performers.

Indeed, according to a 2013 survey conducted for the IRF, only 15% of respondents indicated doubt as to whether offsite business meetings have a positive impact on their job performance. In terms of behaviors and attitudes, more than three-quarters said that good information and being better informed were positive, motivating outcomes of offsite business meetings. Most tellingly, where respondents had participated in offsite meetings used at least partly to recognize and engage high performers, almost 95% felt they worked as motivating tools.[14]

BUSINESS TRAVEL

According to a 2012 *Economist* Intelligence Unit survey conducted throughout Europe, more than 80% percent of organizations believe business travel is critical to boosting their sales, building customer relationships and remaining competitive – and more than two-thirds believe that business trips are likely to meet these objectives.[15] And a U.S. Travel Association report published in 2013 says business travelers believe that, on average, 42% of customers would eventually be lost without in-person meetings.[16]

In 2009, Oxford Economics USA conducted research that found the ROI for each dollar invested in business travel was $12.50 in incremental revenue. Moreover, the report's findings suggest that reduced business travel has significant long- and short-term impact on organizations' sales, revenue and profitability. Respondents estimated that in-person sales meetings converted prospects to customers at more than twice the rate of telephone or other "distance" meetings.[17]

The Oxford report also contains interesting data about motivation and engagement. Executive respondents suggested that the impact of incentive travel is so large, that to offset it they would have to raise salaries by 8.5%.[18] Employee respondents to the survey said travel is: "… key to professional development (66%), job performance (58%) and morale (56%), and more than 40% of travelers perceive a strong relationship

---

12 - Striking the Balance: The Integration of Offsite Business Meetings and Incentive Group Travel. Allan Schweyer and Lynn Randall, Incentive Research Foundation, May 2013
13 - Ibid
14 - Ibid
15 - *Business on the move: How Globalisation is Changing the Travel Plans of European Executives*. EIU, 2012
16 - The Role of Business Travel in the US Economic Recovery, US Travel Association, 2013
17 - The Return on Investment of U.S. business travel, Oxford Economics USA, Sept 2009
18 - Ibid

between travel and staff retention."[19] Executive respondents put those figures even higher.

In a survey of more than 500 employees across all industries in 2013, HfS Research found that even though 29% percent of respondents said less time spent traveling would increase their engagement and empowerment, 32% said more travel time would increase it. And 43% were looking for more time at events and conferences versus 24% who sought less."[20] The report also found that significantly more employees felt that business travel would make them *more* engaged and productive and were frustrated with cost-cutting measures that reduced or eliminated travel.

Bottom line: Despite the inconveniences of travel, it seems clear that many employees welcome it. They believe it contributes to their effectiveness and success and, as a result, they're engaged by business travel – especially when they are able to enjoy personal experiences once business is done.

A fast-growing trend – one travel managers and corporations are struggling to define – is so-called "bleisure" travel or "biztravel" where employees, especially younger ones, are combining personal travel with business-related trips. In 2014, BridgeStreet Global Hospitality polled 640 international travelers and found that mixing business travel with leisure travel ("bleisure) improves engagement and loyalty.[21] Given that employees typically pay the incremental costs of remaining in a destination longer, this arrangement can be mutually beneficial, provided there's no compelling need for the employee or partner to return to work immediately. In fact, "bleisure" travel may help to address a growing phenomenon among U.S. workers – the reluctance of many to use their full allotment of vacation days.

VACATION TRAVEL
Ironically, despite all the advantages of travel for individuals and businesses, one of the most obvious avenues may be the least utilized: vacation time.

A study commissioned by Office Team in 2013 found that about one-third of Americans don't use all of their vacation time each year.[22] Another study in 2013, by Oxford Economics, put that number at 40%.[23] The most recent study of its kind, a Harris Interactive survey in 2014, found that a full three-quarters of U.S. workers with paid vacation don't use all of their vacation days.[24] *Time* magazine says that works out to about *429 million unused vacation days a year* in the U.S. alone.

According to the Oxford Economics study, the impact of employees foregoing vacation time costs the U.S. economy 1.2 million jobs and $52 billion in spending each year.[25] The greater impact however, may be to worker health. According to researcher Jessica de Bloom and colleagues,

> 'A growing body of scientific evidence explains what many of us have learned from unpleasant experience: Push yourself through too many hours or days of work, and your brain starts to push back. Ideas that once flowed easily dry up, and tasks that you should be able to perform quickly become excruciatingly difficult.'
>
> ~ Minda Zetlin, Inc. magazine

---

19 - Ibid
20 - *Traveling For The Best: Examining Engagement And Travel Policies In The World's Best Places To Work*, Jay Campbell, March 14, 2014
21 - *'Bleisure travel' popular among younger workers, surveys find*. CTV News, Sept. 2014
22 - Here's Why So Many Americans Don't Use All Their Vacation Days, Jacquelyn Smith, Business Insider, August 2014
23 - An Assessment of Paid Time Off in the U.S, Oxford Economics, Feb. 2014
24 - *Why Your Mind Breaks*, Sandra Bond Chapman, Psychology Today, June 2014
25 - Ibid

"research suggests that not taking annual vacations is associated with illness or even premature death." [26] Based on studies conducted in 2013, the U.S. Travel Association claims that vacations can cut the risk of heart attack in half, and the same report says that myriad psychological, neural and relationship benefits accrue as well. [27]

Health and wellness play an indelible part in engagement. Most of us believe in the positive mental and physical effects of vacation and travel, but research is helping us to understand the relationship of vacation time to employee well-being, productivity and creativity, even after people return to the office. *Psychology Today* says away time on vacations and experiences during travel lead to heightened mental engagement, which in turn leads to innovation, or what *Psychology Today* calls "breakthrough thinking."[28]

> *"The frontal lobe brain networks that are responsible for reasoning, planning, decision-making and judgment work for you in creative ways when the brain is quiet, not while you're fully engaged in trying to find a solution to a problem. Moments of insight increase as the brain unwinds. Why? When not actively tackling a task, the brain connects random ideas and consolidates these with prior knowledge into exciting new thoughts, ideas, directions and potential solutions. Vacations are important because our bodies and brains are just not equipped to maintain the chronic stress that is a part of 21st-century life."*
>
> – Dr. Sandra Bond Chapman [29]

In other words, healthy employees with the downtime to process information will function better in an organization. And employees who take their vacations – particularly those who combine the positive effects of vacation with travel – appear to do even better in terms of engagement and creativity.

As Susan Adams, Director of Engagement at Dittman Incentive Marketing, says: "The effect of travel is the subject of a good deal of research, much of which is centered on the concept of liminality. Being in a liminal state or place is often explained as 'in-between-ness.' Writers on travel use this concept to express a state of mind in which day-to-day constructs are left behind in a separation phase. Travelers step out of their normal habits and thinking, then re-assimilate with new perspective."[30]

In other words, time away from work lets employees' reset, re-energize and re-engage. Problems that might seem insurmountable at work might become solvable from the distant and different perspective travel brings.

Unfortunately, economic conditions have discouraged many workers from using all of their time off. Workloads and fear of creating negative impressions mean many Americans are working harder than ever with longer hours and fewer days off. Well-intentioned career advice that centers on how workers must become "indispensable" at work is seemingly incompatible with taking vacation time.

Adams recommends that for employees to feel they can actually take vacation time to recharge, companies must let them know it's acceptable and actively encourage them to

---

26 - Vacation (after-) effects on employee health and well-being, and the role of vacation activities, experiences and sleep, Jessica de Bloom, Samuel Guests and Michiel Kompier, Journal of Happiness, 2012
27 - The Benefits are Everywhere: The Personal Benefits of Travel and Taking a Vacation (see: https://www.ustravel.org/sites/default/files/page/2010/02/benefits_of_travel_08_pdf_87080.pdf)
28 - *Why Your Mind Breaks*, Sandra Bond Chapman, Psychology Today, June 2014
29 - Ibid
30 - EEA Interview with Susan Adams, November 2014

take the time they're entitled to. "The workforce needs to hear that it's okay to stop, to put down the cell phone and the laptop for a few days," she says.[31]

SUMMARY
While much of what is reported in the media portrays travel as a "necessary evil" for many American workers, its effects are actually quite positive for both organizations and travelers. Well-designed incentive travel remains one of the most sought-after rewards organizations offer, and is among those with the greatest proven returns. Even business travel – for meetings, customer relationships and sales – is often engaging for travelers, especially when reward elements are deliberately built in.

Travel brings people together physically. The benefits to relationships, sales and other business measures are well documented. But travel can also create incentives for sustained performance and lasting memories that forge deeper bonds between organizations and their stakeholders. While not the least expensive reward option, the returns on well-designed and flexible business travel programs are well established and irrefutable.

---

31 - Ibid

Enterprise Engagement: The Textbook

Chapter 26

Designing an Engaging Environment

By Paula Masters

Studies show that most of the top-performing public companies – the Container Store, Google, Zappos, Whole Foods, etc. – are the ones that understand the importance of engaging every stakeholder in the organization, starting with employees. And one of the first steps to this engagement is right under your nose: the workplace environment itself.

It's no secret that the modern business world is changing. Productivity goals are up, the mobile workforce is booming and employees are getting younger by the minute. That's why it's critical today to construct a physical environment that encourages, supports and, most importantly, engages employees.

There's a rich body of literature and studies from various disciplines that demonstrate the impact of the physical environment on the perception, behavior and performance of employees in the workplace. According to recent research, about 20% of an employee's productivity is directly influenced by their workspace. Emotion, fun and a sense of collaboration within work areas are critical to engagement and productivity. If you're experiencing a lack of motivation and innovation within your company, perhaps it's time you turn your workplace into a catalyst for profit and consider a redesign.

> **According to recent research, about 20% of an employee's productivity is directly influenced by their workspace.**

EVERYTHING IS ON THE TABLE

Making the move to a new workspace design and environment requires consideration of many moving parts, but it essentially boils down to budget and aesthetics – and as we all know they often rely on each other. Capital is required for new furniture, room rebuilds, flooring, lighting and paint, just to name a few key elements. But the money you save in the long-run by eliminating unused space, together with productivity gains and a happier, more efficient workforce, tends to even out the score. In the end, a business will more than likely come out on top. International company Citrix is proof: It was able to reduce its real estate costs by about 2.5% when it switched to an open plan office, among other savings.

The goal is to create more "we" space as opposed to "I" space – locations where employees can engage and interact to work in a relaxing and, more importantly, inspiring atmosphere. It's about creating innovative high-performing flexible workspaces that will serve multiple functions while still being functional and engaging.

As you explore all the options to transform your workplace into a space that will engage your talent and better support your key business initiatives, you should consider and embrace the following concepts:

- **Engaging Environment.** The workplace must engage and inspire existing talent, as well as attract new talent. Studies indicate corporate environment is a key factor when making a career decision. In fact, it has become a competitive advantage for those companies that understand this all-important concept.
- **Real Estate Utilization.** Making the most of your real estate not only allows you to more effectively support your office and the type of work your employees do, studies also show that spatial comfort affects productivity just as much as workspace size and configuration. A well-thought-out space plan can boost innovation, collaboration and overall productivity.
- **Brand Alignment.** The arrangement and design of all your spaces should leverage your organizational culture, management style, mission and company's brand personality. A high-tech company's corporate environment should look and feel much different than the environment at a bank.
- **Employee Well-Being.** Looking at the big picture, well-being goes far beyond exercise and a healthy diet. It's also about the quality of the most important parts of life, which includes the workplace. As such, it's important for companies wishing to engage their employees to create an atmosphere that supports personal well-being.

LAYOUT ISSUES
The first step when planning an office redesign is to determine a layout: open plan versus traditional enclosed. An open plan office functions without most walls and cubicles and organizes different groups of workstations for employee use. Traditional workspaces have the cubes and offices all put together in an orderly fashion, but can use low cubicle walls and relaxation/conversation stations throughout the office to foster engagement and interactivity. A combination of the two is also possible, with part of the floor having cubicles and offices and the other having group areas and a movable work environment.

Using a balanced approach in providing both collaboration and concentration spaces within the workplace is very important. The ability to choose where and how to work is a motivating and inspirational force. Formal and informal meeting rooms, work lounges and other group-oriented and collaborative spaces draw employees in and facilitate brainstorming, spontaneous interaction and problem-solving.

Keeping conference rooms in one location on the floor is a good idea. A cluster of places to meet creates a more interactive and inspiring area without disrupting the flow of the rest of the floor. Inside the rooms, ensure everything is functional and inspiring. Utilize projectors, whiteboard walls and large pads of paper on the table. Comfortable seating is essential.

If you welcome visitors and clients to the office frequently, keep the entryway and foyer in mind as you craft your redesign plans. This space is the initial introduction to the company and should be welcoming, interactive and a sound representation of your brand. Adding a back-lit logo in the reception area or an accent wall painted in your company logo color not only adds interest and excitement to the space, it also serves to reinforce your company brand in the design.

ABOUT FURNITURE

Office furniture can either inhibit or encourage connectivity, productivity and a culture centered around engagement. Traditionally, businesses have designed workplaces with high-walled cubicles from corner to corner. And although they serve their purpose, there's now a push to completely abandon cubicles in favor of more open and flexible furniture that encourages collaboration and engagement. Lower panels with use of glass open up a workspace and accommodate both privacy and collaboration while letting the natural light shine through. No matter what type of workstation is used, it's a must to must to provide multiple and comfortable seating options for employees so they can alter their working posture throughout the day.

Within the open office setting and collaborative spaces, flexible and easily-moved furniture will facilitate quick transformation of space and accommodate multiple meeting styles. Movable screens and walls, beanbags, adjustable tables and couches are good choices to optimize and support a reconfigurable environment.

LIGHTING THE WAY

Studies indicate that something as fundamental as office lighting can have just as great an impact on the success of your business as hiring the right person. Poor lighting can negatively affect overall performance and engagement in the workplace. In fact, employees may not be putting forth their best effort at work because they aren't motivated or inspired, all because of something that may not be obvious to anyone: poor office lighting.

Office lighting should accomplish more than just the task of providing light. It should be energy- and cost-efficient, controllable and well-integrated. Choosing the right office lighting for your workplace, coupled with optimizing natural light in every workspace, is critically important, whether it be the perfect lamp, the optimal cubicle lighting, or an ultimate high-definition solution.

COLOR AND DECOR

Spaces that are welcoming and have a great aesthetic inspire individuals to come to (and stay at) the office. Mixing materials, colors and textures throughout the space stimulate the imagination and become a motivating force. Neutral colors are boring, boring, boring. That means you should add pop colors, colored accent pieces and lots of visual interest.

In a 2011 study, the University of California found that employee productivity skyrocketed when walls were painted bright colors. Red and yellow lead to faster decision-making abilities. Blue is relaxing and puts people at ease. Green becomes bland and distracting over time. And absolutely stay away from white walls. Another recent study, this one by the University of Texas, showed that workers in white rooms were more prone to make mistakes – the lack of color starved the employees' brains of sensation.

Add unique art pieces, decals and storyboards to the walls, and the office will be a powerhouse of productivity spurred by the creativity of the space.

ACOUSTICS
Critics of open plan workspaces often take note of noisy environments. Everyone works differently, and that means some employees operate better in a quiet environment. Be sure to include some quiet zones in the plan, as well as soundproofing or padding for the walls to dampen the din of productive chatting. The use of carpet versus hard surfaces is also helpful.

Take note of where each department is located as well. A loud Call Center should probably be on the other side of the floor from the quiet Accounting Department.

LETTING NATURE IN
Numerous studies have established a link between office settings that have a connection to nature and good health, job satisfaction, productivity and engagement. Consequently, every effort should be made to use natural building materials like bamboo or hardwood, and even to open up outdoor spaces as work areas. A 2013 survey by the Earthing Institute showed that people connecting with real, natural materials like wood and grass felt healthier over time, were able to sleep better and experienced less stress and anxiety.

> **Numerous studies have established a link between office settings that have a connection to nature and good health, job satisfaction, productivity and engagement.**

And don't forget to let in natural light wherever possible. Use of glass walls serves a dual purpose – increasing natural light and providing accessibility to those who require a private office. The addition of artificial skylights, water sculptures, live plants, or even artwork with views of nature can be added to the workplace to capitalize on this phenomenon. Live plants will help eliminate pollution while increasing oxygen levels. Employees will feel more alert and hence be more productive. A happy and healthy employee equates to a happy and healthy business.

STORAGE SPACE
In all the redesigning excitement, don't forget about storage space. File cabinets and drawers are still necessary to hold client information and other documents. Well-organized environments are said to enhance employee engagement and productivity. Many companies with open floor plans, like Kraft Foods, use colorful banks of lockers for employees to store their things. Kraft also uses file cabinets as space dividers, allowing the form of the cabinet to become a functional design element.

MORE OPTIONS, MORE ENGAGEMENT
Also keep in mind that one of the keys to innovation and productivity is making time to play and relax. Employees need to recharge throughout the day. When Kraft Foods redesigned its office space in Illinois, cubicles were ripped out and replaced by treadmills, pool tables, reading nooks and video games. As a result, according to a 2011 company report, more employees want to be in the office than at home, the company eliminated 45% of unused space in the office, productivity increased by as much as 30% and time spent in scheduled meetings decreased.

A similar phenomenon occurred at Steelcase in Michigan. Cubicles and offices were removed, making way for a free-flowing workspace where executives sit among lower-level employees and no one has an assigned desk. The company also redesigned its cafeteria to have a more coffee-shop-like vibe, combining work, food and collaboration space all in one. Allowing employees to choose the way they work instead of forcing them into a "cube farm" cut Steelcase's required floor space in half and led to 72% of workers choosing to work from their office over their homes.

Red Bull has established a number of inspirational office spaces around the world, challenging architects to re-imagine contemporary working environments when designing a new project. The complex includes a cricket pitch, rooftop bar and informal meeting rooms where employees meet and collaborate.

Googleplex, Google's headquarters in Mountain View, CA, is a sprawling complex where shuttles are provided to travel between meetings, and the buildings feature massage chairs, relaxation rooms, pool and ping pong tables, a climbing wall and volleyball courts. Fun is part of Google's brand personality, so it's only appropriate the company provides places to have fun.

SAS is #1 on the *CNN Money* "100 Best Companies to Work For" list and has been for the last 14 years. Why? One reason is their attention to creating spaces within the work environment that encourage employee well-being. SAS features a beauty salon and a state-of-the-art, 66,000-square-foot gym.

COLLABORATIVE SPACES
No matter what type of business you're in, the single most important space in the workplace to fuel employee engagement is its collaborative spaces. They should support a shared sense of purpose, focus on long-term improvement and fuel innovation. They can also provide substantial and meaningful settings in which employees form a deeper connection with the company and their co-workers. And it's not just spaces specifically identified or designed for collaborative work, such as a conference room. It's also about spaces that may potentially be used for casual interactions.

Providing collaborative work spaces that are highly diverse and accommodate – even celebrate – the value of giving employees lots of choice in where, when and how they work will be invaluable. The spaces should be well equipped with anything and everything that inspires and supports innovation and creativity, such as white boards, AV equipment and movable and comfortable furniture.

YOUR BUSINESS REFLECTED IN YOUR SPACE
While open floor plans and interactivity are all well and good for specific corporate environments, any design should be dependent upon business function. A business handling confidential health information, for example, still needs desks and cabinets, but may be able to enjoy the social benefits of lower cubicle walls. Take stock of what type of work is being done and how your employees engage with their tasks and each other on a daily basis.

Aside from assessing the needs of the business function itself, you should ask yourself three key questions:

1. **Is productivity teamwork-dependent?** When work is assigned, does it go to an individual, or to a project team? Are job tasks only able to be completed by one person from start to finish? If the level of teamwork needed to complete standard daily job functions is low and employees need quiet to work, cubicles may be a better option.
2. **What are current productivity rates?** Do employees seem happy and fulfilled in their current environment? Is work already getting done quickly and efficiently? You may not need a change in that case.
3. **Is private space a requirement?** Are executives handling sensitive information that requires a degree of secrecy? Do clients come to visit and share personal

information? Depending on who and what is coming into the office, private spaces may be necessary.

Whether or not you fall into the open-space mold doesn't change the fact that you can still optimize and enhance your space. In the end it's all about using the office as a tool. Include your staff in the redesign every step of the way – they'll have the best input for making the space more useful and interactive, and they'll be even more motivated with their own ideas in play.

These are just some of the ways to enhance your spaces and improve employee engagement. Whether you're working with a small or large budget, adding a small coffee or employee wellness lounge, or building an outdoor play space with a flower and herb garden with hammocks, such enhancements will ultimately prove to be a sound investment.

An office designed around the principles outlined in this chapter can and will increase collaboration, innovation, productivity and engagement. It will also enhance company culture and brand manifestation, which in turn will increase the retention and attraction of top employees, ultimately creating a people-centric business.

Enterprise Engagement: The Textbook

Chapter 27

Trade Shows & Conferences Engaging the Stakeholders

By Robert Hughes and Allan Schweyer

The global trade show business is a multi-billion-dollar industry.[1] In 2013, U.S. business-to-business exhibitions alone passed $11 billion in gross revenues; in 2012 trade shows contributed almost $70 billion to the US economy.[2] Moreover, trade show attendance in 2013 surpassed the height of pre-recession attendance for the first time. By other key measures, including net square feet, number of exhibitors and revenues, the U.S. trade show industry has been growing significantly since the official end of the recession in 2009.[3] Live trade shows are big business, and despite the emergence of virtual options they are predicted to keep growing – indeed, at the strongest pace ever recorded – as the economy expands over the next several years.[4]

On the other hand, the statistics above largely reflect the experience of the largest trade shows and conferences. Each year in the United States, about 9,000 trade shows take place, and perhaps 1,000 of them can be described as "large" – those with hundreds or thousands of attendees, often held in big city convention centers. The rest, about 8,000 in total, represent the majority of the shows American consumers and businesspeople attend each year. In comparison to large shows, small to mid-size shows are, on average, struggling. They must find new and innovative ways to engage their key stakeholders.

For smaller trade shows, the meeting planners who organize them and the exhibitors who sponsor and pay for them must come together to understand each other's perspectives. This is the surest way to make the shows work for both attendees and exhibitors. As much as the satisfaction of attendees at trade shows, the financial return on investment (ROI) for exhibitors determines the ultimate success and future viability

---

1 - Michael Reinhold, Stephan Reinhold and Christian Schmidt, *Exhibitor satisfaction in business-to-business trade shows* (European Marketing Academy, ~2009)
2 - CEIR 2014 Index Report, 2013 Exhibition Industry and Future Outlook
3 - Ibid
4 - Ibid

of a show. Thus, meeting planners and exhibitors should seek to understand the other's needs and priorities. In short, exhibitors and organizers have to start talking with each other prior to the design of the show.

Fortunately, trade show exhibitors and attendees' needs aren't as diametrically opposed as might be assumed. For exhibitors, trade shows have taken on new importance as an engagement tool. Since the advent of voice mail, call identification, the Internet and social media, salespeople have experienced increasing difficulty in reaching corporate decision-makers. Live trade shows give exhibitors a unique opportunity to reach decision-makers directly and in person.

Moreover, though one can find information on almost any product in seconds using the Internet, this has, in fact, helped reaffirm the importance of trade shows as a way to get to know people personally. It turns out the Internet didn't eliminate the desire for people to know and meet the people with whom they do business.
Trade show attendees go to trade shows to learn what's new and what's on the horizon in their industry. This information and education can be provided both by knowledgeable speakers and by exhibitors – especially those exhibitors who arrive ready to share the latest in innovative practices. Meeting planners must devise the best means to integrate exhibitors into the show itself – as providers of the critical information attendees desire – rather than marginalize and minimize them.

A CHANGING LANDSCAPE

While trade shows offer powerful engagement opportunities, the field is still in danger, particularly for small and mid-size players. Trade show organizers need look no further than the retail and media industries to understand where their business is headed unless strong counter measures are taken in the very near future. In 2014, the real estate analytics firm Green Street Advisors announced that 15% of U.S. malls "will fail or be converted into non-retail space within the next 10 years." [5] and half of America's malls will likely fail within the next two decades.

The reason? Kit Yarrow, a psychologist who last year wrote *Decoding the New Consumer Mind*, says, "Retail is in a massive transformation period. Consumers have lost their enthusiasm for trolling through massive stores hunting for a bargain. They can do that online." [6]

Of course, trade shows do more than provide attendees a place where they can shop and kick tires. Most attendees, in fact, attend trade shows to collect new, trending information that they get both from speakers and exhibitors. Unfortunately for organizers, much of that information is abundantly available and more conveniently accessed online in the form of articles, white papers, videos and even virtual trade shows.

To keep attendees coming and, it follows, to keep exhibitors interested, trade show formats must evolve. In a January 2015 article in *USA Today* in which more store closings for retail giants such as JC Penny and Macys were announced, the author argued: "The only big department stores that will remain relevant to consumers are those that incorporate tricks and treats into the shopping mix – like product offerings you can't find online, special demonstrations or sampling, cushy or fun relaxation areas."[7]

---

5 - America's Shopping Malls Are Dying A Slow, Ugly Death, Hayley Peterson, Business Insider, Jan 31, 2014
6 - J.C. Penney, Macy's to shut stores, lay off scores, Gary Strauss, USA Today, Jan. 8, 2015
7 - J.C. Penney, Macy's to shut stores, lay off scores, Gary Strauss, USA Today, Jan. 8, 2015

Beyond stunts, endless "door crasher" sales and the like, agile retailers have become good at returns. A growing number of shoppers buy their merchandise online and only enter the store to return it. Wise retailers see this as their opportunity for engagement, perhaps to educate consumers about other products or to get feedback. Though quite different animals, some of the lessons from the retail industry apply to trade shows as well.

FROM PLUSH TOYS TO REAL CONVERSATIONS

Without a doubt, we're in the middle of one of the largest psychological buying shifts in recent history. Ask any audience whether they have ever bought a pair of shoes online, for example. Chances are a third to a half of the audience will raise their hands. Then ask them whether they know what a "shoe last" is. It's unlikely that any hands will remain up. A shoe last is the mold on which a shoe is built, an important part of the process to ensure that a shoe fits properly – well beyond the typical information given online.

The point is, consumers often buy online believing they know as much or more than the salesperson in the store. In some cases they might, in others they take their chances. But the fact that they buy online may also say something about the quality of their experience with retail salespeople. After all, the convenience of ordering online is quickly negated when an item arrives that has to be returned. Savvy retailers today are enhancing shoppers' live experiences and also investing more in the knowledge and credibility of their salespeople.

It's no different at trade shows. In most industries, products, services and business contracts are far more complicated than consumer products. Buyers and sellers eventually want to meet one another, and by enabling them to meet many people at once, trade shows continue to provide a convenient way to engage.

> **Buyers and sellers eventually want to meet one another, and by enabling them to meet many people at once, trade shows continue to provide a convenient way to engage.**

Yet, too often, exhibitors send their most junior people to trade shows. They arrive armed with glossy promotional materials, polished product videos and cheap, usually irrelevant, giveaways. Tradeshow attendees want rewarding interactions with senior product managers and designers who can answer questions that aren't provided online. According to the International Association of Exhibitions and Events, "In-booth, face-to-face engagement skills will increase exhibitor success and encourage continued investment in exhibitions and in-person events. It will be incumbent upon all aspects of the exhibitions, meeting and events industry to encourage exhibitors to train their in-booth staffs in both the benefit of face-to-face marketing and the skill sets necessary to succeed on-site." [8]

At the same time, organizations often send junior people to attend events as a form of reward or recognition, and/or to learn. While this is good practice, it does nothing for exhibitors when junior people with no decision-making authority visit their booths looking for giveaways. Organizations should send junior employees as part of a larger team that includes senior decision-makers. Still, to attract senior leaders, trade shows and their exhibitors must offer something that can't be found elsewhere.

WHAT EXHIBITORS AND ATTENDEES WANT

In 2014, researchers at Cornell University surveyed more than 2,500 trade show

---

[8] - Future Trends Impacting the Exhibitions and Events Industry, Francis J. Friedman, IAEE, 2013

exhibitors and attendees to determine their preferences and priorities. The good news is that despite new RFID and social media technologies, virtual tradeshows and the like, "the basic objective of a trade show remains unchanged," according to the researchers. Trade shows must still "...facilitate interaction between exhibitors and attendees so that all participants can have a better business outcome."[9]

Exhibitors want access to the buying community, and attendees want to know what represents the leading-edge of their industry. Serious attendees don't want to find the same information they could have seen or downloaded online any more than exhibitors want to cater to employees on junkets seeking freebies.

Given the realities of the vendor-consumer relationship, it's up to exhibitors and trade show organizers to lead the charge. Product managers should staff booths instead of junior salespeople. They should take potential customers through informed product demonstrations. If exhibitors are going to give things away to attract people to their booths, they should make sure those giveaways align to their product or service. Exhibitors must go beyond stamping an email address and phone number on a plush toy to attract attendees who may not care about anything else. Instead, they should attract qualified and interested attendees who seek real engagement with the organization, even if there are fewer of them. Instead of polished but contrived corporate videos, exhibitors should show attendees raw "You Tube"-style videos of real customers using the product or service. And instead of high-level screen shots, let attendees interact with the real product wherever possible.

As above, planners and organizers should do away with the separation of the exhibit hall and the speaker hall. Instead, they should work with exhibitors to turn the traditional exhibitor hall into something like a "sandbox" – a place where attendees can try out new technologies, for example, and sample innovations that might soon change the industry. Speakers and exhibitors should be interspersed and linked. Organizers should educate speakers on the technologies and innovations on display at the booths. Chances are, some of the latest things speakers refer to in their talks are available for hands-on demos just a few feet away at exhibitors' booths. Organizers should ask and expect speakers to refer attendees to those booths.

Research reveals that neither exhibitors nor most attendees travel to trade shows for recreational purposes. Attendees are not primarily concerned about the social technology in use at the events either. The top purpose and goal for attendees is education. Technology makes the biggest impact at trade shows when it provides memorable, hands-on experiences.

Using the "shoe last" example above, imagine a mid-size trade show in the work boot industry. Imagine a vendor who sets up a 3D photography booth with a 3D printer alongside. A speaker presents on the future of mass customization in the industry and a future, just months away, in which any worker can get a custom boot made to order at a price close to what he or she pays today for a generic boot. The speaker refers to the vendor located just a few yards away and says, "...in fact, you can start the process today. Visit XYZ Boots booth and get a free 3D photo of both your feet. They will upload the image to their servers and then you can order a made-to-fit boot whenever you like from the comfort of you own home. They can even show you how it's done using their 3D printer to make a shoe last, which is a perfect model of an individual's foot."

---

[9] - *The Future of Tradeshows: Evolving Trends, Preferences and Priorities*, HyunJeong "Spring" Han and Rohit Verma, The Center for Hospitality Research, Cornell University, June 2014

Though their priorities are very different, the bottom line for attendees *and* exhibitors is content. So clearly, the interests (and potential engagement) of attendees and exhibitors centers on content. Both parties are interested in the educational qualities of the trade show in that it drives attendance. Attendees want qualified speakers with the latest information and knowledge of trends. And, as above, they want to meet with exhibitors (as many of them as possible) who can speak credibly about their products and services and trends – where they believe the industry is headed and, preferably, with interactive displays and use of technology and other innovations.

A TRADE SHOW BUSINESS PLAN

As one of the most critical ways to engage with customers, employees and suppliers, trade shows warrant a formal business plan with ROI measures. Exhibitors' plans should include:

- The specific goals and objectives in terms of leads or contacts, and a clear system of follow-up and accountability
- The specific benefits for attendees who visit their exhibit and how will these be communicated and when
- A return on investment objective and budget
- The sales, marketing, learning, communications, promotional products or rewards, and other components to be incorporated into the experience
- How the event will be used to foster organizational alignment in a measurable way
- A post-event follow-up and relationship-building plan with prospects.

SOCIAL TECHNOLOGY

Though the highest priorities of attendees are the quality of event content and education, the appropriate use of social technologies to enhance a trade show and drive better exhibitor and attendee engagement is also becoming critical. Among other things, organizers should attempt to differentiate the trade show experience from what can be accomplished in a simple online search for information. Doing so requires organizers and exhibitors to get creative.

> **The appropriate use of social technologies to enhance a trade show and drive better exhibitor and attendee engagement is becoming critical.**

While only large events, for the most part, can afford to be creative with RFID-enabled badges equipped with sensors and the like, even small events today should feature free wi-fi throughout the venue rather than just an Internet Café. Organizers should seek sponsors that will pay for the free wi-fi, or work it into the cost of the hotel rooms. Either way, with wi-fi organizers can connect show attendees through private social media and communities set up for the event and can connect exhibitors to attendees in the same way. Attendees will also be able to "tweet" from the presentation sessions and help organizers drive interest beyond those in attendance. Moreover, because attendees (especially senior, qualified buyers) want information and content, exhibitors might give away product apps or eBooks at the event loaded with the latest specs, white papers, video and other information about products or industry trends.

Small and mid-size events might, like their larger counterparts, consider mobile event apps offered by various providers to facilitate organizer and exhibitor contact and information sharing with attendees and exhibitors before, during and after the event. Such apps can bring attendees together with speakers, exhibitors and each other based on mutual interests. An event app's predictive matchmaking technology based on algorithms can even predict attendee interest, so that suggestions are made as discretely and unobtrusively as possible. In reality, however, it's unlikely that a large percentage of attendees will install and use a complex app, even if it's free. Most expect to use it for only two or three days, so it isn't worth the investment of their time to learn. Smaller events might find the expense and time associated with providing complex event apps impractical given the payoff. For many event organizers, simple apps that require minimal learning are often the best bet.

As above, the best use of technology at trade shows is that in which exhibitors and organizers work together to use technology to create a more relevant and engaging experience for attendees. Rather than the typical putting green or ball toss games one sees frequently at trade shows, exhibitors should strive to build the "sandbox" experience referred to above. Again, some uses of technology – especially expensive social apps and the like – apply better to larger trade shows where the costs can be distributed among many exhibitors and sponsors.

INTEGRATING SPEAKERS, ATTENDEES AND EXHIBITORS
Whether with technology or otherwise, events must be re-imagined to eliminate the barrier between the exhibit hall and information sessions with speakers. Planners must see the event from the point of view of the exhibitor. Simply putting exhibitors and lunches together doesn't make the grade any more. The survival of many small and mid-size shows depends on exhibitors, speakers and attendees sharing the same space.

Thoughtful organizers have long realized that when the barriers are removed, far greater traffic flows in and out of the exhibitor space. This might simply mean removing the walls between exhibit halls and speaker rooms in smaller events. In larger events, non-plenary sessions might be conducted inside the exhibit halls, with stages and seating erected strategically throughout, for example.

Organizers should make it clear that the exhibit hall is part of the content – the place where the latest information is available on products and industry trends. For their part, if exhibitors send their best product people, organizers can promise attendees that, far from being sold to, they can expect to be educated at exhibits. After all, attendees are at events to network and learn, and exhibitors possess much of the information and knowledge they need. Indeed, where an exhibitor is qualified, organizers should consider integrating them into the event further as speakers, presenters and panelists.

THE CHANGING ROLE OF THE EXHIBIT
In the old days, exhibits were seen like retail storefronts, with bigger and grander always being better. Today, with the focus on content experience, the emphasis isn't on having large, expensive and heavy exhibits that wall people off but on open, interactive formats with strong visuals and other efficient ways to focus attention on the benefits of engaging with attendees.

In addition to getting face-to-face with potential clients, trade shows offer a unique opportunity to create greater alignment in an organization by having in attendance not only salespeople, but general management, marketing, operations and other key management personnel, not to mention the suppliers exhibitors do business with. By getting everyone together out of the office at a sales event with leading customers, competitors and multiple learning opportunities, trade shows provide an opportunity to create greater understanding of the marketplace by key people in all parts of an organization, and to make sure everyone remains focused on customer needs.

Trade shows are the perfect way for salespeople, sales management and other executives to meet with customers. These events provide a great opportunity to get people together to learn about the marketplace, key product differentiators and gather other competitive information that people need to work more efficiently and effectively across the entire enterprise.

Live trade show attendance, particularly for large events, is predicted to grow by a very healthy 3% annually over the next several years,[10] but virtual trade shows are expected to double in attendance each year at least through 2018.[11] Market Research Media suggests that, "it is just a matter of time before the virtual events world and the trade show world merge to create the next generation of events – a hybrid of the old and the new."[12] Wise organizers are already broadcasting their events to larger virtual audiences and designing better ways to integrate live and virtual components.

> **Live trade show attendance, particularly for large events, is predicted to grow by a very healthy 3% annually over the next several years, but virtual trade shows are expected to double in attendance each year at least through 2018.**

MEASURING RESULTS

With the new technologies and cutting-edge tools available today, the science of measuring event success will soon undergo a complete renaissance. The data generated by RFID-equipped badges, for example, will produce terabytes of unbiased data about each and every attendee and exhibitor, including their interactions and behaviors.

Mobile apps will give organizers tremendous insight into the individual preferences of attendees and exhibitors, including what they download, what they attend, what they eat, who they talk to and for how long, and potentially even the quality of conversations they engage in at events.

Today, organizers rely mainly on surveys and evaluations, which are inherently biased and often annoying to participants. Moreover, surveys are very limited in the type and depth of information they can generate. With modern badges and apps, near limitless, "honest" and irrefutable data will be available to organizers concerning every aspect of the event.

The opportunities new data-capture and analysis technologies present stretch as far as any organizers' imagination. It will soon be possible to know and understand individual attendee preferences, for example, enabling an organizer to tailor the marketing of his or her trade show to each potential attendee and exhibitor differently, based on their observed likes and dislikes. And once the organizer knows who plans to attend, they can create as many versions of the event as there are participants, thereby exponentially increasing the odds of creating an "engaged experience" for more attendees and exhibitors.

At the most basic level, however, measurement goes back to having a good customer relationship management platform; a system for making sure data is meticulously entered into the system and used according to the trade show business plan.

SUSTAINABLE TRADE SHOWS

The trade show industry, not unlike many others, is shifting toward a focus on sustainability. Environmental concerns and proper stewardship remain at or near the top of engagement drivers in the United States, particularly among younger workers and consumers. While it's often impractical to audit an entire supply chain to look for "non-green" actors, it is possible to minimize one's own footprint. Trade show

---

10 - CEIR 2014 Index Report, 2013 Exhibition Industry and Future Outlook
11 - Virtual Conference & Trade Show Market Forecast 2013-2018 (See: http://www.marketresearchmedia.com/?p=421)
12 - Ibid

organizers and exhibitors can source locally, use lighter-weight exhibits, send fewer (but more senior) people to staff exhibits, use sustainable and environmentally-friendly materials at the event, including less paper and more electronic distribution of information, source organic and free-range food locally, etc. The key is for organizers and exhibitors to give deliberate thought to the sustainability of the event and do what they can to minimize the impact of the show on the environment.

SUMMARY & CONCLUSIONS
Trade shows can be a powerful engagement tool if organizers and exhibitors understand what attendees need today – valuable new content and cutting-edge information they can't easily find online. The key to success is having a clear business plan, budget and ROI.

- Look to involve general management, sales, marketing, human resources, operations and financial management to foster greater alignment around customer needs and what's happening in the marketplace
- The focus should be on sharing useful content, addressing needs and building useful relationships by sharing problem-solving and creative thinking that can't be easily duplicated in even the most interactive Internet experience
- Exhibits are no longer about heavy real estate but lightweight, eye-catching and inviting visuals
- Despite all the exciting new ways to measure booth interactions and engagement, the best place to start is a database of everyone who attends, a focused follow-up effort and an ongoing communications and relationship-building process.

The three C's – content, community and connection – are only starting to emerge as priorities for most organizers, even though they have long been craved by participants. And predictive analytics and "Big Data" for trade shows remain in the realm of the "bleeding-edge" for all but a few organizers. Yet, the industry may not have the luxury of incremental, slow change. To survive the rapidly evolving preferences and habits of B2B and B2C customers, it may require fast and substantial change.

Planners and organizers can't solve the trade show design problem all on their own, they must collaborate with exhibitors to arrive at new solutions. Ultimately, the more trade shows can engage their primary stakeholders – and the sooner they do so – the more likely the industry is to survive and prosper in the digital age.

Enterprise Engagement: The Textbook

Chapter 28

Engagement Technology: The Heart of the Problem, The Core of the Solution

While the emergence of customer relationship management (CRM) software, the Internet, and social media are contributing to the growth of Enterprise Engagement, technology is ironically a major impediment to strategic implementation. Even though technology offers a plethora of solutions related to specific engagement drivers, it can also stand in the way because of technology silos similar to those that exist in organizational management that impede the ability to integrate all of the key contributors to engagement, no matter what the ultimate goal of the effort.

On the one hand, technology has made it possible for organizations to measure customer, distributor, employee and even brand engagement like never before. The chapters on Big Data and Measurement clearly show the potential for technology to provide revealing information related to levels of engagement across the organization. And now, as a result of social media, companies can get a three-dimensional sense of the level of customer and employee engagement never before possible. In addition, because the Internet has significantly leveled the commerce playing field, making it possible for almost anyone to sell anything in a highly automated way, many organizations are forced to pay more attention to people because it's now the human interaction between customers, distribution partners and organization that can provide the competitive edge in a way that can be measured better than ever before.

> **As a result of social media, companies can get a three-dimensional sense of the level of customer and employee engagement never before possible.**

In terms of Enterprise Engagement, the problem isn't that there's too little technology, the problem is that there's too much. Unlike in the world of smart phone apps or even sales automation, in which people can integrate various activities on one platform, there doesn't exist in the engagement space a single platform making it easy to integrate all of the technologies that research indicates contribute to engagement. A review of the Enterprise Engagement framework (Part IV, Applications of Engagement) indicates that there's a technology to address almost every type of engagement lever; the challenge is that few if any of these solutions are well integrated.

ENGAGEMENT TECHNOLOGY CATEGORIES

Almost anyone involved with implementing new technology across an organization knows the human element is almost as challenging as the logistics. People use but a small fraction of the technology at their disposal, and adoption rates vary widely in any organization because of the human element. Therefore, any technology implementation strategy has to include a means of engaging people to use it.

Here are some of the key elements of the engagement framework and an explanation of the types of technologies involved with each. Keep in mind that most of these descriptions tend to focus specifically on the engagement element being addressed by technology and don't take into account all of the drivers of engagement in an integrated way. Since it's not the purpose of this textbook to recommend technology, we suggest that people use search engines or association websites in the various fields below to locate and research corresponding technology.

Leadership: A variety of software options are available to provide one-on-one coaching to managers at all levels, in some cases based on engagement scores, most often from companies that provide these services. This technology can include engagement surveys, electronic messaging, videos, useful articles and/or one-on-one communications between a trained coaching professional and individuals.

Assessment: The cost of regularly surveying various audiences continues to go down as a result of technology. (see Chapter 13 on Assessment) The key, of course, is obtaining useful, actionable data that gets into the right hands fast. No matter what form of technology a company is using to achieve a particular engagement goal, assessment is an essential part of the equation.

> The issue is getting all of this information organized for the right audience; easily leveraging communication across the organization so that it's easy to find it when people need it.

Communications: There's a wide variety of software options to choose from for communicating information. Most organizations of any size have some kind of employee intranet or customer information center. Social media players have also gotten into the corporate act; Yammer social media technology is used by many organizations to help foster dialog across the organization, and many recognition platforms include a social media component. Of course, YouTube and other video technology has created an entirely new application for videos due to the low cost and ease of distribution. The issue is getting all of this information organized for the right audience; easily leveraging communication across the organization so that it's easy to find it when people need it.

[A note on content. For communications to break through the clutter, it has to be perceived as relevant, useful, entertaining or necessary. When developing your content strategy, consider how to "pull" people into your information by addressing these key factors. Organizations often "push" information at people or focus on selling, rather than thinking like publishers, authors and editors whose job it is to "pull" people into information so that they're fully engaged.]

Permission Management: Organizations, especially those dealing with consumers, have to make sure they get permission to communicate with people by media, which not only heads off any marketing compliance issues, but also in most cases results in higher response rates.

Learning: The training industry offers a plethora of online learning options, with the focus most recently on "gamification," or using games and points to reinforce and reward learning. There is technology not only for different types of learning styles, but also for testing in particular.

Collaboration and Innovation: A number of companies offer technology that focuses on promoting ideas, sharing and innovation. These technologies manage all of the elements of submitting, reviewing, sharing, communicating and in some cases rewarding suggestions or innovation. Generally, the technology is packaged with the support services of these vendors.

Rewards and Recognition: Probably no aspect of engagement has a broader selection of technological possibilities, from online catalogs to multiple types of recognition and points-based programs to fully-automated back-of-the-house management and fulfillment platforms. So-called "manager-to-peer" and "peer-to-peer" programs have become quite popular, as have social media tools that enable all employees to see news feeds of reward activities. Most of these technologies are proprietary to the solution providers that offer them, meaning that you have to use the services or awards of that company to access the technology.

Measurement: Because all of the above activities are usually managed by multiple technologies and platforms, it becomes extremely challenging to collect all of the data coming out of them, let alone correlate it. In theory, it would be highly useful to correlate customer, distribution partner and employee activities with their respective interactions using the above technologies. It would be useful to know how often a manager participated in a coaching session and how the engagement scores of his/her employees changed over time. How well have customers, distribution partners and employees absorbed key messages? How engaged do customers, distribution partners and employees feel, by territory, and how does that correlate to various financial or other results? What is the correlation between performance and test scores? Or participation in innovation programs with employee retention? The data-mining potential is almost endless – if the data were available in one place to analyze.

THE LEGACY CHALLENGE

Further compounding the problem is that many organizations have intranets or customer websites that go back a decade or more, many of them with miscellaneous information provided by multiple managers over time and often not well maintained. In many organizations, IT professionals are hopelessly bogged down with pressing issues and don't have time to regularly maintain information.

Many of the above technologies often are provided by third-parties in such a way that it's not possible to integrate them with other technologies except in the most rudimentary ways. It's difficult at most organizations to set up a system for strategically rewarding points for different behaviors because most of the technologies through which those behaviors would be tracked don't talk to one another.

To fully integrate its engagement technology and reward platforms, a company not only faces major logistical issues, but also organizational issues because different people are usually in charge of management coaching, assessment, learning, rewards and recognition, innovation and collaboration.

> **Many organizations have intranets or customer websites that go back a decade or more, many of them with miscellaneous information provided by multiple managers over time and often not well maintained.**

STRATEGIC AND TACTICAL
The issue of technology arises at both the strategic level of an organization and at the tactical level where division or department heads need to engage specific audiences to achieve specific goals.

At the strategic level, the discussion about technology is secondary to the issues related to developing an overall engagement strategy that encompasses the enterprise brand, leadership, culture, communications, learning, collaboration and innovation, rewards and recognition and measurement tactics.

This process usually involves creating an executive committee representing leadership of each organizational group (including IT) who meet annually to agree upon an overall engagement plan based on organizational goals and then communicate regularly in follow-up meetings to make sure everyone's operating in agreement with the plan.

After this mechanism is set up, it becomes possible to begin to look at engagement technology from an organizational standpoint. The engagement team should address such questions as:

1. What will be the "authorized" communication channels with each organizational audience, from customers and distribution partners to employees, vendors and other communities? Who's in charge of each and who can influence how those channels will be used?

2. How do we make sure that customer and employee messaging are aligned on the various platforms for overall branding consistency?

3. Is the content being offered customers and distribution partners helpful to them? Does it provide useful information in addition to just selling the virtues of the organization? What about the employee portal – does it contain all of the information employees need to understand organizational values, the types of behaviors important to the organization and all of the resources available to them to continually advance through learning? How easily can individual department managers use the platform for their own communications needs?

4. What type of engagement surveys are conducted and what is done with the results? How is this information made actionable? Are all of the right people receiving this information?

5. How are customer and distributor websites used to make sure people have the knowledge they need to best interact with the company or utilize its products and services?

6. What types of learning and testing strategies are used with the various audiences and how are results tracked across the organization? What kinds of tools are available for use by department heads for specific purposes?

7. What types of collaboration and innovation strategies exist? What is being done to encourage people across the organization, including customers and distribution partners, to encourage suggestions? How are those ideas processed and communicated back to the contributors and organizations? How is any of the technology for these purposes integrated with other technology, such as rewards platforms, learning centers, or assessment to track participant engagement?

8. How well are rewards and recognition technologies integrated with the above efforts? Can the organization reward people for returning surveys, passing tests, exhibiting desired behaviors and actions, etc.?

9. How well is all of the data coming from the above activities being correlated, analyzed and fed back to management at all levels? Is there any way of correlating such information? Who is responsible and how will the information be used?

A TANGLE OF TECHNOLOGIES

Many department or division heads are tasked with achieving specific objectives – customer loyalty; distributor commitment; employee service, quality, productivity, knowledge, wellness, safety, etc. They usually can't wait for top management to develop an organizational infrastructure to provide for all of their technology needs, and rarely can get the access to necessary IT resources. They therefore routinely select particular technologies based on their specific needs. As a result, most large organizations have a tangle of technologies that are very rarely integrated beyond featuring a single log-in experience for participants.

Until a centralized platform emerges for engagement as has emerged for sales force automation and enterprise management, managers selecting any of the above technologies should take the following factors into consideration:

- How easy will it be to connect software with your portal so there's at least a single log-in experience?
- How easy is it to address other elements of engagement beyond the specific behaviors being tracked or managed to make sure people are fully engaged with using the technology for the desired purpose?
- Who will need to be trained on using the technology and how will training be conducted?
- What will be done over time to make sure people properly use the technology and take advantage of its capabilities?
- How will data obtained from the technology be correlated with desired outcomes?

THE MOBILE ISSUE

With the proliferation of smart phones and applications, engagement is increasingly defined, in part at least, as the time people spend using an organization's social media, smart phone apps, or websites. In fact, the web advertising and social media businesses define customer engagement almost exclusively on this basis, rather than on the broader definition that includes "net-promoter scores," a term created by loyalty expert Frederick Reichheld that measures the willingness of someone to recommend an organization, or other indicators of commitment to an organization.

That said, with people using their smart phones so often today, the more that can be easily accessed via a smart phone the better, especially when it comes to delivering messages, useful information, standings, results, tips, etc. With people increasingly using smart phones to fill idle moments, organizations want to make sure they're present when people are receptive. This doesn't mean organizations need to have apps for their various engagement strategies, but certainly it's now beneficial to have re-sizable content so it displays effectively on all screen sizes.

Enterprise Engagement: The Textbook

Chapter 29

Measuring Enterprise Engagement and Performance

There's a lot of truth in the old adage: "You can't manage what you don't measure," as anyone who has ever tried to run a business will tell you. But it's also true that you can't manage what you measure *only once a year*.

When it comes to employee and customer engagement, most of us collect information through annual surveys, analyze the results, share them in a high-level report and perhaps devote part of an executive meeting to discuss the implications. Like performance reviews, this is usually done once a year – if at all.

Engagement, however, fluctuates day-to-day and week-to-week. Employees and customers, like our suppliers and partners, are complex and unique human beings. Measuring their engagement once a year – while better than nothing – is like getting an annual weather report. It provides a large-scale overview, but the data are insufficient for making critical, focused decisions.

Remember also that your broader constituency – the key groups that you depend on for success – include your employees, your suppliers, your channel partners, your customers and to some extent the communities in which you do business.

MEASURE, ANALYZE, REPORT, TAKE ACTION
When an organization strives simultaneously for better engagement across all of its key constituencies, truly exponential gains can be achieved (see Gallup's *Human Sigma* for a detailed explanation). So how can you effectively measure and demonstrate these gains? In order to make informed decisions based in fact, managers need to:

- Regularly monitor trends in employee, customer, supplier and partner engagement
- Analyze those trends
- Share the information across the organization
- Set goals
- Mobilize executives, managers and supervisors to take action

A manager's incentive plans should be aligned to the achievement of engagement goals. Taking action normally means devising and implementing initiatives aimed at improving one or more areas of engagement.

Effective measurement requires that certain fundamentals or principals be observed. Meaningful measurement will normally require an estimate of business impact at minimum and, in some cases, a Return on Investment (ROI) calculation. Following the policies and procedures below will ensure that you develop credible and defensible estimates of the business impact and ROI (where necessary) of your engagement initiatives:

Baseline data. To measure performance change, there must be meaningful "before and after" comparators. For engagement metrics, this means having or creating a reliable benchmark *before* you begin your initiatives. In most cases, the benchmark data will come from your first or previous engagement surveys, or from performance data you've accumulated from a previous, comparable period.

Number and ease of measures. The number of performance measures should be limited and their tracking not overly complex. For example, employee engagement, customer engagement or channel partner engagement scores are singular measures. More granular measures might include scores by division or even by team and manager.

Involvement. It's important to gain participants' input and feedback in the development of the measures. Off-the-shelf engagement surveys are readily available for employee and customer surveys. The Enterprise Engagement Alliance (EEA) offers its Enterprise Engagement Benchmark Indicator (EEBI), which includes measures for employee, customer, channel partner and supplier engagement. In using these tools for measurement, be sure to collaborate with your various constituents in explaining how you'll measure progress and what you intend to do with the data. Encourage their input and suggestions, especially in the collection of data and dissemination of results.

Another option is to get input from some of the participants via a "nominal group technique." Using this method, a facilitator works with selected representatives from the people you're measuring to identify their views related to the most effective performance measures or related opportunities or obstacles. You can also use this phase to help identify any outside issues that could affect results (see Causality, below).

Conservative financial assumptions. Though difficult, you must place a value on the unit measure of performance or engagement. In doing so, err on the conservative side when making financial assumptions and confirm all financials (assumptions and numbers) with colleagues in the Finance or Accounting department. Calculating financial ROI from intangible benefits such as increased engagement is an imperfect science. By making conservative estimates and by assigning only a portion of the gains to your engagement initiatives, your results are more likely to be considered credible by the CFO.

Causality. You may see positive results from your engagement or performance initiatives such that even conservative estimates of the dollar value appear quite high, especially when all of the gains (in sales, for example) are attributed to your engagement initiatives. The impact of your initiatives takes time to surface, so you must consider external influences that might be partially responsible for the gains (or losses, as the case may be).

If your sales team engagement initiative occurred between January and March, for example, you might have had to wait until October for sufficient data to measure its impact. In between, the economy might have changed, demand may have increased or the competition may have suffered a setback. These influences have to be considered and factored into your equations.

One means to limit the effect of external influences is frequent measurement. For example, suppose you've held an event for channel partners. You measure its impact at the time of the event (reaction), then a month or two later (application), and then again after six months or so to determine the business impact and ROI (i.e., greater sales). Still, if prices of products have changed during those six months or if demand has changed, consider these factors in determining causality.

Linkage. Measures should ideally be linked to organizational goals and geared to driving organizational success. When developing your measurement plan, always think about corporate objectives and strategy. For example, one of the organization's goals may be to earn more "share of spend" from existing customers. In this case, correlate customer engagement measures to the metrics being gathered on share of spend. Did an initiative drive better customer engagement scores? Did better customer engagement result in more share of spend?

Demonstrating ROI. The financial impact of poor engagement, or conversely, the opportunity for significant financial gain where engagement is improved, is often large enough to warrant a measurement strategy that goes all the way to an ROI calculation. Where this is the case, measures and metrics chosen must support the calculation of ROI.

Targeting. Select high impact metrics to demonstrate that scarce resources are being applied in such a way to maximize business impact and ROI. For example, metrics aimed at tracking sales increases or reducing customer attrition are ideal. Both are easy to convert to dollar values in a credible manner and both are easily understood, high impact measures.

Ongoing monitoring and feedback. As noted, effective measurement provides not only the opportunity to track your engagement efforts at the end of a program period, but also along the way. Make sure you build into your measurement effort a means to collect and analyze information on a regular basis, and make adjustments accordingly to your strategy and tactics to address performance or engagement gaps.

Predictive analysis. In making the case for spending money on engagement initiatives, a predictive analysis of *expected* ROI can be very useful. Metrics need to support management's ability to understand the relationship between improvements in the measure and impact on organizational success (i.e., if goals are achieved, what is the value to the organization versus the cost?).

USE OF TECHNOLOGY
Measurement and analysis are no longer as time-consuming and difficult as they once were. With today's low-cost, cloud-based software and Enterprise Engagement surveys with polling, tracking, analysis and dashboard reporting tools, organizations have the ability to connect daily with their key constituents (employees, customers, suppliers, partners, etc.).

Daily interaction through engagement software is designed to be non-intrusive. Naturally, you can't survey people every day, but as a result of web-based recognition technology, it has become easier to track the engagement of constituents – not only their performance, but also their website visits, including the content viewed, learning, innovation, participation in social networks, etc. Moreover, engagement technologies provide a dashboard of performance on an individual, department and enterprise level, as well as for individual customers, suppliers and re-sellers.

Allowing employees, and partners in particular, to view the progress of their peers toward goals and program utilization connects employees and partners to the brand, the engagement portal and their performance objectives. The key is to build the community and share data not just at an administrative level, but also at the participant level.

SUMMARY

The measurement of engagement can't be based on an annual cycle; it must be an ongoing process. This allows an organization to see the immediate impact of its actions (for example, the effect of a price increase on customer and channel partner engagement), leading to a "decision science" that permits better strategy and faster action based on actual data.

> **Tracking and sharing real-time performance against goals ideally leads to more high-level leaders taking action and buying in to the process.**

Tracking and sharing real-time performance against goals ideally leads to more high-level leaders taking action and buying in to the process. Real data based on business impact and ROI helps your organization identify issues and opportunities. For example, if the data reveals a negative trend in channel partner engagement, procedures to reverse the trend can be implemented, measured (often with ROI calculations) and adjusted quickly until the desired impact is achieved. Whether the tactic is additional training for employees who manage channel partner relationships, a richer incentive program or an event for top-performing channel resellers, decisions can be made in the light of metrics and initiatives can be evaluated on data, business impact and even ROI. They can then be adjusted, expanded or terminated based on measured, defensible evidence.

Ongoing measurement – where the engagement of key constituents is quantified – can ensure success now. There is no need to wait months for the next employee or customer engagement survey results or, worse, take a stab in the dark based on a hunch. Because so few organizations are tracking engagement data today, an enormous competitive advantage awaits those that do, and especially those who build it into their day-to-day business platforms.

Enterprise Engagement: The Textbook

Chapter 30

Big Data and Analytics

By Charles Scherbaum and Roy Saunderson

It is impossible to navigate today's business media without encountering at least some mention of Big Data and analytics. Everyone's talking about how quantitative data analysis is being used to fundamentally change some aspect of research, business or life. The rate at which books, conferences and information are proliferating is astounding. Many describe Big Data and analytics as transformative and a key source of competitive advantage in today's business environment.[1] Some have even argued that competing on Big Data and analytics has become a core strategy for many organizations.

Professor of IT and Management at Babson College and MIT Center for Digital Business research fellow Tom Davenport and his colleagues[2] suggest that companies can be classified based on their developmental state of analytical competitiveness, ranging from companies that are "analytically impaired" to those that are 100% analytical competitors. According to this view, the use of Big Data and analytics (hereafter collectively referred to as Big Data) as a core strategy will define the winners in the marketplace, both now and in the future.

> **For those of us who are not data or computer scientists (which is most of us), the nature, uses and potential of Big Data isn't always intuitively obvious.**

Despite the pervasiveness of the talk about Big Data, it's not something that's typically well defined or articulated. It's as if you're just supposed to know it when you see it, as well as how to use it to drive business success. For those of us who are not data or computer scientists (which is most of us), the nature, uses and potential of Big Data isn't always intuitively obvious.

If you've found yourself wondering what all the hype is about and how it can help you, you're not alone. The goal of this chapter is to provide readers with a working understanding of what Big Data is, why it's

---

1 - McAfee, A. and Brynjolfsson, E. (2012). Big data: The management revolution. *Harvard Business Review*, 90(10): 60-68. Mayer-Schonberger, V. & Cukier, K. (2013). *Big Data: A Revolution That Will Transform How We Live, Work, and Think*. Houghton Mifflin Harcourt.
2 - Davenport, T. & Harris, J. (2007). *Competing on Analytics: The New Science of Winning*. Boston: Harvard Business Press. Davenport, T. & Harris, J., & Morison, R. (2010). *Analytics at Work: Smarter Decisions. Better Results*. Boston: Harvard Business Press.

important and how it can be used to generate insights on creating, maintaining and building Enterprise Engagement.

DEFINING THE TERMS
Imagine a world in which your organization's managers can anticipate who is at risk of leaving and take actions that prevent it, your vendors can anticipate your supply chain needs and take action on them before you tell them, or your marketers can send customers advertisements containing exactly what they want or need before they know they want or need it. Although this may sound far-fetched, this is the world that Big Data strives to create (and it's a lot closer to reality than you might think). The problem is that the conversations and discussions about the brave new world of Big Data typically presume that everyone is an expert. As a result, neither Big Data nor analytics are usually defined in a way that's useful to those outside the fields of data or computer science.

Simply put, Big Data is a tool for gathering information and generating insights to make decisions – with the emphasis on decision-making. Big Data isn't an endpoint in and of itself. Making decisions and taking action based on data and analytics is the endpoint. In essence, they're methods for leveraging your data, finding the needles in the haystack and gaining insights to support decision-making.

Although there's no one definition of Big Data, it's often referred to as data that's too large to view in a relational database such as Excel or Access. Big Data, on the small end of the spectrum, is at least several terabytes in size and may include millions of database rows and columns. To appreciate the size of this data set, consider that personal computers at the present time typically only include hard drives that are less than one terabyte. To handle and leverage Big Data, dedicated IT infrastructure and approaches (e.g., Map Reduce) are needed.

Venturing into the world of Big Data is an enterprise effort and will require the collaboration of numerous internal and external stakeholders. With the exception of the government and organizations in the logistics, sciences, retail and financial industries, most of us work with data sets that are much smaller. This doesn't mean, however, that it's less important or useful, especially for understanding and driving Enterprise Engagement).

Analytics, on the other hand, are statistics. Statistics are procedures and rules used to reduce large amounts of data into more manageable forms that allow one to draw conclusions or generate insights about patterns in the data. Statistics is a broad field, but when discussed in the context of analytics, the focus is on statistical techniques that allow us to predict, classify and/or condense data into a metric, or evaluate the impact of a program, activity or practice.

Regardless of the specific use or technique, the goal is to use data to derive insights. As Michel Lewis' *Moneyball* or Ian Ayer's *Super Crunchers* aptly demonstrate, the insights derived from analytics can be very different than those derived from conventional wisdom or the proverbial gut instinct.[3]

The most common and basic forms of analytics are descriptive statistics. Descriptive statistics can be used to condense large amounts of data in a smaller set of numbers that represent what is typical in a set of data and the amount of variability that exists in a set of data. Examples of descriptive statistics include frequencies, the average, the median,

---
3 - Lewis, M. (2004) *Moneyball: The Art of Winning an Unfair Game*. New York: W. W. Norton & Company. Ayers, I. (2008) *Super Crunchers: Why Thinking-By-Numbers is the New Way To Be Smart*. New York: Bantam.

the variance and the standard deviation. Descriptive statistics underlie most reporting on business metrics and performance.

Related to descriptive statistics are analytics that examine differences between groups on an outcome or set of outcomes. For example, these analyses might be used to examine the engagement of suppliers who had been contacted by a company representative within the last three months versus those who had not been contacted. These analyses typically examine differences in averages between groups and include the t-test and the analysis of variance. This type of analytics is used whenever one is interested in knowing if a policy, practice, activity or program is having the intended effect.

More common in marketing are analytics related to classification. Classification analyses are used to group individuals into homogenous sets that share particular behavioral, attitudinal or demographic characteristics. In marketing and business intelligence, these analytics are referred to as "segmentation analyses."

Often, when analytics are discussed, the focus is on "predictive analytics." Predictive analytics are a class of statistical techniques (based on regression methods) that allow one to use historical data to develop an equation that can be used to predict or forecast some outcome (e.g., community engagement, supplier engagement) based on set of inputs (e.g., number of community or supplier complaints). The excitement around predictive techniques is that they hold the potential to reduce uncertainty about the future. These methods aren't a crystal ball and will never produce perfect predictions. However, the predictions produced by these methods will lead to better decision-making and insights in the long run. As Eric Siegel eloquently puts it in describing his prediction effect, "a little prediction goes a long way."[4]

Even though we describe them separately, there's a symbiotic relationship between Big Data and analytics. The availability of Big Data has made analytics pervasive, and analytics has unleashed the transformative power of Big Data. Although analytics can be useful without Big Data, Big Data will never be useful without analytics. As we have mentioned, most of us operate in the small data world, and with a little creativity we successfully leverage the transformative power of analytics.

REVOLUTION AND TRANSFORMATION

For us, an oddity of the hype about Big Data in the business media is that it's treated as if it's a new revolution sweeping the world. The reality is that the revolution started long ago and countless aspects of the business world and our personal lives have already been transformed by it. Consider the use of balanced scorecards and dashboards. Since Kaplan and Norton popularized their use in the early 1990s with their books and papers on the scorecards used at Sears,[5] they've become a pervasive management tool.

At their core, dashboards and score cards are simply descriptive statistics (and occasionally dashboards are based on predictive analytics). Most managers today are well versed in the use of dashboards and scorecards without even knowing they're users of analytics. The bottom line is that analytics aren't new, and many managers already use them everyday driving their teams and businesses forward.

---

4 - Siegel, E. (2013). *Predictive Analytics: The Power to Predict Who Will Click, Buy, Lie, or Die*. New York: Wiley.
5 - Kaplan, R. S., & Norton, D. P. (1996). *The balanced scorecard: translating strategy into action*. Harvard Business Press.

Hard Drive Cost per Gigabyte (USD)

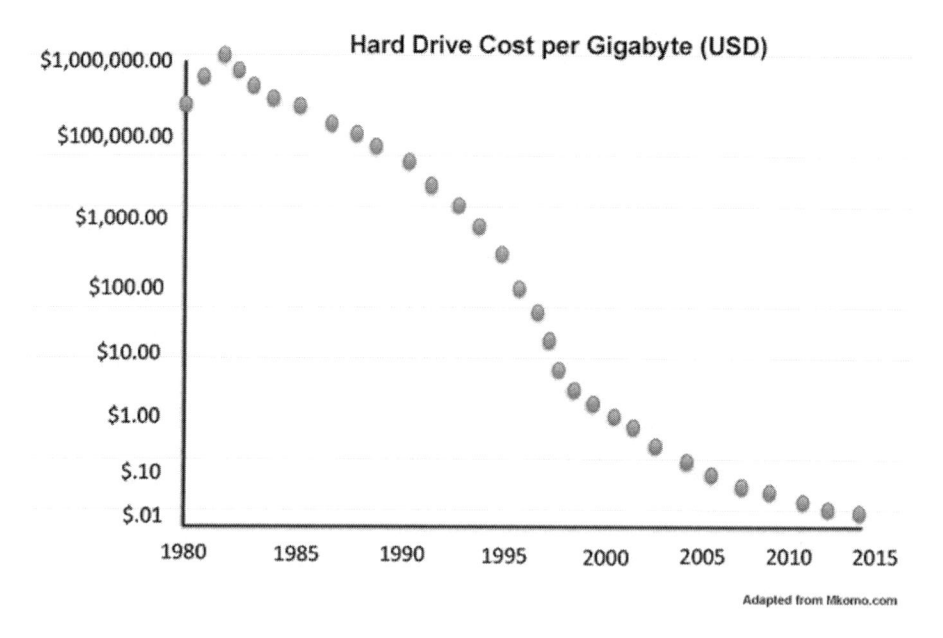

Adapted from Mkomo.com

What is new and truly revolutionary is the number of data sources available and our capacity to integrate information from multiple stakeholders in an enterprise. It was once the case that data sat in silos disconnected from other data that sat in different silos. In this environment, analytics were limited to the data available in an independent, siloed database. If the necessary information wasn't in the database, not much could be done. Questions spanning different parts of an enterprise, such as how supplier engagement impacts operations or how customer engagement impacts sales, couldn't be effectively addressed with analytics.

Modern IT infrastructure and software systems (e.g., ERP, CRM, HRIS) have essentially eliminated the silos and allow data from very different sources to be linked and subjected to analytics. What is powerful about this is that it's not just data internal to an enterprise that can be linked, but also data external to an organization. Also, it's not just structure data (i.e., quantitative data) that can be leveraged, but unstructured data (i.e., text, tweets, social media posts, documents or customer comments subjected to text analytics[6]) as well.

Therefore, analytics can be used to examine the relationships between stakeholders who are internal and external to an enterprise. Data can be obtained from a variety of existing sources or gathered for a specific purpose to generate insights about the connections and relationships that may exist.

WHAT'S ACTUALLY IMPORTANT
The reason these developments in Big Data are important is that they provide a different basis on which to make decisions. No longer do we need to rely on our limited experience and instinct. We can use data to identify facts and generate insights into what's actually important, since it removes any pre-existing biases about what's important and why/how things work.

---

6 - Miner. G., Elder, J. Hill, T., Nisbet, R., Delen, D. & Fast, A. (2012). Practical Text Mining and Statistical Analysis for Non-structured Text Data Applications. New York: Academic Press.

One of the most visible examples of analytics having a positive and transformative effect is Michael Lewis' *Moneyball*. Although there are many dimensions to this story, one of the most important is how the use of analytics removed pre-existing beliefs about the nature of talent in baseball. The talent identified by the analytics was in many cases very different than traditional beliefs about what constituted talent in this sport.

For the teams that have wholeheartedly adopted analytics, such as the Oakland Athletics and Boston Red Sox, the results have been quite impressive. Boston has won two World Series, and Oakland has become a regular in the playoffs with one of the lowest payrolls in baseball.

PRACTICAL EXAMPLES
In addition to professional sports, the impact of analytics can be seen in every industry. Here, we highlight a couple of organizations that are truly competing on analytics.

In the gaming industry, Harrah's Entertainment has long used analytics to help it understand and engage its customers. Using the Big Data from its loyalty program, Harrah's has been able to identify who its most valued customers are (surprisingly, those who are most valuable do not fit the stereotype of a high roller), the point that they will leave the casino and what will make them stay.

The use of Big Data has led to some of the most loyal customers in a very competitive industry where many other casinos have newer and more luxurious facilities.

More importantly, the use of analytics has helped Harrah's casinos go from underperforming to a three-fold increase in revenue in just a few years' time. Much like the Oakland Athletics in the *Moneyball* story, analytics can turn companies who are struggling to compete into some of the fiercest competitors in their industries.

Perhaps no industry has been more impacted by analytics than retail. There isn't a large retailer in the United States that's not aggressively using data and analytics to better understand customers – and in many cases suppliers and employees too.

For example, Wal-Mart uses analytics to help its suppliers optimize their sales. They can provide their suppliers the most detailed of information on what is selling, when it's selling and who it's being sold to. Given the razor-thin margins that many of Wal-Mart's suppliers operate with, additional insights on how to increase volume or better target their products to the right customers can have a substantial impact on their bottom line.

> **There isn't a large retailer in the United States that's not aggressively using data and analytics to better understand customers – and in many cases suppliers and employees too.**

Analytics are such a core part of Wal-Mart's business model that they have their own Silicon Valley technology operation called Wal-Mart Labs that focuses on innovations in analytics and technology.

TREMENDOUS PROMISE
With success stories like these, it's easy to see why people get so excited about Big Data. For those that truly compete on analytics, the promise is tremendous.

We would argue that the potential of Big Data and analytics to contribute to the field of Enterprise Engagement is particularly great. As we'll elaborate, Big Data can help generate novel insights into the complex systems and the relationships between the parts of these systems.

This is the situation we find ourselves when we attempt integrated management of customers, distribution partners, employees and other stakeholders at the heart of engagement.

Particular pockets of Enterprise Engagement are no strangers to using analytics to engage key stakeholders. For example, most organizations apply analytics to data from employee engagement surveys and human resource information systems to identify how engagement impacts important people and business metrics, as well as how organizational factors and leadership impacts employee engagement. Likewise, market researchers apply analytics to customer purchase behavior, loyalty data and customer engagement data to better understand how to engage their customers and increase their purchases, as well as the value of those purchases.

What's often missing is a consideration of a more holistic approach that links employees, customers, vendors and others. However, to take a holistic approach requires there be a clear articulation of an organization's value chain, the various stakeholders, the role they play in that value chain and what engagement of these stakeholders in particular parts of the value chain would look like.

For example, what role do vendors or the community play in the value chain, and what would vendor or community engagement look like? Although the insights generated by the analytics will be clearly valuable, the articulation of what Enterprise Engagement means and what it looks like is equally, if not more, valuable. Without it, truly insightful analytics may not be possible.

Once the value chain, stakeholders and the definition of engagement have been identified, one can begin the process of collecting direct (e.g., surveys, operational data) or indirect (e.g., behaviors, outcomes) indicators of the engagement of various groups. Some of this data will likely be internal to the organization, while other data will be external (e.g., social media, supplier data). The data needed will likely come from many different areas within an enterprise and offer an opportunity to engage stakeholders in the efforts to maintain and build their engagement. The importance of the data cannot be understated. Without some data that can serve as an indicator of engagement, analytics in support of Enterprise Engagement are not possible.

THREE QUESTIONS
Assuming that data is available, one can then use analytics to explore three types of questions about enterprise engagement. First is the relationship between the engagement of different stakeholders in the enterprise. For example, one can ask questions about the link between community engagement and employee engagement. That is, are employees more likely to be engaged when community stakeholders are engaged? Essentially, these are questions about establishing the interconnections of the parts in Enterprise Engagement. These interconnections help identify how the entire Enterprise Engagement system may suffer if one part of it becomes disengaged.

Second, one can ask how the management of the stakeholders in the enterprise is related to their engagement. In other words, what organizational actions predict the engagement of various stakeholders? Understanding how the actions of the enterprise contribute to the engagement of its stakeholders allows the enterprise to take actions to maintain and build engagement. These types of analytics provide a road map when specific stakeholders in the enterprise aren't as engaged as needed or desired. More specifically, these analytics can identify which sets of actions may have the greatest impact. Then the right actions can be applied to the right stakeholders at the right time.

Third, one can ask questions about the benefits of Enterprise Engagement. The implicit belief behind this strategy is that it's critical to the success of an enterprise. Although one can find a variety of reports supporting this belief, there's a need to understand how and why it matters in any given enterprise.

Engagement matters for different reasons and has a different impact in different organizations. For example, one can ask questions such as: Are engaged distribution partners predictive of operational effectiveness and sales? Do engaged employees predict more frequent customer purchases? Do engaged community members predict lower operational costs? Applying analytics to these types of questions provides the type of evidence-based recommendations that are likely to lead to true Enterprise Engagement that's maintained over the long term. Moreover, it perpetuates a culture of data-driven decision making when it comes to engagement and the enterprise's success.

GETTING STARTED
There are a number of considerations for getting started with applying analytics to Enterprise Engagement. As noted, one will need data that can serve as direct or indirect indicators of engagement. Careful thought should be given to the degree to which the data are actually an indicator of engagement.

The data also need to be at the right level of aggregations. If there's a desire to conduct analytics on the engagement of individual customers, then data at that specific level is needed. Often data exists at aggregated levels. These data can be very useful, but keep in mind that conclusions from data are limited to the same level of aggregation.

Data on engagement is only part of the equation. One will also need to obtain sales, operational, employee and customer data that may not be related to engagement. It's likely that this data is held in different parts of the organization, and obtaining it will require close partnerships with multiple stakeholders. The process of gathering the necessary data to conduct analytics on Enterprise Engagement can serve to build engagement among the stakeholders owning the data.

In addition to data considerations, one needs to consider the enterprise's ability to execute analytics and its appetite to do so. The ability considerations include talent in the organization with the capability to execute analytics as well as generate insights from the analytics. Many enterprises will find that they have people who can manage data and execute analytics. However, talent that can simultaneously understand analytics and draw insights that are meaningful to the enterprise is much more difficult to find.

Using analytics to maintain and build Enterprise Engagement is an ongoing effort. Therefore, the collection of the necessary data must be a continuous process. Not all organizations will be willing or able to manage and maintain the continuous acquisition of this data. Of course, the organization will need to develop the internal infrastructure to support the acquisition and analysis of Enterprise Engagement data.

Many organizations believe they want and need analytics. However, some may not have the appetite for it. As noted, analytics applied to Enterprise Engagement or any other area is a considerable undertaking. It requires a lot of resources and management attention. It also requires a possible change in an organization's culture and decision-making processes.

Once data is available on Enterprise Engagement, decision-makers lose a degree of control in telling the story about how Enterprise Engagement works, why it matters and what needs to be done to build and maintain it. Also, whether the opinions are correct or incorrect comes into clear view. In other words, there's a much greater degree of accountability that comes with the use of analytics. The old management adage of "what gets measured gets managed" clearly applies. Not all organizations may be ready or willing to adopt these aspects of analytics.

SUMMARY
Big Data and analytics have become one of the major competitive differentiators in the 21st Century. The Cinderella story of a struggling company turning to analytics and becoming a dominant competitor in their industry has been playing out over and over across the globe. When fully embraced, the impact of analytics is transformative. It's increasingly difficult to imagine how an enterprise can achieve success in today's environment without some use of analytics.

We live in a time where success requires the engagement of all the stakeholders in an enterprise. Analytics can help identify how the engagement of different stakeholders is interrelated, the specific actions that can be taken to increase the engagement of certain stakeholders and how enterprise engagement is impacting business success. To leverage these possibilities, one will need to take a holistic approach that requires there be a clear articulation of an organization's value chain, the various stakeholders and the roles they play and what engagement of these stakeholders in particular parts of the value chain would look like.

The future of Enterprise Engagement hinges on every stakeholder aggressively adopting the power and insights available to them from Big Data and analytics. Only as we draw upon the decision-making capabilities behind analytics will we truly be able to engage all facets of an enterprise. Clearly, this isn't an endeavor for the faint of heart. However, for those who accept the challenge, the payoff is considerable. Mastering the use of analytics within Enterprise Engagement can reveal the symbiotic relationships between the engagement of each stakeholder and their impact on business results.

Enterprise Engagement: The Textbook

Chapter 31

Case Study: UnitedHealth Group

By Ira M. Ozer

Serving more than 75 million individuals, UnitedHealth Group (UHG) is one of the largest insurance and wellness management companies in the U.S. Its two major divisions, UnitedHealthcare and Optum, employ 77,000 people who work in six business units. In each of these businesses, there's an innovation team that works to design and implement new products, services and efficiencies, all aimed at improving the quality of healthcare and driving down costs.

Robert Plourde, Vice President of Innovation and Research & Development, says the key is to focus on root causes, noting that the U.S. spends as much as 10 times more on disease management than it does on prevention.

"It's critical for healthcare providers to educate people and provide them with the tools, incentives and coaching they need to actually implement the behavioral changes necessary to adopt healthier lifestyles," he says, adding that ample information is available, but very few people take the time to seek it out.

Consequently, UHG has pioneered exciting ways to educate people about their health needs, specific diseases and courses of action by using technology and "gamification" techniques, along with incentives, to both engage and encourage them to take the necessary actions.

> Robert Plourde, Vice President of Innovation and Research & Development at UHG, says the key is to focus on root causes, noting that the U.S. spends as much as 10 times more on disease management than it does on prevention.

ENTERPRISE-WIDE SOCIAL WELLNESS
In the fall of 2010, UHG piloted an enterprise-wide "social wellness" program using what it called the ShapeUp platform, in which employees enrolled in a 12-week challenge to lose weight, increase the number of steps they walked and increase the amount of time they exercised daily.

To participate, employees input their progress in the online platform, encouraged others to join them and compete together, and invited others to join as well.

The results: the social reinforcement and team-based structure drove 30% of employees to engage and participate. More importantly, 70% were first-time wellness users, and 40% were at high risk for obesity-related diseases. Overall, participants lost 25 tons of excess weight and recorded more than 1 billion steps. On average, individual participants exercised 30 minutes daily, lost 3.7 pounds and reduced their body mass index (BMI) by 0.6%, with some achieving dramatic and life-saving results.

Then, in November of 2010, OptumHealth launched "OptumizeMe," a health and wellness platform that allows users to create a series of challenges using mobile apps, social interaction, recognition, intrinsic rewards and extrinsic rewards for goal achievement.

MOTIVATION THROUGH GAMIFICATION

According to Karl Ulfers, Vice President of Consumer Solutions for OptumHealth Care Solutions, it's critical to help people navigate the system so they can learn about their specific conditions and health issues, find the right doctors and give them tools to help take the necessary actions, such as losing weight to reduce hypertension and diabetes risk.

Ulfers explains that because many people don't have immediate access to their computers while at work, a restaurant, recreational activities, or while exercising, OptumHealth will be launching a new mobile coaching experience in December of this year that incorporates elements of gaming. As people take actions to improve their health – eating the correct foods, drinking water as directed, etc. – they'll earn "badges" and unlock levels that will provide them with more features and functionality. For example, if they earn a bronze badge, they'll be able to post on their friends' walls and see more content (including articles and videos) and receive surprise rewards, such as congratulations from celebrities.

The OptumizeMe system also includes a "loyalty engine," which awards points for participating, learning and accomplishing required outcomes. In one case, if a participant's BMI is below a targeted number, they will earn points; if it's above, they can still earn points, but only by taking remedial training and coaching.

REWARDS AND RELATIONSHIPS

Although this platform is designed and managed by OptumHealth, it's customized for and sold by the 1,700 payers, providers and employers who are their customers. Award points can be used for insurance premium reductions, incentive merchandise, travel packages, or retail gift cards, depending on the goals and objectives of a particular program sponsor. Some employers believe that offering their employees reduced premiums is more motivational and will result in greater participation and better results (e.g. save $300 for taking the specified actions), while others believe that tangible incentives have greater perceived value, especially merchandise items and gift cards that relate to health and wellness (such as branded athletic gear and apparel).

> **Sweepstakes are also used as a promotional tool to generate interest and awareness for specified activities such as taking a Health Risk Assessment (HRA) or Biometric Screening.**

Sweepstakes are also used as a promotional tool to generate interest and awareness for specified activities such as taking a Health Risk Assessment (HRA) or Biometric Screening. Ulfers believes that OptumHealth has experienced high participation rates because people are motivated by the "aspirational" travel and merchandise prizes that are being offered.

In addition, UHG deploys devices that help improve wellness, such as kiosks that allow employees to test their weight, blood pressure and body fat at work in order to keep themselves on track and tie in to workplace education, coaching and support groups. UHG is also partnering with consumer electronics companies that are bringing products to market that are designed to help people get more fit, as well as with nonprofit health-related organizations and community groups to improve health and wellness education.

BUILDING A CULTURE
In addition to encouraging all of its employees and channel partners to participate in health and wellness programs, UHG fosters a culture of innovation ad engagement that allows everyone to submit ideas for new products and processes, both individually and in teams. Participants can submit ideas in writing, via email, using an online community collaboration platform and even over the phone to reps who forward them to the appropriate reviewers.

And it doesn't stop there, because if an idea is accepted the initiator can choose to become the "idea champion" to bring it forward – in some cases, even as their new full-time position. This culture of wellness, recognition and innovation drives passion, empowerment and engagement – and that comes from the top, because the company's CEO promotes the program, issues challenges (such as a recent one to focus on childhood obesity) and recognizes top ideas and implementation teams at formal recognition events.

Erin Carnish, Senior Vice President of Innovative Health and Technology Solutions for OptumHealth Care Solutions, heads a team that's focused on developing next-generation solutions to drive medical cost savings. She explains that while there are certain generalities that apply to the population as a whole, healthcare education, treatment and management for people with specific diseases must involve customized programs that are sensitive to their unique needs, while at the same time complying with strict privacy regulations.

OptumHealth also continuously gathers insights from patients and physician panels covering various specialties to improve its solutions. Carnish notes that they recently conducted focus groups with employees of a large retailer to learn why they visited the E.R. as their primary source of medical treatment. They learned it was because many of them couldn't get to regular doctors for scheduled appointments. Acting on this information, "virtual doctors" were made available in the employee break room, which allowed the employees to explain their condition via a video conference and then get the proper treatment immediately or be directed to the most appropriate healthcare provider for their needs.

The division is taking this idea further, working on a program with doctors and other healthcare providers to provide an online scheduling service that will allow members of all groups, not just this retailer, to find the right type of doctor for their needs.

CUTTING WASTE, INCREASING CARE
OptumHealth is also launching a major initiative to create a system of Health Advisors who will work in conjunction with people, much like financial advisors, to assess their needs, help direct them to education and providers and coach them to make the recommended behavior changes to live a healthier lifestyle. This cuts out wasted visits to inappropriate providers and maximizes the time of specialists who can help with specific conditions.

In 2010, OptumHealth piloted a program in its Golden Valley, MN, location to integrate all employer healthcare and wellness best practices. This included adding a gym with a variety of exercise classes; making thematic design changes, such as painting some of the office walls and common areas with the GOh! program logo and green color; adding motivational messaging throughout the building, especially in the stairwells; adding a ping-pong table and other equipment to the break room to encourage physical activity; introducing a nurse or other health professional as each employee's wellness "concierge" to coach and guide them; revamping the menu in the cafeteria to eliminate foods with high fat and calories and replace them with fresh, whole foods that have high nutritional value; and coordinating monthly educational and fitness events.

Their key objectives are to lower healthcare costs, change the way employees use the healthcare system, provide an environment where a healthy lifestyle is easy to achieve, and improve employee health with a comprehensive onsite health management solution.

The results have been outstanding. Some highlights:

- medical savings increased 35 times over the prior year
- wellness program engagement rose from 7% to 22%
- employee engagement scores increased by 6 points
- 31% of employees say their workplace productivity has increased
- 67% say that they are placing a higher priority on improving their health.

The healthcare system might seem broken, but United Health Group is one of many companies leading the charge to fix it through continuous innovation and Enterprise Engagement.

Part IV
Applications of Engagement

Enterprise Engagement: The Textbook

Intro: The Enterprise Engagement Framework

Internalizing and organizing all of the information in this textbook may seem like a daunting task, but it's nonetheless essential in order to move ahead into the implementation phase. This outline provides a basic framework for building an Enterprise Engagement strategy and monitoring its progress. Let's start with the basics:

ENTERPRISE ENGAGEMENT DEFINED
A management and marketing process for achieving organizational objectives by fostering the proactive involvement of everyone critical to success, inside and outside the organization.

FOUNDATION OF ENGAGEMENT
Based on dozens of research studies, here are the fundamental elements of engagement that this framework is designed to address:

- Clear sense of mission – What the organization stands for
- Clear goals – Where do we want this relationship to go?
- Emotional bonding – A sense of community and camaraderie
- Capability – Do people have the resources and knowledge to do what is asked of them?
- Fun – A sense of humor and good-naturedness
- Support – A sense of being valued and that someone human is overseeing the process
- Task value – A sense that what I'm doing has purpose
- Feedback – Meaningful suggestions on how to improve.

THE ENGAGEMENT FRAMEWORK
The basic building blocks and constituencies of a successful Enterprise Engagement strategy should include:

Leadership. Clear goals, objectives, and performance measurements.

Assessment. Engagement surveys; the nominal group technique to gain input from key groups.

Recruitment. Identifying ideal employee skills and characteristics; talent identification and management.

Collaboration and innovation. Invite participants to contribute ideas, case studies, best practices, how-to articles, or whatever content can enhance the program.

Recognition. Enable managers to recognize employees, and peers to recognize peers for specified results, behaviors, actions.

Campaign. A business plan (often with a theme) with goals, strategies, tactics, and measures.

Communications. An Intranet site or Engagement portal that is the focal point for the campaign: a launch kit and/or poster or handout; ongoing use of available organization media; meetings, emails, promotional products, etc. to distribute news, case studies, contributed content, highlight winners and best practices, and get attention.

Technology. Find various ways to automate and integrate assessment, communications, learning, collaboration, rewards, and measurement, etc.

Learning. Incorporating the program into ongoing training and distributing periodic tests.

Rewards. Use non-cash rewards to distinguish from compensation; use low-cost "treats" to broaden participation and fewer high level rewards to draw attention to top performance.

Return on investment. Try to assign a value to the results, behaviors, or actions being promoted; track results of ongoing engagement surveys and tests; look at web site engagement metrics; track level of participation in recognition program and surveys, etc.

Enterprise Engagement: The Textbook

Chapter 32

Keys to Implementation

While there may be dozens of different definitions of engagement, all of them are very similar in their most important aspects. All agree that engagement goes beyond mere satisfaction and that it involves a level of commitment from employees, customers, partners and suppliers that surpasses simple respect for an organization or mere contentment within the relationship.

Engagement is reached at a higher level – an emotional one – and that makes all the difference. True engagement must translate into enhanced performance. Engaged customers, employees, partners and even suppliers are remarkably similar in their attitudes. They're more enthusiastic about the organization's success, they share ideas, they relate to the brand and are proud of their association with it. Most of all, they contribute *discretionary* effort beyond what might be required to simply maintain the relationship.

Current estimates of employee and customer engagement hover around the 30% range across all industries nationwide.[1] Similar benchmark data for supplier or channel partner engagement doesn't exist, yet any organization that can engage the majority of its key constituents – employees, customers, suppliers and partners – can expect to reap tremendous advantages and results.

The relatively new field of Enterprise Engagement seeks to promote and quantify the benefits of gaining emotional commitment from all key constituencies across the organization and applying that approach consistently throughout the enterprise.

In this chapter, we examine a critically important element of Enterprise Engagement – moving from strategy to execution. The main objective is to provide practical, clear and readily-available techniques, practices and tools to implement an Enterprise Engagement process.

SETTING THE STAGE
Investment in engagement beyond employees and customers is still a fairly new idea. While the key ingredients are baked into the management and marketing principals of

---

1 - For the most recent data, see Gallup's U.S. Employee Engagement Survey results 2010-2012 (www.gallup.com).

well-known companies such as Whole Foods, the Container Store, Southwest Airlines and many more, this business discipline remains in its early stages – which makes the rewards for early adopters all the more enticing.

Enterprise engagement doesn't require a huge leap of faith. Any employer knows they can't be successful without their employees and customers. For that reason, employee and customer engagement have moved beyond buzzwords to best practices. But organizations cannot maximize results without all their partners – resellers, the people who supply them and even the communities in which they operate. For any organization to make the most of its potential, it must engage all of its key constituents.

CONSTRUCTING A STRATEGY

Before a plan can be implemented, it has to be documented. The plan should communicate the strategy in enough detail to allow the "doers" to craft tactical action plans from which initiatives can be implemented. An Enterprise Engagement strategy has two basic components:

- An integrated strategy to include at least four key constituents – employees, customers, partners and suppliers.
- A strategy to ensure that the activity, methods and processes are consistently known, understood and applied across the enterprise.

Culturally, an organization needs to be prepared for change on a large scale. Even if executives "get" employee engagement and customer engagement, is the organization ready to truly embrace engagement on an enterprise-wide basis? Is it ready to start building trust with employees? Can it engage the people from whom it buys goods and services by treating them the way it would like to be treated by its own customers? Is it ready to emotionally engage customers and channel partners in the business by really connecting with them, listening to their concerns and ideas and even involving them in decisions?

> **An Enterprise Engagement strategy will include a baseline survey to gauge current levels of engagement throughout the organization and across constituencies. This is necessary to establish a benchmark for strategy development and planning.**

For most organizations, the first part of the strategy is aimed at changing organizational values. Despite the rhetoric, changing or evolving values (hence adapting the culture) is not exceedingly difficult; it just takes time and commitment.

An Enterprise Engagement strategy will include a baseline survey to gauge current levels of engagement throughout the organization and across constituencies. This is necessary to establish a benchmark for strategy development and planning. A broader SWOT analysis should also be considered to uncover current strengths and weaknesses, as well as an analysis of outside forces that might impact the strategy and initiatives.

The executive team needs to have honest conversations about the current realities of the business, identify the barriers that have prevented it in the past from being successful and gain agreement and conviction on what the organization's future state should look like This may also include identifying which behaviors the leadership team needs to "throw out" and which they need to embrace and embody to ensure they set the standard for the rest of the organization.

Document a vision for the organization in a high-level strategy. In this case, executives should know what an "Enterprise Engagement organization" will look like so they can paint the picture for the rest of the business. To better understand what the organization might look when it achieves the vision, strategists and planners should have an understanding about each element of engagement. Books, papers, articles, videos and webinars with leading experts are accessible on the web. Relevant conferences are useful, both to hear and meet the presenters and to network with professionals who are trying to accomplish similar goals.

Craft a communications element to the strategy, including, in most cases, a call for initiatives to change attitudes and adjust values. Recognize that communication likely will have to take many forms and require a variety of solutions that incorporate the different ways that people learn – visual, auditory or kinesthetic.

While many organizations may assess employee and customer engagement, and some might actually implement initiatives to improve engagement, very few organizations have a broad "culture of engagement." Where that culture exists, employees, managers and executives all see the value in engaging key constituents and approach every relationship with this attitude. A survey will quickly determine the degree to which such a culture exists in your organization.

Address the consistency of commitment to engagement and engagement practices across the enterprise. A culture of engagement cannot be developed and sustained if engagement practices are inconsistently understood and appreciated, and applied differently from department to department.

Create and implement a learning strategy that understands what customers, distribution partners, different types of employees and even vendors need to know in order to do what is asked of them. Collect resulting data to see how they correlate with performance.

Identify the appropriate innovation and collaboration strategy to foster ideas, suggestions, and other forms of participation from all of your audiences. Determine the appropriate rewards and recognition strategy to foster feelings of support, an atmosphere of fun and to reinforce the values being promoted.

Provide detailed goals and objectives that can be measured so you can make improvements continuously. Planners should quantify the improvements desired in the first year – better engagement scores in the next survey, better customer retention, higher "share of spend," lower absenteeism among employees, faster supply times from vendors, better knowledge of products, more sales from partners, etc.

Determine how technology can help with all of the above. Most companies start with an "engagement portal" where all of their audiences can interact with an organization through a single touchpoint.

Ultimately, an Enterprise Engagement strategic plan is created in much the same way as a strategic plan for any other part of the organization. It should be aligned with and support the broader corporate strategic plan and provide clear guidance to those who are tasked with implementing the strategy. Where multiple strategies arise from the exercise, forecast ROI for each and use the results to prioritize various phases for roll-out.

IMPLEMENTATION ISSUES

Like many other enterprise-wide initiatives, engagement requires buy-in from leadership and a senior executive sponsor – ideally the CEO or CFO.

Enterprise Engagement implementation faces the additional challenge of having no natural leader other than the highest ranking executives – few, if any organizations currently employ a Chief Engagement Officer[2]. Responsibility for employee and customer engagement, for example, tends to fall to executives in HR and Sales, respectively – people who may rarely, if ever, talk to each other. If official responsibility for channel partner and/or supplier engagement is assigned, it very likely involves two additional executives.

> **It's critical that the CEO or CFO appoint the equivalent of a Chief Engagement Officer as part of the strategy or take on this role on himself/herself.**

It's critical, therefore, that the CEO or CFO appoint the equivalent of a Chief Engagement Officer as part of the strategy or take on this role on himself/herself. Whoever is in the role must have the authority and support necessary to drive a consistent, organization-wide effort that will most likely require cultural and values change to succeed.

For organizations that can overcome the chief obstacles to an effective strategy outlined above, the remaining hurdles might seem minor. With a properly empowered and resourced Chief Engagement Officer in place (who enjoys enthusiastic support from the CEO or CFO), the right participants can be recruited to help devise and document the strategy across the organization.

The heads or senior representatives of Sales, HR, Marketing, Account Management, Vendor Management and Channel Partner Management (where applicable) are "must-haves." The VP Communications, the Chief Operating Officer and others pulled from the ranks of management across the enterprise might round out a team of a dozen or so individuals.

In addition to internal members, the team will benefit from senior representatives of the employee, customer, supplier and partner communities who might be attached to the team as guests when required. It's vital to hear from the key constituencies during strategy formation. Traditional or online focus groups may be useful in getting input from key constituencies inside and outside the organization. As noted above, with the right representation in place, the team should be able to craft an Enterprise Engagement strategy much the same way it would any other strategic plan.

A REALITY CHECK

It's been said that nothing worthwhile is ever easy, particularly where you're dealing with uncharted territory. Organizations that design an Enterprise Engagement strategy (much less execute it) are trailblazers; there are few case studies or checklists. Those who execute an Enterprise Engagement strategy will become the discipline's early adopters, beta-testers and pioneers.

The rewards for doing so are touched on above – performance improvements, better retention of customers, more committed employees and partners, special treatment by suppliers ... the list goes on. To monetize those advantages, by even the most rigorous and conservative standards, would result in significant sums for most large organizations.

---

[2] - A June 27, 2012 search of the entire U.S. Monster jobs database resulted in no openings for "Chief Engagement Officer". A search of the U.S. resume database returned only one candidate with that title (who was employed by a small employee engagement consulting firm).

The process, while difficult at first, is likely to be worth the investment. The question then, is how does an organization execute their Enterprise Engagement strategy through specific tactical initiatives?

5 KEY TACTICS
The need to garner executive buy-in and support from other key leaders is addressed above. Yet even with active CEO sponsorship, senior leadership team commitment and adequate resources, roughly 60% to 90% of plans aren't executed.[4] Why? Partly because between 70% and 75% of employees aren't engaged.

A strategic plan to engage the workforce (and other key constituents) has one clear advantage over other change initiatives: most employees will offer less resistance to plans that are intended to benefit them. That said, change is still required, and wherever change is a factor, resistance can be expected.

In this case, resistance might come from those who will be held accountable for results (managers, executives) or from those who view the strategy as an insincere attempt at engagement, meant mainly to extract more effort and output from the workforce. No matter the situation, here are five key tactics that can help ensure support and follow-through:

> Even with active CEO sponsorship, senior leadership team commitment and adequate resources, roughly 60% to 90% of plans aren't executed.[3] Why? Partly because between 70% and 75% of employees aren't engaged.

1. THE RIGHT MESSAGE
Some organizations have built a level of trust with their employees over time that makes change initiatives much easier to implement. Employees trust their leaders, so they're less likely to be suspicious about ulterior motives. Their trust also translates to openness and a willingness to say what they're really thinking about the strategy and ideas for execution, thereby streamlining the process of getting it right.

In most organizations, employees are reluctant converts; they have to be convinced, and part of that process means helping them arrive at the same conclusions as the leadership team on their own – enabling them to understand not just the "what," but the "how" and the "why" as well.

The best approach is to be honest and clear about the strategy. Transparency is at the heart of breaking through to people. Discuss the real issues to get an honest assessment of where you are and where you want to go. Make it safe to talk about "the elephant in the room." The time spent up front in addressing objections will pay off tenfold later in the project. Plowing through people's objections or achieving rapid consensus by being closed or defensive about the strategy will almost invariably cause it to fail somewhere down the line.

Communication is also required to get the word out beyond those involved in implementation. Perceived need and backing for the initiative across the enterprise is the ultimate objective. Describe the strategy in the context of the overall corporate strategic plan. How will Enterprise Engagement help the organization achieve the objectives of the corporate strategy? What are the goals of the initiative? How will it impact the workforce? How will it benefit the various constituencies?

---

[3] - A 1999 Cover story in Fortune Magazine referenced its research showing that 90 percent of organizations fail to execute their strategic plans. Other studies have estimated failure frequency of 60-90 percent.
[4] - A 1999 Cover story in Fortune Magazine referenced its research showing that 90 percent of organizations fail to execute their strategic plans. Other studies have estimated failure frequency of 60-90 percent.

Communications should include visioning – painting a picture of what the organization will look like after it has embraced Enterprise Engagement, thereby helping create a shared vision.

2. THE RIGHT TEAM
If possible, the implementation leadership team should include the same people as the strategic planning team discussed above. The heads or senior representatives of Sales, HR, Marketing, Account Management, Vendor Management, Channel Partner Management, the VP Communications and the Chief Operating Officer are key.

At the hands-on level, the implementation team will be much larger than the strategic planning group. In addition to those mentioned above, Communications, Legal and Union Reps may be required. Team leaders should be identified for each segment of engagement – employees, customers, suppliers and partners. It's critical that the team is given ownership, as well as responsibility for results.

3. THE RIGHT SKILLS
Enterprise engagement will touch the entire organization, but there will be key players who are largely responsible for carrying it out – both in the implementation stage and in sustaining the initiative moving forward.

For employee engagement, front-line supervisors and managers are the most critical. For customer engagement, account managers, salespeople, customer service specialists and others will be directly involved. Buyers, procurement specialists and vendor management staff will be critical for supplier engagement. Channel partners are in regular contact with sales managers and others. These individuals will carry out the plan, and to do that they'll need resources and training.[5]

4. THE RIGHT GOALS
For each component of Enterprise Engagement, set clear and realistic stretch goals. If employee engagement is near the national average of 30%, make it an objective to achieve greater than 50% engagement after year one, and greater than 75% after year two. If customer attrition is 20% per year, make it a goal to reduce it by half. Set a realistic higher goal for channel partner sales agents, and so on.

Make the goals clear and easily measurable. Where goals such as increased sales are concerned, external factors will have a bearing on the results, so use simple tools such as the ROI Methodology to provide accurate estimates of the contribution your engagement initiatives made to increased sales.

In addition to goals, set milestones for the implementation project itself – the number of people trained, number of initiatives launched, progress in implementation across the organization and among each element of engagement, etc. Also plan to make adjustments and refine processes/operations based on various checkpoints.

5. THE RIGHT INCENTIVES
It's crucial to make sure that incentives are aligned with actions. Unless employees have real incentives to implement the engagement strategy, they won't commit to it. Simply put: Reward good behavior, correct bad behavior. This thread must weave through daily communication at all levels and include performance reviews, salary adjustments and bonus configurations. This is why your goals have to be clear and measurable.

---

[5] - The potential range of training required will vary from organization to organization. Many will benefit from investment in the soft kills that enable managers to more successfully manage frontline employees, for example. Other training might include equipping frontline employees to make customer-first decisions and ensuring that partners and channels have the same skills.

Employees responsible for implementing your engagement strategy may love the plan and the vision behind it, but if they're not recognized, rewarded and held accountable for it, it's certain to receive lower priority. Also remember to recognize success on the team itself, to celebrate milestones and call out people who have made significant contributions. Recognize them publicly and reward them based on their individual needs and interests to achieve maximum impact and effectiveness.

SUMMARY
The implementation of an Enterprise Engagement strategy is similar to strategy execution elsewhere in the organization. It should be viewed as a three-stage process with strategy informing tactics and tactics driving tasks – with necessary adjustments being made through constant measurement and analysis. However, given the organization-wide scale of Enterprise Engagement – and the fact that it must touch multiple stakeholders and constituencies – it requires significant change in both culture and values.

Enterprise Engagement is as much a mindset as a series of practices and protocols. And the stakeholders of such an ambitious and comprehensive effort must maintain constant vigilance, including measurement, to sustain it.

As noted above, things of great value are rarely achieved easily. Any organization that wishes to become a trailblazer in the field of Enterprise Engagement should expect a long road fraught with challenges, setbacks and frustration. Yet the potential rewards are likely to surpass what is to be found elsewhere in business.

Indeed as, Gary Rhoades, Ph.D. has said: "Engagement is one of the most powerful emerging business opportunities of the 21st Century." A similarly wise observer, Thomas Friedman, said recently: "The new model in business is that you involve your community and customer in an ongoing conversation about every aspect of your business."

Enterprise Engagement: The Textbook

Chapter 33

Budgeting and ROI

One of the first issues that comes to mind when considering any business strategy is: What can we expect in terms of a benefit and what will it cost?

So where do the budgets for engagement come from? The answer is simple – from the traditional budgets organizations create to define their brands and establish their cultures; attract and retain customers; engage retailers and distributors; encourage employees to fulfill the brand promise; to innovate, work smarter, contribute ideas and improve wellness. Engagement is simply a more holistic, systematic approach to addressing how to maximize the chances that people will do whatever's necessary to meet and exceed their goals and the goals of the organization.

ENGAGEMENT INTEGRATES
Engagement programs are funded from budgets allocated for branding, leadership training and coaching strategies; customer, distributor and employee assessment; advertising and social media; leadership and training; corporate communications; innovation and collaboration tactics; rewards and recognition; and data analytics, because engagement integrates all of these to ensure that organizational efforts are specifically aligned to achieve specific objectives.

The fundamental premise of Engagement is that it lowers costs because it allocates resources based specifically on the desired business result and the people needed to accomplish it, not on supporting the wishes of organizational interest groups and silos promoting their own agendas.

It took decades for marketers to more strategically integrate all of their marketing programs from advertising to promotions, events, direct marketing, etc., and it will take time for organizations to better integrate their overall engagement efforts as well.

LOOK ACROSS SILOS
Another primary premise of this textbook is that business management should look across silos whenever possible to find tactics they can leverage – such as communications platforms, learning systems, collaboration programs, etc. – that might be currently managed by someone else in the organization. Perhaps there are ways to utilize those resources in a way that can easily be applied to a specific need.

Executives who understand the importance of integrating engagement efforts across the organization can facilitate this process by ensuring regular collaboration between business group leaders and a commitment to aligning efforts across the organization.

CALCULATING ROI OF ENGAGEMENT

The best known, most broadly implemented and most successful method for measuring the impact and ROI of business initiatives is the ROI Methodology™ developed in the 1970's by Dr. Jack Phillips.

By applying the principles of measurement and using the ROI Methodology™, organizations can effectively measure engagement initiatives. The key steps are as follows:

1. Determine the goals and objectives of your engagement program and ensure that they're aligned to corporate strategy and objectives. This can include goals related to improving engagement scores by a certain amount, as well as to payoff goals that are tied to ROI, such as a goal to increase customer retention by 10%.

2. Create a plan to both collect your data and evaluate it. At this stage you must also have baseline data for comparison. Before moving on, you should be able to identify: 1) the data you're collecting; 2) how you'll collect it; 3) the method(s) you'll use for analysis and evaluation; and 4) what you will compare the data to for benchmarking purposes

At this stage, the program initiatives are underway. You might, for example, be seeking an improvement in employee engagement among your consulting group. Your initiative may be manager/supervisor training for those who lead the consultants, for example. In this case you'll collect data on the managers' reaction to the training, what they believe they've learned and what they plan to do with it.

Later, as they go back to work, you'll collect data on whether they've actually applied the learning and have taken specific actions to improve engagement among their reports.

Engagement ROI Calculator

Step 4: Bottom Line Impact of All Employees

What is the current financial impact on our organization financials?
NOTE: Change the numbers within the YELLOW shaded cell.

A typical 1,000 employee firm with 1/3 of employees engaged. Average salary is $60,000+ benefits. From employee disengagement alone, the firm loses over $14 million each year in productivity. This does not include the cost of turnover or other human capital costs.

The Bottom Line Impact of Employee Engagement

	(A)				
Total Employees	1,000				
Average Salary and Benefit Cost	$ 79,200				

(B) % Employees at Each Level	Engagement Level	Performance Delivered	(C) Bottom Line Impact of Engagement		(A) x (B) x (C) Financial Impact
13.0%	Level 4: Fully Engaged	122%	Organization GAINS	$ 17,424	$ 2,265,120
20.0%	Level 3: Engaged	100%	Employee delivers an organization "value" equal to the costs (Salary + Benefits)		
55.0%	Level 2: Somewhat Engaged	75%	Organization LOSES	$ (19,800)	$ (10,890,000)
12.0%	Level 1: Disengaged	40%	Organization LOSES	$ (47,520)	$ (5,702,400)
			Current Bottom Line Impact of Employee Engagement	$	**(14,327,280)**

Depending on the nature of the training, you'll collect data on the application of the learning and its impact – perhaps at intervals of several months after the training. This may include the results from an employee engagement survey and its linkage to better, measurable financial goals, for example.

3. Now that you have your data, isolate for the effects of your initiatives. For example, you've measured the reaction, implementation and impact of a manager training program. Suppose an improvement of 41% has been achieved in the benchmark employee engagement survey (among consultants) over the most current survey period. That's an impressive gain, but how much of the gain should be attributed to the training? Several months may have passed between the courses and the results from the latest survey.

The easiest and most effective means of determining attribution is to ask. Ask the managers, ask a sampling of the consultants, ask senior managers and executives. Each group should be presented the summary findings and asked how much of the improvement should be attributed to the initiative. After you've received your answer, ask them one more question: "How confident are you in your estimate?" After you've consolidated your responses, a simple calculation will determine your attribution level.

For illustration purposes, suppose the individuals you canvass estimate, on average, a 55% attribution level, meaning after considering all the things that occurred between the training initiative and the improved engagement results, they would attribute 55% of the gains to the training. Then suppose they were only, on average, 65% confident in that estimate – after all, many months have passed and a lot has happened at the organization that could have impacted employee engagement.

Once you have your data to calculate attributions, it's time to convert the gains (41% better engagement scores) to actual dollars.

4. Do the conversions. Conservative estimates are critical, since converting any form of engagement results to money is imprecise and therefore subject to the skepticism of financial executives and the CEO. In this example, consider the impact of employee *dis*engagement. For example, is employee attrition higher among disengaged employees than engaged employees? What is the average cost of replacing an employee, including recruitment, onboarding, training, etc.? Are performance review results better for engaged employees versus less-engaged employees? Can you analyze several groups of employees (salespeople, for example) and calculate the difference in productivity and performance between those who are engaged versus those who are disengaged and then extrapolate throughout the organization?

Using measures such as these, it's possible to convert engagement gains into hard dollar equivalents. Suppose your organization is a professional services firm that employs 1,250 people. Among them, the consulting group is 800, with an average of $178,000 in salary
and benefits. We will also assume that each consultant generates, on average, $350,000 in annual gross revenue for the firm. Next, assume that you've suffered 50 fewer unwanted departures and benefited from 3.2% higher productivity (based on billing increases, adjusted for any changes in fees), on average, across the consulting group based on the 41% improvement in employee engagement. Now, in this highly simplified example, you're ready to calculate dollar value and attribution levels as follows:

Multiply 50 fewer departures by your organization's average cost of replacement. Common industry standards range from 100% to 150% of salary, but suppose you choose a far more conservative estimate based on hard dollar recruiting and training costs, plus loss of productivity (billings, etc.) while the position was unfilled – let's say $50,000 per person:

$50,000 x 50 = $2,500,000

Next, estimate the hard dollar impact of 3.2% better productivity for all 800 consultants:

800 x $350,000 x 3.2% = $9,000,000

The subtotal of $2,500,000 + 9,000,000 = $11,500,000.

You already know that attribution of gains is 55%, therefore:

$11,500,000 x 55% = $6,325,000

And you know the confidence level is 65%. As such, your next calculation will be as follows:

$6,325,000 x 65% = $4,111,250

After discounting, your gross Return on Investment is about $4.1 million in round numbers.

5. Calculate the entire, fully loaded costs of your initiative. For example, did you purchase the course? Was it delivered by an external trainer, or do you have to calculate total compensation divided by days spent on the training by internal instructors? What were the costs of materials, promotion and communication? Did you account for taking all of the organizations' managers away from their work for the duration of the course, the value of renting the facility (even if it was onsite in a room that would have otherwise been unused), catering costs, etc.? Try to factor in all costs, no matter how small, to determine "fully loaded" costs.

6. Calculate the ROI of the engagement initiative by subtracting the fully loaded costs from the hard dollar benefits. For the purposes of this illustration, let's say the fully loaded costs were $550,000. To arrive at an ROI then:

$4,100,000 - $550,000 = $3,550,000

ROI = $\frac{\$3,550,000 - \$550,000}{550,000} \times 100\% = 545\%$

The hard dollar ROI from the engagement training initiative can be calculated at 545%, a very good return based on conservative calculations, and not including all possible tangible benefits (such as reduced absenteeism, etc.) nor intangible benefits such as happier employees, who may speak better of the organization to colleagues, customers, friends and family.

Enterprise Engagement: The Textbook

Chapter 34

Engagement Careers

In 2007, British business author and consultant Thomas Smythe coined the concept of Chief Engagement Officer, using it as the title of his book on employee engagement. While the title could suggest that every Chief Executive Officer should be the Chief Engagement Officer, it also begs the question: Is Enterprise Engagement a skill, a business field, or both?

Clearly, the successful CEO will have to understand Enterprise Engagement, but he or she surely won't be responsible for tactical implementation connecting engagement efforts to desired organizational results. Who then is responsible for implementation? And what types of solution providers will these people draw upon to design and implement engagement strategies? Will an industry of such solution providers emerge as it has in advertising, direct marketing, event marketing, etc. to create both a set of skills and a business field?

The answers to these questions have significant implications, not only for organizations struggling with how to make Enterprise Engagement part of their business plans, but also for people interested in mastering these skills and applying them for professional satisfaction and profit. While it's too soon to say exactly how the field of Enterprise Engagement will emerge, the history of other fields that have crystallized over the past decades, such as direct marketing, loyalty, event marketing, etc. provide some predictive insights.

ENGAGEMENT MANAGEMENT
One sign that a field is emerging is the creation of new job positions related to it. In some cases, the CEO maybe believe that Enterprise Engagement is his or her role and that developing the overall engagement strategies and seeing that they're effectively implemented stops and starts at the executive's desk.

Others may create positions specifically related to engagement, and a few companies have begun to do so. Consistent with the tendency to create silos, many organizations create those positions specifically in customer, employee, or distributor realms. Because

> **Clearly, the successful CEO will have to understand Enterprise Engagement, but he or she surely won't be responsible for tactical implementation connecting engagement efforts to desired organizational results.**

no one until the publication of this textbook has ever formally defined the concept of engagement from a strategic point of view, many companies define it in different ways.

In the consumer world, customer engagement almost always focuses on digital and social media, even though it's obvious that digital and social media aren't the only ways to engage customers. For example, how about engaging people by providing customer-friendly policies, or engaging employees to continually deliver the brand promise, or managing effective loyalty or referral programs, or event marketing? The budgets and power of the search engine advertising and social business fields have warped the conversation to focus on the mobile revolution, when in fact customer engagement is far more involved. Adding to the confusion, customer engagement also sometimes refers to the position as being in charge of onboarding new customers.

EMPLOYEE ENGAGEMENT
In the human resources arena, the employee engagement manager position has a broader definition, more in line with the definition of this textbook, but still in many cases siloed from other key areas. Here's an example of a 2014 job posting for Employee Engagement Manager at the University of Minnesota:

The Employee Engagement Manager will work with the OHR Service Teams and the unit HR Directors to create a University-wide engagement strategy. The manager will also work with those responsible for supervisor training to integrate engagement concepts into existing and future supervisor training so that strong supervisors become the primary conduit for increasing engagement. The manager will be responsible for the execution and overall communication as it relates to employee engagement initiatives.

The job calls for a Master's degree, five years of human resources management or related experience (including five years of staff management experience), as well as strong communication, public speaking, financial analysis and event management skills – a combination that reflects many of the elements of Enterprise Engagement, with the notable exception of helping to develop an enterprise brand.

Ironically, the job doesn't require prior experience as an Employee Engagement Manager, probably because that would rule out most candidates.

> **More and more management-level jobs with the term "engagement" in them are emerging in both marketing and human resources, but not exponentially at this point.**

It does appear that more and more management-level jobs with the term "engagement" in them are emerging in both marketing and human resources, but not exponentially at this point. PepsiCo has a Senior Vice President of Customer Engagement, but his focus appears to be on the social media side rather than defined strategically as in this textbook. A recent search on Monster.com yielded not one result in either category. To the extent that these positions exist, the best candidates will require an understanding of all of the potential engagement tools applicable to any particular organization and know where to find, and how to manage, the resources to implement them.

Clearly, people qualified for these jobs will need to have at least a four-year college education, traditional marketing or human resources experience and a grasp of as many tools of engagement as possible to obtain expertise through learning or, better yet, experience.

It is by no means clear that numerous organizations will be creating new job positions in enterprise-wide, customer, or employee engagement. What is much more likely is that traditional executives and managers in human resources, sales, distribution management and consumer marketing will be called upon to have an ever-diverse set of skills as organizations discover the wide variety of engagement tactics and how they work together to get the best results.

ENGAGEMENT SOLUTION PROVIDERS

Because engagement involves so many different types of tactics, much like advertising, promotion, or direct marketing, it appears increasingly likely that a field of engagement solution providers will adapt their businesses to meet the demand. Traditional providers of leadership coaching, assessment, communications, learning, collaboration and innovation, rewards and recognition, and measurement will have to tailor their approaches to selling and implementation to better understand how what they do either integrates with or addresses all of the areas of engagement necessary to drive human actions. They will need salespeople and account management teams who have an equal understanding of engagement and how specific tactics contribute to success. Whether or not these various types of engagement solution providers will see enough common interest to coalesce into an industry, such as the advertising, direct marketing, or loyalty fields, remains to be seen.

As of 2014, it's safe to say that Enterprise Engagement is a valuable skill that can set any job candidate apart from others applying for a management position or a job with an engagement solutions provider.

Obviously, skills are what people need to perform specific tasks – writing could be considered a skill with very broad application; the ability to operate a lathe a much narrower one. Almost every skill has multiple educational opportunities associated with it. A skill becomes a field or industry when there are not only people who specialize in that skill, but when demand arises for a variety of businesses to support that skill beyond education, such as the design and manufacture of equipment or other products and services related to it.

History would suggest that Enterprise Engagement is not only a skill, but also a field, because it requires not only knowledge and expertise, but also the understanding of a variety of tools, tactics, products and services addressing everything from assessment and coaching to innovation, software, rewards and recognition, among others. Traditionally, these businesses have defined themselves within the narrow confines of their specialty. Only time will tell whether or not they will find common interest to define themselves under a new engagement umbrella.

Enterprise Engagement: The Textbook

Chapter 35

Engagement and Nonprofits

Although *Enterprise Engagement: The Textbook* focuses primarily on the for-profit sector, the principles are no less critical for nonprofits and not-for-profits – in fact, they're probably even more important. Many people involved with nonprofits and not-for-profits (although certainly not all) work for less than the going rate for their profession, and many of their constituencies are volunteers and donors. Charities may have the toughest engagement challenge of all: getting people to donate their time and money.

By nonprofit or not-for-profit, we mean any organization that qualifies for such designation under relevant tax laws and whose prime goal is to advance a cause, candidate, group, or other related effort. For purposes of brevity, we will hereafter refer to all such organizations as "nonprofits."

The Enterprise Engagement framework is entirely relevant to nonprofits, as are all of the tactics outlined in this edition, and some others not yet covered. What differs is the nature of the constituencies or audiences and their relationships to the organization rather than human nature.

THE NONPROFIT FRAMEWORK
Here's a quick overview of how the Enterprise Engagement framework applies to nonprofit organizations.

Leadership and Coaching. If leadership and coaching are important in the for-profit world, they're mission-critical in the nonprofit world. The driving force for people willing to work for nonprofits often is their conviction that they're doing good. On the one hand, nonprofits have to engage people based on a vision and purpose. On the other, since nonprofits don't always pay as well as organizations in the private sector, they often have to recruit people who lack the critical management skills to properly engage people at the front lines. These front-line people are critical to fundraising, recruitment and volunteer/people management. They need even more coaching and assessment than typical managers because in this case the

> On the one hand, nonprofits have to engage people based on a vision and purpose. On the other, since nonprofits don't always pay as well as organizations in the private sector, they often have to recruit people who lack the critical management skills to properly engage people at the front lines.

audience they're managing often consists of over-qualified, under-paid employees or volunteers.

Audience. The audience in the nonprofit sector is obviously different because it includes volunteers and donors who have no direct financial reason to engage. And in the case of those nonprofits that can't pay rates competitive with for-profit organizations, they have to find other ways to attract quality people.

Assessment. Because engagement is so critical to the success of nonprofits, gauging how people feel can provide invaluable information for executives in terms of detecting problematic front-line management or other issues affecting performance. A non-intrusive strategy for "taking the temperature" of your organization and donors and identifying the best ways to engage with them provides invaluable insight into potential problems and solutions.

The Engagement Business Plan. Just as with any other business process, engagement strategies merit a formal plan that addresses all of the applicable issues in the engagement framework with the best possible tools. Generally, top management representing all parts of the organization determines the strategic vision and "brand" proposition – i.e., what the organization is promising people it will do. Then each department is charged with having a plan for its own group related to its specific business goals, from volunteer recruitment and fundraising to delivering the promised services of the organization, etc. As with any engagement strategy, it pays to have not only a specific objective, but also single out a couple of behaviors critical to achieving that objective. The key to connecting these is to have department heads in regular contact to maximize alignment and minimize obstacles.

> **Giving all employees the opportunity to be part of a continual brainstorming process provides a welcome break and fosters task value, more positive work communication and invaluable ideas for organizations.**

Communications. Nonprofits face all of the same communications issues as for-profits, except even more so in the sense that resources are often limited. Social media has created a powerful new tool to build communities and communicate on a permission basis, but it also places a greater burden on providing true value to the participants. Again, engagement forces a fundamental shift in communication from the old focus on selling to engaging, informing and empowering people and providing the satisfaction that can come from being part of a community. Having an engagement web portal for the community is critical to engagement, because it becomes the focal points for assessment, learning, collaboration and other tactics that foster alignment and commitment.

Learning. One of the great benefits of working in any capacity for a nonprofit is the opportunity to learn. Because of some of the factors outlined above, these organizations sometimes put relatively inexperienced people in relatively important positions, creating the opportunity to address higher-level issues than what that person might encounter at a larger, for-profit organization. This in turn means nonprofits shoulder the responsibility to continually focus on how best to equip people with the capabilities they need and who can realistically apply to their jobs. Building learning into nonprofit engagement strategies can have long-term benefits by creating more capable people.

Collaboration and Innovation. Almost no engagement tactic is better suited to the nonprofit community than collaboration and innovation. Many nonprofit positions require laborious work. Giving all employees the opportunity to be part of a continual brainstorming process provides a welcome break and fosters task value, more positive work communication and, even more importantly, invaluable ideas for organizations.

Recognition. By itself, recognition can appear an ineffective band-aid; in fact, it's a critical part of an overall engagement strategy when it's built in the culture, overseen by well-trained managers and sincerely attempts to make people feel good in a way that also rubs off on their significant others who so often are affected by one's work.

Rewards. No empirical evidence better supports the importance of rewards than the role they play in the nonprofit sector, where compensation is often below average compared with the for-profit world. Because of this, nonprofits have to be particularly mindful of how they use rewards, as the risk of success and failure are heightened. It's also a challenge to justify their use to board members concerned about, budgets, compliance with tax laws and ethical behavior. The most effective nonprofit reward programs are those used as part of formal programs available to all audiences – create special lasting experiences, memories or carefully selected rewards that live on in their homes; become reminders of accomplishment; use inventive rewards tailored to the demographics of the organization. There's an entire industry of rewards program providers that specialize in this domain.

Return on investment. The same ways of measuring engagement and its benefits apply in all sectors. Engagement strategies yield highly meaningful data on actual behaviors and provide measurable results in terms of fundraising, membership, volunteer activity, etc. Having such data is also important in terms of compliance with possible ethical standards related to efforts to engage donors, employees and volunteers.

Enterprise Engagement: The Textbook

Chapter 36

Implications for Government

Enterprise engagement combines strategy with a set of tactics and tasks that is as relevant in the public sector and government as it is in the private sector. And while this textbook was written in the United States, it is intended for use beyond North America. It is difficult to conceive of a best practice, tactic or strategy offered anywhere in these pages that is not applicable worldwide – to workers, clients and stakeholders across all industries and sectors.

People are people, whether you're a mid-manager in Mumbai, a customer in Hong Kong, or a member of the community in Boulder, Colorado. You're likely to respond to the same fundamental elements of engagement – respect, fair treatment, purpose-driven work or causes, rewards, recognition, appreciation and inspiring leadership. For government, however, the scope of the engagement challenge and opportunity is greater than even that of the world's largest companies.

In the U.S., direct government employment constitutes more than 21 million full-time jobs[1],[2] and at least twice that many if full-time equivalent government contractors are counted.[3] U.S. government spending constitutes a full 40% of the nation's GDP, an enormous chunk of the economy.[4] Moreover, government is unique in that its stakeholders include everyone in the country and, arguably, millions more beyond its borders.

Enterprise engagement means something more to governments than employees and the citizens they serve. Often overlooked is the fact that governments must also be concerned about engaging employers and talented people that might be attracted to their jurisdiction (or leave it). Today, state and local governments across the U.S. compete almost as aggressively for talented people as they do for businesses. At the international level, many nations promote their benefits and attractiveness abroad and use numerous tactics to entice the world's best and brightest people and companies to their shores.

---

1 - https://www.opm.gov/policy-data-oversight/data-analysis-documentation/federal-employment-reports/historical-tables/total-government-employment-since-1962/
2 - http://www.forbes.com/sites/mikepatton/2013/01/24/the-growth-of-the-federal-government-1980-to-2012/
3 - http://www.prepareandprosper.net/how-many-americans-work-in-government-would-you-believe-40-million/
4 - http://www.usgovernmentspending.com/us_20th_century_chart.html

Where a local government or a nation fails to attract and keep the best and brightest, it invariably declines and even disintegrates (witness the recent tribulations of Detroit) much as any business would. History demonstrates that good government sets the conditions for sustainable economic advantage. And where governments succeed in attracting and keeping talent and businesses, the economy thrives, colleges and universities blossom, new industries are formed and standards of living increase, attracting more talent to the city, region or country – a virtuous cycle that requires ongoing engagement at all levels.

THE CHANGING WORKFORCE
Until very recently, at least by historical standards, the global economy was agrarian. In 1789, when George Washington became the first president, eight of ten people lived on farms and New York City had a population of 22,000.[5] But with the Industrial Revolution – starting in the early 1800's – the highly independent, self-employed farmer began giving way to the collective and highly fungible factory worker. The exodus from the farm to the factory was followed by a migration of workers from the factory to offices in the second half of the twentieth century. In all, between 1800 and 2000, the world's per-capita income rose 1000% and the population grew 600%[6] attesting to the widespread prosperity (in relative terms) brought by an evolving, more productive economy.

With the Industrial Revolution, new methods of workforce efficiency emerged. Henry Ford's assembly line and Frederick Winslow Taylor's research into industrial workforce productivity radically changed how people worked. It also gave birth to the science of management, a legacy that we still see today and many elements of which are still taught in business schools and practiced by today's leaders, despite their having been created for a workforce that has long ceased to dominate.

Today the U.S. and other developed nations rest between what might be called a creative economy and a knowledge economy. What is clear is that it is evolving more and more toward innovation and creativity each year.

In 2010, McKinsey & Co. estimated that only 30% of job growth in the U.S. came from algorithmic (routine) work, while 70% came from heuristic work (artistic, creative, emphatic, non-routine). In 1975, 83% of a typical organization's worth was based on tangible assets (land, factories, inventory).

By 2009, the value of firms had switched entirely, such that 81% of their value now rested on intangibles. Organizations today are valued (in the stock market or by those that might wish to acquire them) mostly on the intangible things that talented people bring – relationships, innovation, patents, creativity and ideas,[7] Which is why firms of fewer than 5,000 people (i.e., Facebook) can in some cases be worth many times that of firms of hundreds of thousands of people (i.e., GM).

Unfortunately, large vestiges of the management tactics designed for the 1920's factory are still used today. Hierarchies and command and control leadership styles work well where routine work is performed – and where one set of hands is much like another – but they are far less effective where creative work is concerned.

Yet, even though the industrial economy was eclipsed by the service and knowledge economies decades ago, change has come slowly. As a consequence, many of the

---

5 - http://en.wikipedia.org/wiki/History_of_New_York_City
6 - http://www.ncbi.nlm.nih.gov/pmc/articles/PMC1291342/
7 - See: http://www.wdc-econdev.com/intellectual-capital-management-abv.html

knowledge and creative workers of today have become increasingly disengaged from their work, largely due to management and leadership styles that haven't kept pace with the times. Nowhere is this more evident than in government.

Most government work today is white collar and requires a college degree. The average federal government worker receives total compensation about 75% greater than the national average for full-time workers,[8] reflecting the nature of their work and the necessary qualifications.

Yet despite competitive compensation and interesting work (for the most part), the government workforce, as we'll see below, remains somewhat less engaged than the rest of the U.S. workforce (which, as reported throughout this book, is itself largely disengaged).

DISENGAGEMENT IN GOVERNMENT
Since the recovery from the Great Recession officially began in June 2009, public-sector employment (among the combined federal, state and local government workforces) has decreased by more than 600,000 jobs.

Our current economic recovery is the only one in memory that has seen public-sector job losses over its first four years. Pay freezes, hiring restrictions, tighter budgets and ineffective managers all contribute to lower morale. Indeed, in its annual *Federal Viewpoint Survey* for 2013, already low measures of employee engagement fell even lower, and for the third year in a row.[9]

2014 Federal Employee Viewpoint Survey

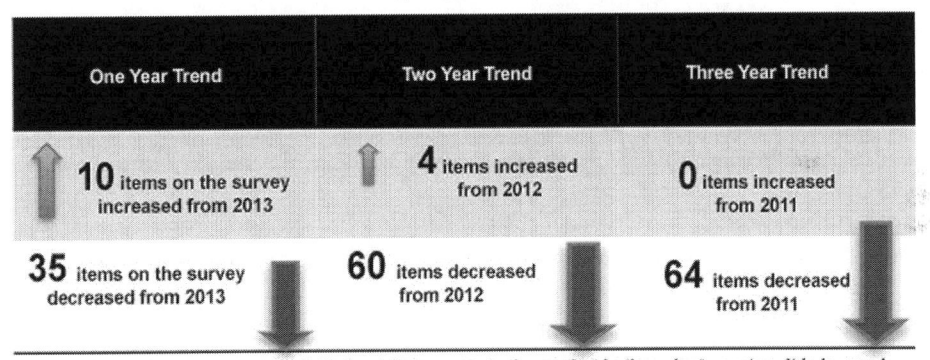

One Year Trend	Two Year Trend	Three Year Trend
↑ 10 items on the survey increased from 2013	↑ 4 items increased from 2012	0 items increased from 2011
35 items on the survey decreased from 2013 ↓	60 items decreased from 2012 ↓	64 items decreased from 2011 ↓

Employee engagement in the US Federal Government mirrors that in the private sector. It is low and getting worse. Of the 71 items measured in 2011, none improved through 2014 and 64 decreased.

Government employee disengagement is only surpassed by the disengagement of its customers – the U.S. public. Americans' approval ratings for the President fell below 40%[10] in 2013, and those who believe Congress is doing a good job fell to just 8% in January 2014.[11] Overall, Americans' faith and trust in government hovers at about 19%, and just 12% say they're "content with the federal government."[12]

---

8 - http://www.downsizinggovernment.org/overpaid-federal-workers and
http://www.cbo.gov/sites/default/files/cbofiles/attachments/01-30-FedPay.pdf
9 - http://www.bbg.gov/wp-content/media/2013/11/2013-AES-Report.pdf
10 - http://politicalticker.blogs.cnn.com/2013/11/12/poll-obama-approval-ratings-drop-americans-say-hes-not-trustworthy/
11 - http://www.rasmussenreports.com/public_content/politics/mood_of_america/congressional_performance
12 - http://www.people-press.org/2013/10/18/trust-in-government-nears-record-low-but-most-federal-agencies-are-viewed-favorably/

Disapproval of government takes a toll on government workers. Throughout this book, evidence has been presented demonstrating that the engagement of one stakeholder group drives the engagement of another.

Unfortunately, the opposite is also true. In government, appreciation comes sparingly. The president is cautious about praising public servants, lest he be branded as soft toward a group the public doesn't sympathize with. Congress routinely bashes the public service, voting against pay increases and tabling bills intended to increase their current benefits. The media rarely sides with civil servants, and the average American, as we've seen, believes government workers are overpaid and under-worked.

Not surprisingly, the latest federal government employee viewpoint survey results paint a depressing picture. Leadership is just one aspect of the survey, but it's clear that the federal government has a steep hill to climb. A strong majority of the federal workforce doesn't believe that federal government leaders can actually lead.

Most tellingly, civil servants report that their leaders don't inspire (or engage) and motivate others to higher performance, which is the most important job of anyone who leads people.

Though it might be tempting to blame government for all of our ills, if we can't figure out ways to drive higher performance and engagement among government employees, the United States' position as a leading nation of the world is sure to erode – it is that critical and that important. Without an effective government, Americans will experience declining standards of living, a less healthy nation and the country will become a far riskier place to live, work, do business and raise children.

THE ENGAGEMENT IMPERATIVE
As important as good government is, political and other public leaders must also be concerned about engagement on a broader level, whether it be the residents of a city, region or nation. For most of the past century, America and its constituent parts have been fortunate. Engagement, or at least contentment for the great majority of citizens, came relatively easily in the United States during a mostly prosperous 20th century.

Today, however, the U.S. and most of the world are still struggling to break from the grip of a long and deep recession. Unfortunately, government has few levers at its disposal. Monetary and fiscal policy has been exhausted in terms of keeping interest rates low, and stimulus spending has hit levels that are not likely to be exceeded, given the depth of the national debt and the prevailing political climate.

The key difference between the economy of 2014 and those of the past 100 years or so is the lack of large economic stimulators. Past economic recoveries gave way to years of growth and abundance, growth that was driven by social phenomena and government programs that are simply unavailable today. The Depression was overcome largely due to government spending necessitated by WWII. The post-war years saw the rebuilding of Europe and Japan (the Marshall Plan) and the GI Bill, both government programs that poured billions into the economy and set the stage for creating the most educated and productive workforce the world had ever seen.

Near the end of WWII, a visionary government devised the GI Bill, essentially offering all war veterans a free post-secondary education. Nearly nine million veterans took advantage, either by going to college or taking training.[13] Management guru Peter

---

13 - http://en.wikipedia.org/wiki/G.I._Bill

Drucker said that providing free higher education to so many Americans changed the world by creating the modern knowledge economy.[14] The original GI Bill, according to the best estimates, returned $7 for every dollar invested, it became a powerful economic driver by placing millions of skilled veterans into the workforce, making the United States the greatest economic power in history. [15]

The GI Bill also introduced the idea of mass public post-secondary education to the world and fired the U.S. economy for a generation. Higher education exploded in the U.S. during the 1950s, 60s and 70s, and continued to grow through the turn of the century.[16] In 1900, one in 400 Americans went to college. In 2011, nearly 40% of American adults possessed either a two- or four-year post-secondary college degree.[17] The U.S. may never again replicate that growth in educational attainment or the productivity that went along with it.

In the decades of the 1960s, 1970s and beyond, the U.S. and developed world economies benefited from another powerful economic stimulus – in this case a social one, but one fueled and supported by government. Women entered colleges, universities and work in huge numbers, effectively doubling the workforce in the U.S. by the year 2000.

Today, women constitute roughly half the U.S. workforce and more than half of all management and professional positions.[18] Moreover, for every two men who get a college degree this year, three women will do the same,[19] and according to the Census Bureau, more women earned advanced degrees in 2012 than men, for the first time ever.[20] While all of this is good news – after all, it produced economic advantages similar to the GI Bill – it is essentially over, women already represent half of all workers.

Lastly, the economy of the last century benefited from a third powerful stimulus – immigrants, and skilled workers in particular. The U.S. and a few other countries (most notably Canada and Australia) have benefited enormously from immigration.

Despite not having a "skills-based" immigration program, the U.S., until 2001, attracted more than half of the world's mobile, skilled workforce. The benefits to the economy cannot be overstated. Yet since 2002, mainly in reaction to the attacks on September 11, 2001, U.S. immigration policy has kept many of the best and brightest out.

More importantly, the slowdown in the U.S. economy and the rise of developing nations has meant that far fewer skilled workers are interested in leaving large source countries like China and India than in the past, and competition for those that are willing to emigrate has intensified worldwide.

Depressingly, some researchers argue that since 2001, the U.S. has lost more skilled workers than it has gained.[21] Despite the end of the recession almost five years ago, the U.S. suffers from what author and professor Tyler Cowen terms, "The Great

---

14 - http://www.google.com/url?sa=t&rct=j&q=&esrc=s&source=web&cd=1&ved=0CCgQFjAA &url=http%3A%2F%2Fwww.marketplace.org%2Ftopics%2Feconomy%2Fhow-gi-bill-changed-economy&ei=negVU_HOG8_LkQfp9ICABg&usg=AFQjCNGPMzaBCS4Xu7cgHq-EXGiFE5JxMQ&bvm=bv.62286460,d.eW0
15 - http://www.columbiatribune.com/business/saturday_business/gi-bill-created-generation-of-business-leaders/article_24848d9f-9988-58a0-9691-f633304028c8.html
16 - http://en.wikipedia.org/wiki/File:Educational_Attainment_in_the_United_States_2009.png
17 - http://www.luminafoundation.org/stronger_nation/report/main-narrative.html
18 - Bureau of Labor Statistics, Current Population Survey, "Table 3: Employment Status of the Civilian Noninstitutional Population by Age, Sex, and Race," *Annual Averages 2012* (2013).
19 - http://www.theatlantic.com/magazine/archive/2010/07/the-end-of-men/308135/
20 - http://www.aei-ideas.org/2013/05/stunning-college-degree-gap-women-have-earned-almost-10-million-more-college-degrees-than-men-since-1982/
21 - See Richard Florida, The Flight of the Creative Class, Harper Business, 200r and David Heenan, Flight Capital, Nicholas Brealey Publishing, 2o05

Stagnation." [22] A condition he sees as more or less permanent, unless something unexpected occurs. As Cowen says in his e-book, *The Great Stagnation*:

"You can only move your smartest people from the farm to the school system once. As for China and India...they're mostly picking the same fruit we've picked - and grown - over the past century, bringing electricity and schooling and modern medicine and management techniques to people who never had them before....the American economy has enjoyed lots of low-hanging fruit since at least the seventeenth century, whether it be free land, lots of immigrant labor, or powerful new technologies. Yet during the last forty years, that low-hanging fruit started disappearing, and we started pretending it was still there. We have failed to recognize that we are at a technological plateau and the trees are more bare than we would like to think."[23]

> "If America continues to make it harder for some of the world's most talented students and workers to come here, they'll go to other countries eager to tap into their creative capabilities – as will American citizens fed up with what they view as an increasingly repressive environment."
>
> ~ David Heenan, Flight Capital

Cowen and others argue that there remains no more "low hanging fruit" to drive growth and living standards in developed nations. But they appear to be overlooking one important factor – the workforce itself. As noted above, engagement levels in the U.S. hover at about 30% of the workforce[24], and employee engagement outside the U.S. is typically no better or worse, on average.[25]

Thus workers are far less productive than they could be, leaving trillions of dollars on the table that could provide the massive boost to the economy that the world needs – perhaps even on the scale of another Marhall Plan and GI Bill combined.

DRIVING ENGAGEMENT IN GOVERNMENT AND BEYOND

Today there's no more influential management guru than Gary Hamel, visiting professor at the London Business School and founder of Strategos. He is perpetually ranked as one of the world's most influential business thinkers and among the world's most sought after management speakers.

In his 2007 book, *The Future of Management*, Hamel argues that we need to innovate in management; we need to move from military-style workplaces to democratic workplaces; we need to supercharge our workforce through better human capital management. "Modern organizations are motivationally crippled," he says, "because they 'coerce grudging compliance instead of inspiring passionate performance.'"

Hamel believes that the primary growth area for 21st-century management is a more sophisticated and nuanced approach to employee motivation and engagement. "I dream of organizations where an electric current of innovation pulses through every activity. I dream of organizations that actually deserve the passion and creativity of the folks who work there, and naturally elicit the very best that people have to give."

If we accept Professor Hamel's message, the federal government has a steep hill to climb. A strong majority of the federal workforce is disengaged and the trend is

---

22 - Tyler Cowen, The Great Stagnation, 2010
23 - Ibid, see also: http://voices.washingtonpost.com/ezra-klein/2011/01/things_that_are_more_important.html
24 - State of the American Workforce Report 2013, Gallup See: http://www.gallup.com/strategicconsulting/163007/state-american-workplace.aspx
25 - http://www.aon.com/human-capital-consulting/thought-leadership/talent_mgmt/2013_Trends_in_Global_Employee_Engagement.jsp

worsening. However, should the U.S. focus on engagement as a national priority – starting with its own workforce – the situation could be reversed in much the same way that organizations spur productivity through strategies, tactics and tasks aimed at driving engagement among employees and their broader stakeholders.

According to conservative estimates based on data from the Center for Talent Solutions, the federal government alone (not counting state, county and local) could save more than 30 billion dollars *each year* by just marginally increasing engagement among its 4.2 million workers.[27]

With modest investment, government could improve engagement levels throughout its workforce, leading to better interactions with customers and a more engaged citizenry. A highly engaged government provides a more attractive place for skilled individuals and businesses to stay or relocate to, keeping towns, cities, regions and nations more competitive.

SUMMARY
The topic of government engagement extending beyond its own workforce is a new one. While a few enlightened politicians and civic leaders may understand the importance of an engaged citizenry at a theoretical level, very little is done by way of implementing engagement strategy and tactics in most jurisdictions. From the attraction and retention of talent and businesses to the participation of citizens in volunteer work, engagement is central to thriving communities and nations. Governments must take it upon themselves to drive community-wide engagement.

The opportunity is immense. Governments should start with their own employees, but plan to spiral their engagement efforts beyond the workforce to include customers and stakeholders throughout all components of their communities.

> **According to conservative estimates based on data from the Center for Talent Solutions, the federal government alone (not counting state, county and local) could save more than 30 billion dollars each year by just marginally increasing engagement among its 4.2 million workers.[26]**

Notes and Acknowledgments

A WORD ABOUT THE ENTERPRISE ENGAGEMENT ALLIANCE

The Enterprise Engagement Alliance is comprised of business leaders, corporate practitioners, researchers, academics and solution providers committed to creating a formal business field dedicated to helping organizations achieve financial and other goals by engaging all of the people critical to success. Enterprise Engagement is unique in that it focuses on helping organizations develop an Enterprise Brand to align external and internal marketing and on integrating key engagement tactics such as coaching and training, assessment, communications, learning and gamification, rewards and recognition, measurement, etc. to achieve organizational goals. The EEA's activities include:

- The Enterprise Engagement Textbook, Curriculum and Certification program created and continually updated and expanded with input from top corporate practitioners and solution providers in all areas of Engagement.
- The online Engagement University and regional engagement seminars at which the Textbook curriculum is both updated and taught based on input from corporate practitioners and solution providers.
- Engagement University Online courses on a growing number of textbook chapters.
- An Enterprise Engagement Certification program based on an online test and other accomplishments.
- The EnterpriseEngagement.org portal, blog, Twitter and Linked in communities.
- The Engagement Strategies quarterly print magazine, website and eNewsletters.
- The Engaged Company Stock Index
- Consulting on enterprise brand development
- Training on engagement program design/business plans
- Public speaking on engagement

FUNDING

The Enterprise Engagement Alliance is funded through:

- Consulting and training related to development of enterprise brands and engagement business plans.
- Sponsorships and support fees from engagement solution providers seeking to become leaders in this emerging field.
- Regional education programs.
- Training and certification fees.

FOR MORE INFORMATION:

Go to www.Theeea.org
Contact Bruce Bolger at bolger@theeea.org
914-591-7600, ext. 230

Made in the USA
Middletown, DE
01 October 2015